CORPORATIONS STRIPPED NAKED 2

Controlling the AQ Virus

Ed Rychkun

ISBN 978-1-927066-07-2
Copyright © 2014 Ed Rychkun

Editing: Hope Rychkun
Cover and Cartoons by Ed Rychkun

TABLE OF CONTENTS

PREFACE

Before you read another sentence, I want you to understand clearly that this book is my own personal satire of the corporate world. It is my view of corporations stripped naked of their glamour and efficiency. When I look back at how I climbed the "ladder of success" to take on positions of CEO, Partner, Director, Owner and Chairman... all those supposedly respected positions, I realize there wasn't really a lot of things learned at University that helped me get there. Perhaps I was lucky but I think perhaps I learned some things that were just not taught in school. What became apparent in the climb was what I saw as the "underbelly" of a corporation and a certain behavior in successful people that went far outside of the normal MBA training. What was so interesting to me was that there was a huge textbook of unwritten material on how people actually succeed to power and position in a corporation without following the traditional management stuff. This book is where I bring this unwritten material to you. It strips companies of their usual look and practices thereby revealing the underbelly. When you look at your company and your experience in this light, I hope that you will get many chuckles and perhaps a different perspective on your journey upwards in the company.

I first began this book in 1986 after spending many years engaging in what many people call climbing the professional ladder. My parents were particularly poor so they spent a lot of time convincing me to go to school so I didn't have to be poor like them. Like a good lad, I set my journey towards corporate life in the business world... with absolutely no idea what I was headed for. My entry into business was fairly easy as I worked part time through University. This business world I was peeking into looked so rewarding. After all, it was the place to be. It was after graduating from University, however, that I really got immersed in this folly. And I got the bug like many others! It seemed that no matter where I was or what I was doing, there was always someone smarter, more powerful, and wealthier than me. There were also more people that seemed pretty stupid with power as well. But through my glasses it was those guys that were better than me that I needed to follow so I began to climb in efforts to be like them. It was only logical that I should climb the same corporate ladder that they climbed up. After all, it got these guys what many strived for... more power and money.

So I climbed for some thirty years. What a struggle! Some years were great. Others were horrible. But with conviction I worked and worked, followed the rules and slowly transformed myself from technical positions in the information industry up into supervisory roles and then into management. Basically, I just followed others, took management courses and worked as hard as I could. I never questioned the process. But I noticed that not everyone worked as hard as me. Some of the guys with power and money seemed such jerks. They didn't even seem to know what they were talking about. Yet they were feared and respected by the others... plus they made a lot of money. Was I missing something? Then somewhere along the journey, I got to know the breed of corporate people called the "executive". These were always the golden guys that we all admired. What was so interesting about so many of these guys was that they seemed to work hard but they didn't really work... everybody else did. Was I doing something wrong? Did I go to the wrong training program? What was it that I was missing? It was only when I started to attend management and executive meetings that the secret started to reveal itself. It became apparent that many of these top leaders of corporations used many unwritten tactics to control and manipulate people. Oh, yes I will admit there are exceptions but I didn't meet too many.

As I ascended the corporate ladders, I began to develop a rather oblique humorous perspective of the business world and these corporate leaders. It was here that I began to materialize a hypothesis that I dubbed as the AQ Phenomenon. Very much like the process called the "Peter Principal", the *AQ process defined how and why so many people get into disharmony with their fellow*

7

employees and how and why, despite the conflict, some still rise in status while so many others failed. It was at that time, as Director of Information Services, that I was beginning to question my sanity and I began to look at things in a different light. The whole process of growth, promotion, career became fuzzy as I began to see conflict with the kind of person I really was. Knowing that I would have to change my personality, levels of aggression, social sphere of influence and many other individual traits if I wanted to rise farther became somewhat disconcerting. Sometimes I had to fire people, even humiliate them because they did not follow directives or rules. Sometimes I was even told by a superior that I had to treat people more horribly. What was becoming bothersome was that I was expected to treat others like assholes as a survival tactic or they would destroy my credibility. Even more troublesome was my changing perception of certain people in the company, and my respect for them, never mind my potential relationship with them. It was difficult to understand why so many of these people had so much power and position entrusted to them when they were really such awful jerks.

It was difficult to see how I could be part of this peculiar culture. What I observed and felt, I began to quantify in this rather obtuse process I called AQ. As I began to reflect and write about my findings I decided that I needed to get out into a new job. I decided to move to Africa and took a senior position in a new area with IBM in South Africa. You can imagine the shock. This time it took me only two years to reach another level of awareness and one of conflict with myself. The picture of what was happening was clearer now, one that allowed me to complete yet another chapter in this book. But there was still something missing... I didn't feel I had climbed high enough in the business world to give credence to my theories. So the book sat in limbo while I climbed higher in the corporate tree.

In 1988, I returned to Canada to take a Vice President position with a high tech company and truthfully forgot about my scribbling. After I became President in 1989 I began to view my interaction with people from a new level and to complete another chapter. When I finally gave up this position up in 1997, I realized that my hypothesis on AQ was even more relevant at the top of the heap. But there was still another level in my progression for being on top. I had realized that as a CEO, you were still controlled by a Board of Directors, shareholders, government and others. So I decided to move into those positions in a quest to be free and get to a situation where no one could tell me what to do and work in my own free enterprise. Now don't get me wrong... I didn't go higher just to write a book, the idea was to attain more freedom. But this is where I became familiar with some new titles like founder, partner, director, chairman.... and so ends the story. That's where it all stopped. I could then report that I have climbed through every major step in the corporate world and beyond. In 2002, I decided it was time to share my findings.

What I had determined was that employees, regardless of position, exhibit certain behaviors and characteristics that are anything but "professional". I discovered that the word organization was really a myth. The word management was really an invisible ability to collect a bunch of untaught techniques to manipulate others. I discovered that the rate of progression (or regression) in a company was actually dependant on a very little portion of time. The progression related to how you relate to others in the company... and more important... how you feel about them.

The whole phenomenon is wrapped up in your AQ, short for "Asshole Quotient". This is simply a measurement of your relationship to others in the company. The reality was that just about everyone in a corporation kept a secret mental list. This list contained other people that they had determined were jerks... more aggressively referred to as "assholes". It is how big (or small) an individual list is relative to the individual's position in the corporation that is the crucial concern. Sound silly? Well first, let me warn you. If you are not endowed with a sense of humor about your job, or you have difficulty seeing anything amusing about corporate life, then you may not want to read this book because it may depress you even further when you realize how ridiculous we are.

Anyone who has lived in the corporate world, and I mean anyone who has worked in some organizational structure, will understand the need to grow as a professional citizen. It becomes apparent quite early in anyone's career that many traumatic experiences will be found along the way. Whether the pathway leads upwards or sideways seems to matter very little, for in either case, various rules and regulations, policies and procedures, cultures and personalities, will be encountered. These, sooner or later, will lead to disagreement or conflict. This process inevitably adds more people to the secret list. What becomes apparent is that this list is actually very important in determining how you succeed or fail in an organization. The use of this secret list is what the AQ is all about.

It is this culture, and the way companies work that is the topic here... but with a different slant than those management books. Call this one "un-management" if you will... it is a look at the silly but true underbelly of a corporation. That's why I call it "Corporations Stripped Naked".

What you will read about is anything but orderly management and organizational efficiency. Rather, you will get a picture of the flip side of a company and its people. The AQ phenomenon is universal. It reveals the untaught secrets of those "successful" executives and managers. The material will vary from serious treatments to satire and exaggeration. It will inject raw humor into the grim realities of corporate life.

Special thanks are given to those many assholes I met from the past. I have met many and you are also about to meet them in this book. Some are purposely exaggerated to make a point. Thanks to them, they have made this book possible.

There is a final note here and it came about when I began to promote the book. On many interviews, after describing the AQ process, people would ask for advice on how to deal with their problems at work. This was not the intent. It was to show how people become "***Corporites***" that acquire the AQ Virus that sucks us into the mire of corporate power and need to use (and abuse) others. It stems from a need to preserve the ego and to protect one's position. It is something that happens to people when they engage in this Corporite addiction which is like ***corporitis***, the power and preservation addiction of a very contagious virus which I call **AQ'ISM.** Once this virus takes hold you begin to lose your real personality and it becomes a ***corporitic*** need to survive.

The intent was to present a funny but true picture so you could laugh, realize you may have caught the virus, and then change that picture which breeds so much conflict, fear and negative emotion.

As it turns out, to be corporitic, you need to be a dead human, like what the Corporation itself is - a dead entity for the sole purpose of engaging in commerce usually for a profit - which is without emotion or a conscience. Typically we call those beings in a corporation assholes but it is because corporations become profitable and grow because of a dependence and interdependence on their employees. And that is where the way we do this - with or without emotion - makes the big difference as to how the AQ Virus has taken hold.

This book is meant to show how employees typically take on this virus and how they shift in their corporitic behavior to become Assholes in other corporite citizens eyes.

The big lesson here is **not** how to teach you to become an asshole addicted by ego preservation and desire for power. It is to see how the AQ Virus is caught, its symptoms, it's common behavior patterns, and to have laugh so as to avoid losing your good side of emotion and happy interrelationship in your job.

The book will refer to many of these behavior patterns as tools. I have observed these as common habits when one gets the virus.

Of course to the one addicted to the power over people and the need to protect money and ego, these tools may be used unknowingly, just like an alcoholic or smoker is unknowingly addicted to the habit.

And so, please do not seek advice on this. Nor should you consider using many of these in a negative way. You do have a choice in applying many of these techniques in a positive way if you insist. It is all to open your heart and avoid the AQ Virus so **you do not become** a Corporate Zombie that uses and abuses others for the sake of egoic pride and the insatiable urge to attain power over others and through commerce.

There are always choices in these dead corporations; to engage others in a good way or a bad way.

When I got to the top, I found that my basic constitution was having a bad time of treating people under the spell of the virus and always being conscious of profit and covering my ass. I was copying what I thought was a successful formula as exhibited by the majority of corporate leaders that eventually gave me heartache and heartburn. That's why I had to exit the corporite addiction of AQ'ISM and retrench my habits.

Once you check out your own AQ and see the folly of the AQ Virus, what will you choose?

And in conclusion, through my own experience, I have ended the book with a Chapter on how to zero out this AQ permanently!

Ed Rychkun

INTRODUCTION

A QUICK SUMMARY

In the **Book Corporations Stripped Naked: Exposing the AQ Virus,** the concept of AQ for Asshole Quotient was brought forward. Here we learned what AQ'ISM was and the basic laws that it abides by. We learned how it works in an example corporation and we got to meet the three levels of Executive, Management and Others to see how they fall into the trap.

We learned what the Executives like to use as their AQ Arsenals that they deploy (sometimes unconsciously) in order to maintain control and to improve their profits

But here is the crux of the matter. Whether you are aware of it or not, the tools are knowingly or unknowingly used to maintain AQ equilibrium and climb rapidly if that is your wish. The AQ measurement is your thermometer to measure your progress. The AQ allows you to measure your relationship to others in the company. But the AQ level is directly related to your position. Behind the scenes is this insidious AQ process that creeps into every corporation. It effectively works against you from the first day on the job. Let us now time to recap the AQ Laws:

1ˢᵗ BASIC LAW OF AQ'ISM: There exists a natural tendency within any one corporation for any one individual to classify another as an Asshole.

2nd LAW OF AQ'ISM: The percent of Assholes within any company, as viewed by any one individual at any point in time is defined as one's Asshole Quotient or "AQ" level.

3rd LAW OF AQ'ISM: Any new entry into a corporation will tend to have an individual AQ near zero.

4th LAW OF AQ'ISM: Any individual AQ, given sufficient time, will tend towards 100.

5th LAW OF AQ'ISM: Individual AQ's have a tendency to rise according to a natural growth.

6th LAW OF AQ'ISM: From the date of entry into a corporation, an individual carefully sets out to prove that he or she is an Asshole.

7th LAW OF AQ'ISM: Sooner or later any individual will freely offer evidence to prove that he or she is an Asshole.

8th LAW OF AQ'ISM: AQ's have a tendency to be reciprocal in motion.

9ᵗʰ LAW OF AQ'ISM: Your local AQ will rise to its level maximum within a period of 2 years.

10ᵗʰ LAW OF AQ'ISM: Your level of responsibility must rise in direct relationship to your AQ level.

Accepting these laws as an underlying process is not such a bad thing if assists you from becoming an asshole yourself. If it is your destiny to become a Big Corporate Asshole, then knowing the process and the means of using these AQ "tools" can of course get you there a lot faster.

What I hope is that you can get a chuckle and you can work it to your advantage by avoiding the virus. Simply build your own resilience against the arsenals and monitor your AQ level. Remember the Peter Principle? It reflects the fact that you become further and further removed from what you knew best... you become incompetent! Sorry but that's reality. It appears that these AQ tools are your means of defeating this and avoiding those devastating productivity slides downward in position and stature.

THE AQ PROCESS

It is no accident that Corporations have the part "corp" in it because it is essentially a dead entity created for the sake of commerce. It has no heart, no emotion, no intelligence and no real life except that which is reflected by those who command this dead vehicle. So the ones best suited to run these dead things seem to be the ones who are themselves emotionless with no heart. After all: "It is just business." And that seems to gravitate to being ruthless and heartless so as to best attain power and profit. Not surprising, the way the corporites move through the six phases of communication is key.

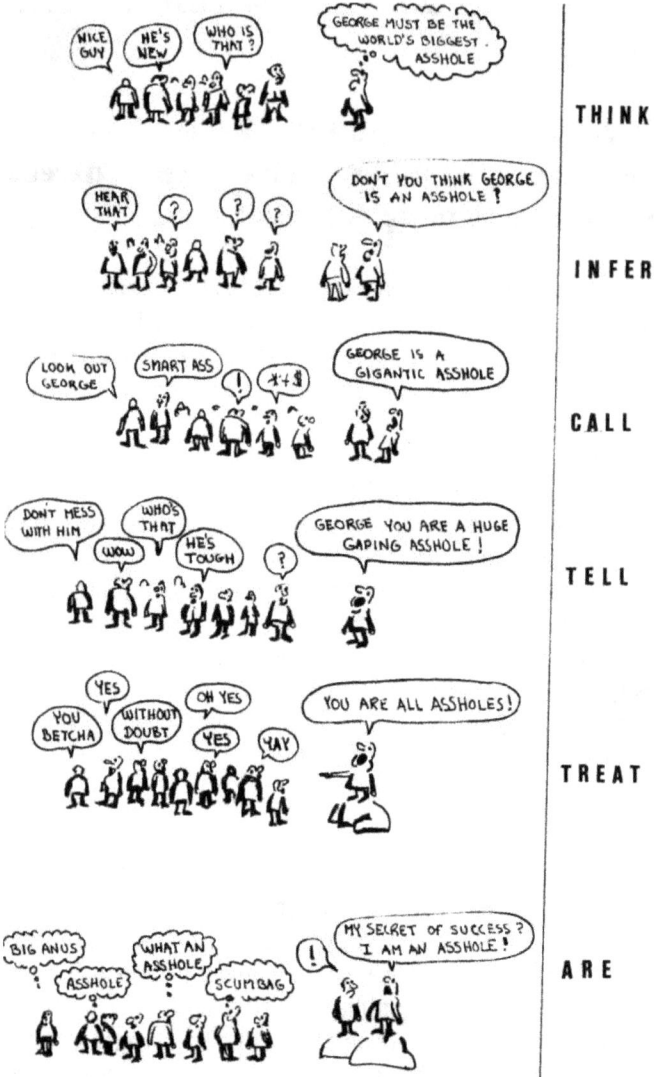

THINK

INFER

CALL

TELL

TREAT

ARE

These stages, directly related to the level of position of power in the corporation - and the level of monetary control is all about getting others to do one's bidding. In the previous book it was shown how the levels of management correlated with the level of AQ. This is shown in the AQ Meter below.

THE ASSHOLE METER

LEVEL	STATE	AQ	METHOD	PROCESS
DECISION MAKERS	PRESIDENT	100	ARE	Rule
UPPER ECHELON	VICE PRESIDENT	90		Power
		80	TREAT	Superiority
DOERS	DIRECTOR	70		Control
MIDDLE MANAGEMENT	MANAGER	60	TELL	Conflict
	SUPERVISOR	50		Change
		40	CALL	Responsibility
WORKERS	SENIOR	30		Confidence
	INTERMED	20	INFER	Exposure
LOWER REACHES	JUNIOR	10		Learning
	NOBODY	0	THINK	Impressions

To recap, a worker (0-40) can infer others are assholes, A manager (40-80) learns to call people asshole, a VP (80-99) can treat people like assholes, and a CEO (100) is usually an asshole so viewed by others. And how this is done is the key to the Virus taking hold. As one moves to the heartless and emotionless side of getting others to do things, one gets more and more infected it seems, and those who have done best seem to be the ones who are fundamentally ruthless, merciless and emotionless, just like the dead corporation.

THE FOUR CHOICES

Here is the bottom line. If these laws are working against you and your AQ is in Dis-equilibrium, (AQ higher or lower than your position) you appear to have three key choices:

1.   **Raise your AQ to be in line with your position.**
2.   **Raise your position to be in line with your AQ.**
3.   **Leave and zero out your AQ.**

AQ Arsenals are used to make 1 and 2 happen as quickly as possible, and the executive, who spends so much time in meetings, has become expert in developing a new expertise to do this.

But there is a 4th choice. You can learn from them and laugh about it once you see this AQ process clearly. It is however, the most difficult.

4. Don't engage in the AQ'ISM addiction

If you have ever grown a business, the most glorious part is in the beginning, when your passion is high, you are eager to learn the business, and the people you work with are like family working and prospering together... together, loving every moment of their engagements and efforts, acting as one unit of heart.

Of course this changes as the AQ Virus takes hold and the need to protect ego, position and profits become different when the corporation grows. We idolize the mighty executive, the pillar of leadership, that has come through the earlier phases of the AQ Progression - through middle management. It is in his travels through middle management that he has picked up other tricks and tools that were needed for AQ Equilibrium - the ones picked up through the Big Transition. These tools helped him move through middle management to the position of Executive and it seems that that original philosophy in choice 4 is quickly left behind to create the AQ Arsenals for survival. We are going to expose more of this in the book, and deal with the 4th choice.

If you have read my book **How's Your AQ Today?**, or **Corporations Stripped Naked 1: The AQ Virus Exposed** you have come to see this as a satire on corporate life. Hopefully you have gained a new perspective on corporations and those pillars of strength at the top. Yes, they were all stripped naked for a while to give you a new look at them. Yes, this was presented as a satire, but in reality I have presented many people and situations that may be more real than we care to admit. In reading all this, you may have wondered what was real and what was fiction. So let us continue to recap book 1:

OUR CORPORATE EXAMPLE

In the previous books, I brought forward an example corporation, the names of which reflect their personalities and behaviors. These in actuality are real characters I have encountered but changed the identities to suit their characters. There are certain prototypes which, like the signs of the Zodiac reflect certain bad and good tendencies. What the AQ virus does is move people to the bad side, even when they begin on the good side.

Here is our list and you will get a feel for their corporate identity and behavior from their names.

EXECUTIVE	POSITION
Boomer Steadfast	Chairman of the Board
Franklin Hardass	President and CEO
Scoot Blastoff	VP Operations
Flash Spreadsheet	VP Finance & Administration
Slink Wirlwind	VP Planning
Herbert Hoyle	VP Engineering
Angus Steadfast	VP Projects
Murk Muddler	VP Legal & Corp. Affairs

MANAGEMENT	POSITION
Marcus Mule	Manager Projects
Fred Fantasy	Manager Planning
Randolf Snooper	Director Personnel
Clepto Superbyte	Director Information Technology
Micro Tabulate	Chief Accountant
Bill Blastoff	Assistant Manager Planning
Donna Dingdong	Mananager Marketing
Grunt Hollowhead	Supervisor Projects
Pomp Crotchley	Supervisor Personnel
Oscar Ostrich	Controller
Kevin Baloney	Sup. Industrial Relations
Prim Strutland	Sup. Administrative Services
Willy Liplock	Assist. Mananager Operations
Cut Thrasher	Sup. Systems & Operations
Gross Fartley	Manager Corporate Affairs
Barf Chapstick	Manager Legal
Slime Mealymouth	Sup. Mechanical Engineering
Horace LaPrick	Sup. Ranch Operations
Clone Mimicker	Sup. Ind. Engineering
Switcho Stumpbrain	Manager Engineering
Wimp Wishwash	Sup. Support Services

THE REST	POSITION
Gayle Grimley	Accounts Payables Clerk
Moose Baxter	Special Serv. Coordinator
Hump Pussywhip	Sr. Financial
Feelo Ballsack	Jr. Draftsman
Buff Windbag	Sr. Financial Analyst
Cirilla Gorilla	Sr. Systems Analyst
Sleeze Huffer	Sr. Engineer
Quirk Multiples	Systems Analyst
Fanny Bumwiggle	Secretary – Legal
Lardo Billobum	Solicitor
Irk Guffer	Accountant
Lila Memomangler	Legal Clerk

Dork Assgrabber	Intermediate Draftsman
Sam LeSlam	Project Account
Oink Freaker	Administrative Assistant
Slip Goofball	Special Projects Engineer
Jaybird Warpmatter	Engineer
Lou Kabbagetop	Sr. Planning Advisor
Viola Broadbum	Int. Mechanical Engineer
Bula Bugle	Business Analyst
Spasmo Mover	Industrial Engineer
Korno Klutz	Engineer
Vera Sparkle	Receptionist
Dudley Dwarfbrain	Marketing Analyst
Fats Gutstuffer	Computer Operator
Birtha Bitchalot	Senior Filing Clerk
Jock Flasher	Supply Clerk
Souse Growler	Int. Mech. Engineer
Tina Tinkle	Operator
Polly Perfect	Personnel Assistant
Wormley Crawler	Jr. Engineer
Slim Twinkle	Designer
Bang Loudmouth	Systems Analyst
Karen Klutz	Secretary – Eng.
Dink Primrose	Sr. Accountant
Moira Mouthpeice	Executive Secretary
Flirt Shameless	Coordinator Office Ser.
Wendy Worker	Filing Clerk
Olga Titwhopper	Executive Secretary
Buzz Bottle	Intermediate Planner
Calc Theorem	Marketing Engineer
Marf Garfle	Accounting Clerk
Grog Stinky	Engineer – Planning
Harvey Hotshit	Planner
Barry Brass	Intermediate Engineer
Blam Featherflash	Marketing Analyst
Warp Monkeynuts	Programmer
Milo Muff	Support Person
Suzy Bubbles	Accounting Secretary

Dork McPork	Coordinator Ranching
Perky Shortwhip	Sr. Advisor
Bark Banana	Legal Assistant
Wino Dingbat	Business Analyst
Rolly Growl	Budget Coordinator
Nose Grindstone	Junior Designer
Crass Farkle	Project Engineer
Moon Flasher	Engineer – Design
Milly De Dilly	Secretary
Brenda Breeder	Personnel Clerk
Piles Bumrubber	Designer
Herf Honker	Solicitor
Ruff Honker	Jr. Programmer
Garfle Greymatter	Systems R&D
Whipply Grizzlepuss	Draftsman
Sac Meddler	Personnel Clerk
Grim Rectum	Planner
Jerk Jerkins	Engineer – Mechanical
Tina Droop	Executive Secretary
Marcus Mule	Financial Analyst
Rhonda Grinder	Secretary
Eric von Shithead	Industrial Relations Clerk

All of these corporites, we learned, have titles that reflect their status (and power over others) in the corporation. All of them are subject to the laws of progression that changes these titles - and their power over others. These simple laws were:

LAW 1: You will progress only when you "do your job well".

LAW 2: Your "job competency" will be judged by someone above you.

THE LAWS OF EXECUTIVE REGRESSION

It is not hard to understand how many executives become outdated and helpless in a family of "eagles" or "condors". Most have forgotten their chosen technology… called a **has-been**. They also require a new area of expertise, called finance. Being novices here makes them **dummies**. This means that has-been dummies are running companies. Think back to the big meeting we had at Steadfast Meats. This not meant as an insult, it means that as you rise up that ladder of positions you have to take on other skills to control people and profits (budgets) so those superiors can be shown you are "improving" or "doing well."

In view of this it is easy to understand why the following laws are in force at an executive meeting?

LAW 1   Information deteriorates as it moves upwards in a pyramid.

LAW 2   Meetings bring together a group of incompetent assholes who attempt to exchange and present ever deteriorating information in such a way as to impress each other so they can become bigger assholes and affect company profit.

LAW 3   The more general or simple the topic is, the more likely it is that it will get blown out of proportion.

LAW 4   Authorization is quickly given when the authorizers cannot be held responsible should the project fail and when all of them can claim credit should it succeed.

LAW 5   The greater the cost of putting a plan into operation the less the chance there is of abandoning the plan - even if it becomes irrelevant.

LAW 6	The higher the level of prestige accorded the people behind the plan, the lesser the chance of abandoning it.
LAW 7	Rationality will prevail only when all other possibilities have been exhausted.
LAW 8	The more distant the participants are from the facts the more likely they are to believe what they hear.
LAW 9	The amount of time spent on detailed discussions can be inversely proportional to the financial commitment.
LAW 10	If a majority of the attendees are responsible for a miscalculation no one will be at fault.
LAW 11	Justification procedures will become more difficult as the cost decreases.

It is because this is rooted in one's own progression in the Peter Principle. Here are the primary issues that take people deep into the AQ Virus away from the corporation where one family works passionately as one unit. This shift is inevitably reflected by these characteristics:

- They usually have forgotten the discipline they used to get the position.
- They have picked some business related education or experience.
- They have developed boardroom brawling techniques.
- They have picked up "bottom line" savvy.
- They have learned to treat people like assholes.
- They are not shy about successfully telling people they are assholes!
- They made it through the Big Transition into management.
- They have somehow successfully come through the Great Transition.
- They have a very high AQ.

Because an executive has moved into a world where boardroom brawling and the use of this AQ arsenal takes up a majority of his time, this distinguishes them in the corporate pyramid. But they have usually elevated the AQ through the AQ phases of calling, treating and telling so they are good at it. This means that they can treat others like assholes and get away with it as part of normal function. It is this aspect that one must pay attention to. The executive arsenals are just the tools that allow the executive to stay in AQ Equilibrium.

It was shown how you can better understand why so many meetings are such a joke. These are the laws commonly working against progress and these are the laws that help AQ's rise quickly. It is this mixture of idealistic approaches and regressive obstacles with which we see executives functioning. This is the corporate playground where the rules are learned and executed by has-been dummies.

We learned that the meeting was the Executives way to convey information, control things, and to get things across rapidly to many others.

Meetings bring together a group of incompetent assholes who attempt to exchange and present ever–deteriorating information in such a way as to impress each other so they can become bigger assholes and affect company profits.

THE SIX EXECUTIVE ARSENALS

We learned that the Executives use various tools which we called arsenals because they are truly weapons executives use and they are consistently applied internationally. I would swear executives have a secret rulebook that comes to them in a flash of light when they attain the title! I have classified them into six major groups, many of which are used in the meetings as a method of control and power/ego maintenance. The arsenals are the ways by which you create assholes rapidly so as to re-align your AQ or impress someone in order to change your position.

Arsenal 1   is the **Offensive Arsenal** used to attack an opponent.

Arsenal 2   is the **Defensive Arsenal** and covers the weapons needed to create a defense against the offensive weapons.

Arsenal 3   is the **Aversive Arsenal** used as offensive or defensive methods. They are there to round out the arsenal.

Arsenal 4   is the **Trouble Makers Arsenal.** It is designed to deal with people who need to be put in their place

Arsenal 5   is the **Cultural Arsenal** and it includes methods outside the boardroom to also align position

Arsenal 6   is the **Manipulators Arsenal**. It is used to get your way.

THE GREAT TRANSITION

We saw how at some point in one's corporate life, if one is to climb upwards into the upper echelon, fly with eagles, sit high up in the tree; one must go through the Great Transition - sort of like a corporate menopause. This happens somewhere in the middle management phase when one has to start letting go of that which he has learned and been trained for - to become immersed more in the methods of business and management. Towards the end of this period, he must also develop his arsenal in preparation for the move into the upper management and executive echelon. If he fails, then the process will be difficult and perhaps even disastrous. Ws saw that The Great Transition involves getting your degree in the second and third levels of training.

If I could possibly summarize the Great Transition, it would probably be that period of time where there is an urgent need to understand and adapt to dealing well with "Boardroom Brawling". I say this because executives spend more and more time in meetings... the boardroom... that is where they jockey for position, power and recognition. If you were to spend most of your time in meetings, it would make sense to gather up a new expertise in performing well at meetings. Clearly, some must be weapons that allow one to survive in the boardroom - that place where executives spend the majority of time. Clearly you can't use your technical skills any more so what can you do when AQ Disequilibrium knocks on your door? My contention is that the majority of the Executive Arsenal is therefore made up of weapons used in boardroom brawling so as to adjust that AQ. It turns out that there are actually six arsenals executives use.

In terms of AQ'ISM these are the secret tools that keep AQ's high. And this little aspect is one of the most significant secrets that executives learn... the art of AQ Equilibrium using the arsenals. How do they do it? Well these tools are very effective in creating assholes so if you need to get the AQ higher to maintain your position, use the tools. If, on the other hand, you find your AQ is too high and you need to elevate your position, try using tools to make yourself look good... at the expense of creating or maintaining assholes. And where is this best accomplished? In the boardroom or in meetings of course!

What we are doing here is quantifying my observations from experience. The people who are deeply addicted to power and control at any means do not even know they are doing these things. To them these tools simply work and if you have to move to the dark side of your nature, "*it is just business*".

In the following chapter we are going to review and detail these Arsenals. Then we are going to look at the tools that the Middle Management Groups have commonly evolved.

Again, I repeat that when you understand what the AQ virus is and how you may be falling to its dark side, you have four choices:

1. **Raise your AQ to be in line with your position.**

27

2. **Raise your position to be in line with your AQ.**
3. **Leave and zero out your AQ.**
4. **Don't engage in the AQ'ISM addiction**

You can learn from all this and laugh about it once you see this AQ process clearly. Remember that:

"If you have ever grown a business, the most glorious part is in the beginning, when your passion is high, you are eager to learn the business, and the people you work with are like family working and prospering together... together, loving every moment of their engagements and efforts, acting as one unit of heart."

In the previous book, we had a preliminary look at the AQ Arsenals of the Executives. We also saw how the AQ'ISM Virus can be measured and monitored. We looked at how the AQ works and got to know the players in an example corporation. It may be usefull to read that book. If you have bought this book 2 and would like to read the first, please send me an email at *ed@edrychkun.com* and I will be happy to send you a free ebook.

Now we are going to look at these arsenal in more detail and also look at Middle Management, then conclude on how to best execute the 4th choice to zero out that AQ and take better control of your corporate destiny.

AQ TOOLS IN THE OFFENSIVE ARSENAL

As we take a good look at the executive's weaponry, we are going to focus on their AQ Tools of the trade. The first toolbox of tricks is the **offensive** group. This is the one that executives use to launch attacks and keep order. The Offensive Arsenal is made up of four main weapons; **Control, Probe, Counter and Attack**, covering the areas of finding, feeling out and attacking victims. There appears to be no mercy in these tactics; all oriented towards control and improving the bottom line. All have a tendency to treat others like assholes, and, of course, be one! Let us deal with each of these weapons in the boardroom arena.

THE CONTROL: ALWAYS CONTROL THE FLOCK

Control is the means of keeping order in a meeting. It gives one the ability to keep any situation orderly by forcing a direct focus on relevant issues. Essentially it is like acting as a policeman who maintains order by simply being present and by also being equipped to enforce the laws if necessary. If we relate this to the boardroom, the laws are not quite as clear but the need for order and focus is critical. Otherwise the issues at hand are not likely to be solved. In addition, the "controller" must be able to coldly attack to enforce order so that a focus is maintained. This is not a place for some babbling pipsqueak. Any meeting can typically be broken into six components:

CONTROL

1. **INTRODUCTION** Starting from a general premise, this is the process of bringing in a general purpose, objectives and summary of what is to transpire.
2. **PRESENTATION** This segment brings in the information to be presented and assimilated, usually within a set time.
3. **DISCUSSIONS** The presentation is discussed with the intent of reaching conclusions and moving toward solutions.
4. **SUMMARY & CONCLUSION** All proceedings are summarized and conclusions are presented.
5. **DECISION** Some decision is reached, either through vote, veto etc.
6. **ACTION** The decisions, conclusions, etc., are acted upon in some way through assignment or delegation.

Executives remember that meetings are supposed to accomplish tasks quickly, provide interaction for collective solutions, create joint commitment, and communicate information quickly. To accomplish this, the Control tactic must therefore focus on the above six meeting components to ensure that they transpire efficiently. Control is therefore executed in such a way as to force members into focusing on these components - in successive order! They are made up of both statements and questions. The statements are designed to police while the questions are designed to force interaction with focus on key matters - moving towards the conclusions and decisions.

There are two distinct processes that should take place in a meeting. These are **Focus** and **Assimilation**. Focus is the means of maintaining direction, policing towards purpose, moving towards conclusions or focusing on results and objectives. Assimilation is the process that, unlike Focus, allows exchange, interaction, discussion, and action to take place. A meeting, for anyone who is to control it effectively, becomes a constant interplay between focus and assimilation. So it is these two processes that allow control - if they are understood!

The meeting components were Introduction, Presentation, Discussion Summary, Decision and Action. The components introduction, summary, decision and action require mostly focus, while presentation and discussion require mostly assimilation. So a meeting will typically move back and forth from focus to assimilation until some action is taken. The meeting will therefore appear to be under control while Focus is active and out of control when Assimilation is active (particularly if volatile discussions take place or no conclusions are reached). Let us look at Control examples of each.

INTRODUCTION FOCUS

"I am your chairman, our topic is..."
"The meeting will be one hour in length, our objective is..."
"We have five issues to deal with after a quick presentation."
"Our purpose is to make a decision on the proposal before you."
"Questions are to be dealt with after the presentation."
"Any smartass comments will cause immediate dismissal"

PRESENTATION FOCUS

"Please welcome George Jerkoff who is here to..."
"We start with a summary of the proposal from Jack..."
"The presentation will conclude on five recommendations."
"After the presentation we will invite criticism from you."
"Does anyone need any further clarification?"

DISCUSSION FOCUS

"Thank you for your presentation Mr. Mouth."
"We will now spend 20 minutes discussing the recommendations."
"This is a participation type meeting with two objectives."
"If you recall our objectives are..."
"That is not relevant to our discussion."
"This is not the place for emotional outbursts."
"Do you understand what the problem is?"
"We are not interested in negative attacks."
"We do not have time for that."

DISCUSSION ASSIMILATION

"Perhaps Mr. Billowbarf can give us his ideas."
"Are there any other comments?"
"Would you explain to us..."
"Since Mr. Willowturd is our resident expert, he should explain."
"What would your alternate course be Sam?"
"We are still unclear of the intent, what is your impression Jack?"
"What do you suppose would happen if..."
"What have we concluded so far?"
"Are there any points that we have missed?"

SUMMARY & DECISION ASSIMILATION

"Bill would you summarize the main objections?"
"So what are the main courses of action?"
"What have we concluded?"
"The main points are..."
"Are there any conclusions that we missed?"

"Is there enough information to reach a decision?"
"What are the disagreements and major concerns?"
"What actions and decisions have we reached?"

SUMMARY & DECISION FOCUS
"We must make a decision on the following points."
"We are not able to reach a consensus at this time."
"A vote must be taken."
"There is not sufficient time to resolve it."
"We will have to defer any decisions on..."
"We must have a decision by upper management."

ACTION FOCUS
"Frik, you are now authorized to..."
"We will continue this on Thursday at 8:00 A.M."
"Jack you will summarize the decisions."
"George you will be given authority to set up..."
"A formal approval will be submitted by..."
"Once you have prepared a more detailed response..."
"Each one of you will prepare the following..."

It will be noted how, if you are in control, you must police activities with statements which focus on direction and objectives. You also police by questions that make people realize that they are off base. The assimilation process, on the other hand, requires that people are drawn out, they understand the problems, they interact and they exchange ideas in an objective manner. The control will mean that you may not be too popular especially if it makes other egos look bad... so they add to the AQ very effectively::

- There is a need to be unemotional and neutral.
- You will keep notes on key issues, conclusions, points.
- Keep a balanced flow moving.
- Protect members from attackers.
- Focus on content and process.
- Understand the problems.

- Maximize interaction.
- Stimulate alternatives, solutions, and ideas.
- You be a strong individual.

The most skilled Corporites are of course the Executive. They have learned to maintain control and focus. Let us look at some of their simple methods, most of which are not very nice.

THE PROBE: PROBE AND FIND THE STATE OF HEALTH

Probing is a boardroom technique which directs a query at the opponents. A Probe is meant to start the ball rolling - focusing on basic corporate objectives and needs. This assumes that you, the Prober, are concerned about the company and are taking the responsibility of looking out for the company's interests. And what are the company's interests? Profit, Results, Efficiency and Control are key company interests. Now by setting yourself up as this shining, concerned company representative, you automatically infer that your opponent has not clearly followed the same interests so he is on the defensive immediately. Probes are also designed to see how well prepared, how healthy or how organized your opponent is. In addition. Probes are usually left until some material, proposal, project, etc. has been presented or circulated. Although Probes are numerous, here are the main thirteen universal probes:

HERB HOW COME YOU'RE SUCH AN ASSHOLE? WAS IT BUDGETED?

THE PROBE

1. *How much will it cost?*

2. How much will it save?
3. How much will it make?
4. What are the benefits?
5. Who is responsible?
6. What is the payback?
7. Is it budgeted?
8. Is this within policy guidelines?
9. Where is the plan?
10. Is this in the company interest?
11. Where is the supporting detail?
12. How is it controlled?
13. What is the bottom line?

Any one of these Probes can open up someone's defenses should a vague answer follow. That is exactly what they are designed to do - so one can focus on any key area which needs more clarification or requires further analysis.

THE COUNTER: COUNTER AND FRUSTRATE YOUR VICTIMS

Countering allows one to take advantage of his position in the hierarchy. Counter weapons are especially capable of placing the opponent on the defensive quickly. The insinuation process that it conveys is that those who are in the authoritative state to make decisions are not yet convinced of whatever someone is attempting to convince them of. The Counter is a move that immediately assures that the one who uses it is superior in position to the one it is directed at.

The effect is the same even if it is a group that a Counter is directed at. Counters will also focus upon the material of the meeting whether it is presentation, report, exchange, or whatever. Although there are many varieties of Counters, here are the main eleven universal Counters that seem to dominate the methods of executives.

1. *I am not yet convinced.*
2. *We are not yet in agreement.*
3. *How can we be sure?*
4. *Why would we believe this?*
5. *We cannot support that yet.*
6. *I am still not clear on the purpose.*
7. *Can you prove it to us?*
8. *How can we approve this?*
9. *What commitments are you prepared to make?*
10. *What are you telling us?*
11. *Explain to us why.*

Note that these Counters are lacking in being specific. They only infer that the opponent has not yet done something. It is left to the opponent to figure out what to do or say - hence, these counters create a frustrated defensive attitude in the opponent if he cannot recover. Just imagine, if after every attempt to convince your boss of something - say five times at ten minutes a crack - he just says "*I am not yet convinced*". How long do you think your mind will remain logical and unemotional? How long before you break the asshole's nose?

THE COUNTER

Well there are counters to this that we will look at later. But note also that, if you dare, you can attach a specific phrase to a Counter. For example Counter 1. could be more specifically worded as "I *am not yet convinced of the 12% rate of return*" or Counter 5 could be "We *cannot support that until you provide backup analysis to your rate of return calculation*". Counters can be used in general or more specifically - the specifics being decided upon from the meeting context.

THE ATTACK: ATTACK AT THE SIGN OF WEAKNESS

Attacking is conducted in various ways but the purpose is the same - to identify issues, which need better analysis and clarification - before decisions can be made and before the company commits to some course of action that it may regret. An Attack is meant to make someone look stupid for not being thorough enough in convincing the members. Although Attacks can be conducted diplomatically, only the positive group of tree dwellers like Eagles, Hawks, Owls, Falcons, etc. have a tendency to do this constructively.

THE ATTACK

The negative group like Vultures, Condors, etc. will use such opportunities to totally disable and sometimes cripple victims quite permanently if possible. Here are some key universal Kill Techniques:

1. *It is obvious that you are not sufficiently prepared.*
2. *You have wasted our valuable time.*
3. *Why did you not consider these ramifications before?*
4. *How did you ever expect us to approve this?*
5. *You have been totally misguided on corporate objectives.*
6. *The quality of your presentation is embarrassing.*
7. *We should have considered your weaknesses.*

Note that an Attack is launched when a failure has been perpetrated. This means that a probe and counter have identified the fact that someone has not "done his homework". Again, an Attack can be done constructively. Attack 1., for example could have been *"Our discussions indicate that we have insufficient material at this time. We should therefore continue the discussion when we have reviewed it"*. Attack No. 2 could have been *"Although we have spent considerable time on this issue, we have at least resolved a few critical items"*.

These are attacks, however, that assume a fatal conclusion. In reality there is never any guarantee that your opponent is indeed totally disabled and that he will take the crap that has been handed to him. The Probes already discussed were a form of indirect Attack method. They just attempted to identify weaknesses subtly. There are many ways direct attacks are used, all of which put the attacker on the AQ list because they can make one look pretty stupid. Here are some of the most popular well executed by executives to put people in their place and to solicit vital information that "supports" the cause::

HOTSEATING: PUT HIM ON THE SPOT

Hotseating involves placing someone else on the hotseat just to see if one can fry this person. If done properly, the victim cannot escape without third degree burns. The procedure involves picking out someone in the meeting and saying something like the following:

"George has been sitting quietly through our discussions saying very little. And yet he is our resident expert in the area of dynamic models. Perhaps he can give us a quick presentation to clarify matters for us."

"Bill you were involved in the detailed analysis on the cost-benefits. Give us a summary of your findings."

The whole idea of hotseating is to first identify the person as an expert and then "spot light" him for a quick explanation. If he isn't an expert he will look silly, either by acknowledging so, or by attempting a stupid explanation. If he is an expert then the attacker will look good for bringing about an explanation. If one chooses the time (confusion) and the topic (something the guy knows only a little about) he may be foolish enough to open his mouth - to destroy his credibility.

Hotseating is used effectively to keep meetings flowing and on focus. This we talked about in the Control discussion.

SHOTS: READY, SHOOT, AIM

Shots are used to "take shots at" an opponent. Taking a shot means that one must be fairly certain that his point is valid or it could backfire. Shots are most effective when one can pick upon some conflict, change of opinion, error, etc. that someone else has made.

Shots can be used to anger someone. The intent is to make him voice wild emotional outbursts, raising his voice, or to look like a fool.

"Jim, just fifteen minutes ago you said that you had supported the idea, now you don't want anything to do with it. Why can't you make up your mind?"

"Flash, you took the responsibility to implement those procedures. The 200% budget overrun cannot be blamed on anyone else."

"Your calculations are wrong Scooter. Do you or your staff take the honors for such stupid incompetence?"

"Frank, you are the chairman, why do we have to listen to this irrelevant dribble that he is giving us?"

It should be noted that the attacker should always carry a calculator so that he can check simple numbers while others argue. It is quite likely that one will indeed find some simple error. But even the simplest of errors, if detected, can annihilate any good proposal. Here are the annihilate statements:

"How many other errors are there in your proposal?"

"Jim you have become emotional about the issue. Perhaps we should ask you again when you have checked your calculations."

"So now that you admit you made the error, tell us why it occurred."

"How can we have any confidence in the rest of the material."

POWER: DON'T SCREW AROUND PAL

Power is used only when one has to use to police something with authority and bring fear into the room. Commonly power is used when things have gone out of control:

"I will say this once and only once. We are here to solve a problem and not exchange emotional outbursts."

:"You are not in charge. You will obey this order or resign."

"I have stated that you have exactly half an hour to resolve the conflict. You have two more minutes."

"Your comments are out of order and irrelevant. You are dismissed from this meeting."

"I am telling you to do it that way. It is not a decision that you can make."

"The next presentation is at 2:00 sharp. At that time you will all be better prepared."

"You are all emotional assholes. Report back in two hours.":

Power is used to maintain order or to squash disobedience. It goes without saying that one must be in a position of power to be able to use it. It is a good way to increase your AQ rapidly as well.

INTIMIDATION: DO YOU KNOW HOW TOUGH I AM?

Intimidation invokes the use of scare tactics to either get commitment, clarification or to get the opponent/victim to back off, even give in. Here are some examples:

"Are you prepared to make a commitment to your stated 25% rate of return?"

"Are you telling us that all these cost benefits are going to materialize within six months?"

"Do you really believe that you can accomplish that target date?"

"Do I understand you correctly when you say that you guarantee the results?"

"Am I hearing you say that if we do an audit that your costs will be in order?"

"Does that mean that you will resign if you cannot meet the objectives?"

"You undoubtedly know what happens to the assholes who fail on their commitments?"

The process infers ominous courses of action should a failure occur. In addition, the statement allows the intimidator to word the commitment the way he wants to hear it - not the way it may have been suggested. A good intimidator will always subtly include an ominous threat to get a commitment or a back down from the position. He is brief, assertive and forceful.

CHALLENGE: PUT UP OR SHUT UP

Very similar to intimidation is the Challenge. It has the purpose of getting a commitment or a back down by issuing a challenge - either directly or indirectly:

"My people suggest that the best you could accomplish is a 4% return on investment, not 12% as you have stated."

"There are three people in this room that say you cannot do it."

"Why do you feel that you can succeed when so many before you have failed?"

"I agree with George - you are not mature enough to handle this responsibility."

"You have not performed this type of work before so why should we believe you are capable?"

Note that the challenge has a tendency to question the opponent's capabilities and even his intelligence. It has a tendency to precipitate commitment from the silly bugger who the comment is directed at - sometimes through sheer emotion - just to prove the challenging asshole wrong. An outburst simply reduces the one who falls victim.

THREAT: YOU BETTER BE RIGHT

The threat also deserves mention, since it has an effect of its own. The threat is a cross between a Challenge and an Intimidation. Here are some examples:

"Do you understand fully the consequences of failure or should we point them out to you?"

"What do you think the executive recourse would be if your target is not achieved?"

"Your annual increase will be set at the amount above your projected return on expenditures. Anything less than that will yield a decrease. Do you agree?"

"The company will not look kindly upon any budget or time overrun."

"Our reports indicate that your costs are out of control. Before we take action what do you suggest as a solution?"

In this case, the threat carries some gruesome connotations should the commitment not be achieved. The threat, however, cannot be executed by anyone without authority. An indirect threat can be made, on the other hand, by suggesting consequences. Sometimes that is just as effective.

FRIGHT: SCARED - OF COURSE YOU ARE

The fright is used in a similar manner to the threat except that you need not have authority. The whole idea behind this weapon is to provoke anxiety in the opponent. The approach is much more indirect than a threat. It is basically left to the individual to be aware of and to decide upon the possible consequences of his folly. *"If you do that you will get fired"* is a threat that will cause fear. *"If you do that you will suffer bad consequences"* is a threat, which will cause anxiety. And Anxiety will slow your opponent down as his mind is considering these consequences. Here are some more examples:

"You are going to regret this action if you persist."

"Better think this out first before the executives hear about it."

"I wish I had enough courage to ignore the potential bad consequences of your plan."

"Suffering shitballs Man! Do you have any idea what could happen?"

"You and only you will suffer if you are wrong."

The more nebulous the threat of consequences, the greater the potential anxiety of the opponent - as his mind works quickly to decide what they could be.

Now we are ready to see some of the defenses used to counter these. This group of tactics is the Defensive Arsenal.

2

AQ TOOLS IN THE DEFENSIVE ARSENAL

Again we follow from the lead of the executive who has evolved some simple nasty tools to keep power, order and focus. The Defensive Arsenal, unlike the Offensive Arsenal, is made up of weapons for defense purposes. Clearly, they are aimed at avoiding, averting, deflecting and confronting offensive weapons that may be used on them. If we look at meetings in general and what can happen, we will see that there are various phases of personal trouble - trouble being when things start going wrong for any individual.

Closer inspection reveals various phases of defense or deception. Consider the example where a report has been prepared for presentation. This document could be prepared to create the air of thoroughness or completeness where, in fact, it is not. This type of possible deception, and the continued cover-up, requires special defensive weapons. The preparation of the deception itself requires special weapons. But even if it is not a purposeful deception, and some spontaneously detected flaws show a weakness, special weapons are needed.

Thus someone may start to uncover or suggest a flaw in some material, argument or whatever. The owner is then in the need of defensive weapons otherwise the attacker will be quick to point out one's weakness. Whether one attempts to hide something one purposely tries to cover, or whether one is defending something being ill-prepared on does not matters once an attack is launched; the process is the same. Phases 1 and 2 involve the cover-up itself - the process of keeping the enemy away from the area being covered up.

The third phase involves the tact taken when penetration actually occurs. Someone is aware of what is the flaw but cannot as yet prove it. The fourth phase exists when one is caught and needs to gain a recovery before being totally destroyed. Let us summarize the four **Phases of Deception**.

> **Phase 1 - Plan or create the means of hiding a weakness**
> **Phase 2 - Keep the opponents away from a weakness**
> **Phase 3 - Divert from the detected weakness**
> **Phase 4 - Recover from the attack**

If you have ever watched a bird protect a nest, you will see the picture quite clearly. First, the bird tries to hide its nest. Secondly, should an enemy approach, it tries to keep it far away from the area by diverting attention to itself- even though the enemy has not yet spotted the nest. Thirdly, when the enemy detects the nest, the bird attacks by dive bombing the enemy or trying to use itself as more desirable bait, even if it could be eaten. If all fails, the bird itself gets caught or it flies off to save itself as best it can. So just as we had the Probe, Counter and Attack in the Offensive Arsenal, we have the **Conceal, Divert, Deflect and Recoup** as main weapons in the Defensive Arsenal.

Now if you happen to find this hard to believe or you just can't see yourself being involved in deception, just think about your own meeting experience. How many times have you had some fat balding buzzard trying to pick away at your material, trying to show that you don't know what you are talking about? How many slick vultures have you seen totally destroy all your good hard work by blowing out of proportion some trivial item on costs? And how many times have you tried to get approval on something as quickly as possible, without imbedding piles and piles of crap that you know is beyond their intelligence anyway? Wouldn't you just love to short-circuit your way through all those assholes that don't know what you are talking about? Wouldn't you just love to put these cockroaches back under their boards? Let us look at some of the ways the executives use for defending themselves..

The Defensive Arsenal, as you will have gathered, is made up of countering weapons - against Probes, Counters and Attacks from the Offensive Arsenal. We have identified these as Concealment, Diversion and Deflection. At the end of the sequence is the Recoup that allows some form of recovery from various wounds that might have been inflicted. I have known many experts at these tactics. You will recognize them I am sure.

THE CONCEALMENT: HIDE THOSE WEAK AREAS

There are various needs for concealment at certain times, regardless of whether such concealment is done on purpose or because someone is poking around looking for a weakness. If for example, you have conducted what you considered a thorough study, written a great report and made a super presentation, then you would expect that the executives would just honestly accept your recommendations - right? That could well be the case but it is not likely, for the various probes, counters and attacks that are aimed at your material could quite easily reveal a weakness or something you just bloody well forgot at the time. You can rest assured that the detection of this - even if honestly admitted - could easily result in a total destruction and refusal of all your hard work. Why else do you have executives? So do you take the chance or do you launch a play to conceal your underbelly? Most likely you will elect the ploy and add to your AQ virus.

On the other hand, if you know that the executives are only interested in whether the idea makes money, then why would you present all of the triple integration formulas from Differential Calculus, which were used to prove new theories in Wave Form Transmission. Anyway, it may be that a consultant did it so why not just reference it with the hope that they will not have some freaky haired Mathematician there to make you prove the idea? So why not launch a little ploy to conceal your underbelly? Most likely you will elect to use the ploy. So it matters not whether you have purposely tried to conceal or you are trying to cover yourself from some vicious probes - the idea is the same.

YES THOSE FIGURES DIDNT ADD UP DID THEY... BUT LET'S JUST LOOK AT THIS FIGURE..

CONCEALMENT

Concealment can work in several ways but is mostly applied to presentations or reports, sometimes both together. Let us consider a scenario where Flick Smoothy is preparing a report for an executive meeting where the material is to be presented. Flick, in his wisdom, has forgotten that his key man who prepared the Appendix 3 on costs, is on vacation. Flick has also detected an error in addition but the right number does not balance with the other number on some following pages. Since the report has been circulated Flick cannot correct it and to his horror he cannot explain the $3.20 error. In the back of his mind he knows about Grizz Buzzard, the Vice President of Finance who just happens to have incredible expertise in finding these little things out and using them to demolish and discredit good work. What is Flick to do? Flick needs to use Concealment because even if he admits it at the meeting, old Grizz will have his nuts in a bag and if Grizz catches the imbalance then Flick is going to lose more than just his nuts.

So when Flick holds the presentation, he uses two concealment weapons, those of Veneer and Flash. The Veneer approach allows Flick to sum figures to the nearest $10,000 so this will quickly eliminate any problems with dollars and balances. This way he can talk about costs without fear. The Flash approach then allows Flick, in his presentation, to scurry through the section just as fast as possible. If he Flashes fast enough, he can skip the section and just mention summary numbers in his overview. Let us look at several of these Concealment tools:

VENEER: NICE LOOK BUT BAD BODY

Veneer is used as we just saw, to give the appearance of a solid body by presenting a polished surface. The Veneer is also useful in superficial explanation of details. Here are some examples:

Conceal Errors -Just as Flick decided to round his numbers to the nearest $10,000. This immediately covers any errors where numbers are smaller.

Conceal Ignorance - It may be necessary because of a lack of knowledge or support, to speak only in general terms but in a thorough fashion.

Conceal Incompetence - Because of incompetence it may be necessary to speak of irrelevant credentials and projects that create an air of competence.

Conceal Incompleteness - Because of a lack of thoroughness it may be useful to have detailed generalities.

Whatever way you look at Veneer, however, it looks good and it makes sense. Here are some ways that Flick would have used Veneer:

"All figures are rounded to the nearest 10,000 since we leave details to more junior employees. Numbers more accurate are not significant nor are they required at this time."

"There are 37 different cost headings only three of which are important enough to talk about here."

"To develop the idea we have had a Mathematician, an Economist and a Financial Analyst all of whom worked in the research area."

"We have 120 headings to cover but time is of the essence. Each will take 20 minutes so we should choose only key ones. I have chosen two for today."

You can see that the whole idea of Veneer is to create a superficial cover up to hide errors, ignorance, competence, completeness or whatever you feel may be inadequate. It is done with polish. Here are some other methods.

FLASH: WHIP IT BY QUICKLY

Once again we saw Flick use the Flash method when he scurried through the bad section as if nothing was wrong and it wasn't important anyway. This way he could avoid anyone nosing around too deeply to find something. He would choose the FLASH sequence, however, so that the next item that he would stop at was a highly important item. What we mean to say is that you cannot give your enemy enough time to look around - move quickly to something that will capture his attention immediately. This will usually be something he specializes in but also make sure that you are also versed in this stop point. You must state that it is a more important section.

AVOID: LEAD THEM AROUND IT

It may be possible to avoid a bad area, especially if you are giving the presentation. Just as the FLASH method was used to whip through and into special topics, one may choose to just lead them around until there is no more time or until they probe. Hopefully they won't probe! And if they do, there are other weapons to use. If you recall the little bird, he would flap around in an area away from the nest, with the hope of getting the enemy further and further away.

VOLUME: GIVE THEM QUANTITY TO CHEW ON

There is nothing more intimidating than a pile of thick volumes and reports. With virtually no hesitation, like a duck to water, Mr. Executive will head for some kind - any kind - of summary to get clued into the relevant financial stuff. It goes without saying, therefore, that these guys prefer not to look through it but rather like to look at it since it suggests that "*the troops have done their homework*". What the ding-dongs are incapable of figuring out themselves is whether all that stuff really makes any sense. Even if the volumes come from outside the company, it will normally be assumed that all the material is "*homework*". This will be true only if the appropriate overviews, summaries, etc. have been provided - up front! If there are no summaries, then the executive will have no choice but to have someone inspect all the homework to evaluate and summarize it. That is when poor material can be detected.

The moral is: Give'm bulk and give'm an overview. But also give them little time to evaluate the bulk. So executives like to use one-liners to reference Appendices filled with details. It most likely will create the air you they need - a thorough study.

REFERENCE: FOOL THEM WITH A REFERENCE

If you have ever picked up a paper, book or bulletin on legislation such as tax laws, you will fully understand the unsurpassed value of referencing for causing confusion and legitimizing pure horseshit. Consider this: "*In accordance with Section 30(a) and in consideration of paragraph 3, item ii under sub-section 306 entitled Gross Negligence, the fourth amendment hereafter classified as pure bullshit (errata 34a(iii) dated July 13, 1985) is expressly prohibitive under Section 10-(a) but notwithstanding clause 13 of paragraph 4, item 2."*

Now who the hell can shovel his way through this and still understand what is being said? Only a few lawyers may be sufficiently demented to flip flop back and forth between 25 different pages and maintain a constant level of ignorance.

There are two notions brought about by Referencing, mainly confusion and substantiation. These are brought about by the cross referencing as noted in the above example, for when you flip to paragraph 3, item ii you will undoubtedly find some equally frustrating dribble that makes you flip again, and again and again and again. If you create a chain of flip-flops it won't take long to lose sight of where you started. Moreover, you will get someone so pissed off they may even forget what it is you were doing. Substantiation means that somewhere at the end of the chain is the crucial document that substantiates the original statement. This could well be an external book, paper or whatever and it is unlikely that anyone will trace, seek or want it.

The illusion of thoroughness, completeness and even competence can therefore be created superficially through a cris-cross network of impenetrable bullshit and a list of some goofy papers. So the idea of referencing is indeed useful and it has its place. Executives can stop everyone dead in their boots with: *"that is not true Mr. Hisser, if you and your four doubters care to read the July 1921 issue of Scientific Horflehuff, you will see that your opinion is a bit out of date."*

DETAIL: SCARE THEM WITH A FORMULA

There are times at which you may want to throw in some details. Details have a tendency to indicate thoroughness and competence, regardless of whether true or not. There are two ways to use detail. The executives typically use deceive and bluff. The second is to convey superiority. As we already mentioned, large reports are not likely analyzed by executives if executive overviews are provided. The awesome volumes of junk that may follow behind the summaries serve to back up the conclusions. Any backup with formulas in them is an immediate means of giving the executives brain seizure - it just won't compute. What it does absorb, however, is an impression that: *"the turkey who wrote this stuff sure does know his business."* Even though such detail may piss someone off for being included in an executive report, he will still wrongly or rightly have a first impression of thoroughness and competence.

The moral is then, that such material can be scattered about through reports, proposals, etc. to create a positive deception - but it must be remembered that come presentation time, it is a deception and it may be better to conceal it. The second use is to convey superiority. Needless to say a quick slide, overhead or handout with equations, formulas etc. may not be what executives want to talk about, but one might want to Flash to such a stop point, provided one is versed in such detail. Executives have learned that if not pushed too hard it will instill the image of technical competence and superiority in their heads. If they know that some member is a bit interested in one of the special areas, the application of Detailing can waste considerable time unless one wants to waste time. So through this second use, a new avenue is available - that of wasting time.

As we look at the weapons of concealment we can see that they can be used quite effectively in a positive sense as well - it just depends upon the needs at the time. In addition, the methods can be applied to presentations and material.

THE DIVERSION: DIVERT THEM AWAY FROM WEAKNESSES

The diversion becomes necessary when the enemy is close to finding your cover-up. The weapon of Diversion is used to keep the foe away from the potential problem area - so that it is not a problem. Sometimes one may have detected the weakness only when the enemy has sniffed around a bit. If that is true, one must act fast to divert him away from any vulnerable area. If for example, one just realized that there is a simple calculation that is wrong - where some totals don't balance - but one is close to agreement, would one not want to keep old Grizz Buzzard, the V.P. of Finance away from his calculator? One surely would, especially when there have been horror stories about the mean bastard demolishing so many proposals that had poor arithmetic. In fact one may even jump on the table and try to make the old fart laugh so it could distract him - in shear desperation! Remember that a diversion is required to get the enemy away from the area where he happens to be sniffing around, but as yet has not found the smell source. Just like the bird, one has to distract him in a different direction - away from the nest.

NOW MISS PRISKET, WHAT DID YOU SAY ABOUT YOUR COST OVER RUN?

THE DIVERSION

To perform a dance on the table may be a bit more than one requires so executives would deploy the Fast Forward method on old Grizz. If all are all obviously looking at some pages in a report that show various cost tabulations. Grizz and others are poking away at the pages. One would want to make sure that Grizz does not look at the table on Page 353, so what do one do to get his narrow mind on to something else? A skilled executive would say this: "*Now that you gentlemen have had a chance to inspect this section, I would direct your attention to the more critical section on rate of return, page 200. Since this is a key area in finance, perhaps Mr. Buzzard will lead off on questions*". Guess who will quickly move to page 200 and guess who just got Hotseated? Here the executive statement just combined a Fast Forward technique with the Hotseat method to divert our dear old Mr. Buzzard - a successful Diversion. There are several ways to execute an effective diversion. Let us now look at these diversions.

FAST FORWARD: FORGE AHEAD QUICKLY

We have seen the Fast Forward technique used on Mr. Buzzard. Clearly, it is meant to dilute any efforts that may lead to an attack. In a presentation, where one is temporarily in control, the fast-forward is executed by just moving quickly to a new item, topic or section. Similar to the Flash, or used in conjunction with it, one can move away from something that may cause trouble, embarrassment or grief.

"We have spent too much time on that issue and should move to the next item."

"This item must be discussed outside of this meeting."

"We do not have time to waste on this item."

"The next item on the agenda is..."

"Mr. Droner, we are wasting valuable time. Can we not move to the next item?"

"Must we expend our valuable time on such Huff and Wind? Let us move on."

"These matters are trivial and irrelevant. We must deal with more serious issues."

The above examples serve to show the use of Fast Forward - just like a video or audiotape - you simply move quickly to pass over undesirable material.

FALSE BATTLE: AVOID THE REAL FIGHT

The false battle is commonly used to throw the opposition off course. Typically this is executed by using some unimportant issue as a decoy. If one can succeed in doing this, several things can be accomplished. First one may find out the strengths and weakness of the opponents and secondly, one may find who the enemies or supporters are. One may also wear out the opposition and lose a minor issue to gain a major point. More important one can minimize the time for a real issue and just waste time if so desired. By raising a good battle, one could embroil others for some time. This is a common executive tactic.

"We appreciate your concern over that Mr. Gripple but what about the error in Section 2?"

"Pork stated at the management meeting last week that you were an asshole. Why would he say that?"

"How can we talk about the cost/benefit analysis when the problem of coffee breaks hasn't been settled?"

"Here we are trying to solve serious problems and the coffee hasn't arrived. We should fire the tardy bastards."

"Before we move on, can someone explain to me why we didn't meet last week when we should have?"

"This waiting around is supreme bullshit. Do we have to put up with this?"

The examples will give you the idea, even if they may be silly. Unless you have a smart chairman, however, the silliest things can be blown out of proportion.

PISS OFF: AGGRAVATE THE EMOTIONAL SIDE

The Piss Off is a severe form of False Battle. The big difference here is that one is not trying to focus attention on some other issue. The tactic attempts to focus on some person to get him pissed off and emotional. Piss offs usually precede emotional outbursts and subjective diversions that an executive can then attack with vigor. This, in turn, can lead to a lack of concentration and destruction of focus. If this can cause someone to blush, stutter, sweat, leave, become hostile or avoid eye contact, then one has succeeded in the aggravation ploy. There are numerous ways to piss someone off and executives are expert at this. Here is a common group called the "**10 DIRTY D'S**"

1. **DISDAIN** - Use disdainful phrases like *"my dear boy"* which imply haughtiness and arrogance. *"I don't think you understand"* or *"look my dear fellow"* are sure-fire methods to aggravate a person.

2. **DEGRADE** - Discredit his credentials. If he has a PhD then say he has a BSc. Say things like "*Mr. Dingdong here, has a BSc. in Goofology so we must heed to his advice."*

3. **DRESS** - Pick on oddities in appearance: *"How can you stand that tie?", "Your suit should be pressed", "How do you get seagull shit on your pants?", "What an awful suit - do you sleep in it?", "Do you know about the company dress code?"* These are sure to embarrass someone.

4. **DECIDE** - Whenever possible decide for him "*Well since you can't decide, you should...",* or "*If I were you I would...",* or *"You should..."* are all ways that will aggravate someone. "*Why don't you make a decision?"* will also create aggression.

5. **DEFACE** - Pick on some habits - personal ones. "*You should see a doctor about your twitch"* or "*Have you seen a specialist about your zits?"* or "*Do you always pick your nose like that?"* or "*What's wrong. Do you have crabs from*

last night?" or "*Can't you ever stop fidgeting?*" are all good ways of making someone nervous.

6. **DEBASE** - Impair the quality of action. Query persistently why action has not been taken: "*Why have you procrastinated?*", "*Why can't you make a decision?*", "*Why don't you move already*", "*What is your problem?*", "*How long do we wait for action?*" These all debase his ability to act.

7. **DEVOTE** - Devote falsely to him with sarcastic expressions such as: "*My good buddy Willy here says...*", "*My good friend Perkly...*", "*My close associate and friend...*". Invent a relationship that he knows is false.

8. **DUB** - Dub a name in and continue the use of it. If the guys name is Ed, call him Fred or anything that is obviously wrong. If you are corrected, apologize and keep doing it. Do it directly to his face and indirectly as well - the more times the better.

9. **DISTURB** - Disturb him by ignoring most of his hints or suggestions. Also deliberately misunderstand him. Grab offers or suggestions from others that were intended for him. All these actions are meant to disturb his mental processes so as to aggravate him. Also disturb him by acting humble, switching back and forth from subservience to aggression.

10. **DIRT** - Throw up some dirt if you can: "*Why did your secretary go out with you last night Sleeze? Is that why you are tired?*", "*Got pissed up last night did you, Slog?*", "*How is your divorce coming, Flasher?*", "*Oh, by the way Jock, some of the girls were commenting on the porn sites you visit.*". There is an endless variety of Dirt, which can be brought up.

You will have noticed that these are designed to cause some form of embarrassment, anxiety or unease. All of these are meant to distract someone away from that which they are hiding. Silly? Not really... these are used all the time.

WORD CLOUDS: CLOUD THE ISSUE IF YOU CAN

Word clouds are exactly what the expression suggests - a cloud (grouping) of words that together makes it difficult to see the rest clearly. The beauty of a word cloud is that it is meaningless to the real drift of a statement but it can confuse or cloud it's meaning. Word clouds are made up of a combination of three heavy words, two adjectives and one noun that means nothing. For example the words approach, options, capacity and activity are general nouns that typically require more specific information. If we then put some vague adjectives before the vague noun, then we have a word cloud. Words like exceptional, integrated, responsive and synchronized, for example are fairly loose adjectives that can be placed before the noun quite randomly. We could say *"exceptional responsive approach"* or *"synchronized integrated activity"* as an example, with virtually no precise meaning to what one is really talking about: *"So in conclusion we have a responsive, synchronized capacity"*, is a sentence which really doesn't say too much. If we would have said something like *"the development of an on-line system requires further study."* and added a word cloud we might have: *"The integrated responsive options and the development of an on-line system with responsive synchronized capacity requires further study."* Try figuring that one out in enough time to ask an intelligent question or not losing track of the conversation.

It will be noticed how the meaning has not really changed - but the complexity has. If you had heard this sentence, you might be spending a few seconds figuring out what the hell the guy said or meant. And this is exactly enough for you to lose the flow of what is really being said. By the time you have realized it, the topic could have been changed and you dare not ask for clarification. Now the clouds in this case were quite simple. Consider two new meaningless nouns like infrastructure and articulation and some adjectives like encumbered, homogeneous and cognitive: *"The cognitive homogeneous articulation and the development of an on-line system with encumbered cognitive infrastructure requires further study.*" How does this grab you? Do you think that you would ponder awhile before you got the meaning? The clouds have done nothing to the real meaning but they most certainly have clouded it. And if you can't understand what someone means, then how can you query anything?

Word clouds are best made up by individuals that become comfortable with them. To illustrate one can create two columns of words - meaningless adjectives and meaningless nouns. Here are some more examples:

ADJECTIVES	NOUNS
individualized	imputation
motoric	development
systemalized	nonresponsiveness
responsive	rationale
incremental	synthesis
optimized	methodology
subordinated	accreditation
motivational	dynamics
supportable	preclusion
hypothetical	contingency
orchestrated	endeavors
multi-disciplinary	proficiency
pragmatic	permeation
encumbered	consultancy
hypothetical	allocation

Now just try taking any two adjectives and sticking them before the noun in the second column. Then stick this cloud into a simple phrase within a simple sentence. You will see how you can confuse your simple sentence but not change its meaning.

Everyone should have his own little arsenal of potential word clouds. And they can be created for specific applications. Consider for example the following as they apply to computers. This is how those sneakered geeks make a mockery out of intelligent mortals:

ADJECTIVES	NOUNS
computerized	system
analytical	procedures
systemized	methodology
technological	development
interfaced	implementation
logistical	input

The simple statement of *"We need some help"* becomes *"The technological interfaced methodology suggests that we need a logistical systemized input for some help."* by throwing in a few clouds. It can be seen how word clouds can be used not only to confuse issues but to also quite effectively create diversions. Crazy? Many use this unconsciously to look good and impress others.

OUTSIDE CALL: GET HIM OUT QUICK

The outside call is a fairly desperate measure that can be difficult to execute. The whole idea is to get the appropriate guy out of the room, so that the meeting can continue. To execute this, one must be able to leave the room so you must be able to temporarily hand off to someone, let things continue, or stop things temporarily to get outside. Once outside the idea is to get a critical message through to him at the meeting. The best way is to leave a message like *"Please call immediately we have an emergency situation which requires critical attention."* Skilled executives leave a long distance number and have the message from some made up name, say Vera or Duke.

The next trick is to get this message to the switchboard or to the guy's secretary or whomever to bring this message to the troublemaker's attention. If the secretary does not know your voice then it is easy to convey it yourself. If she knows your voice then you may want to drop by his office to pick up his messages so you can 'slip one in' for him and give them to him at the meeting. If this cannot be done then call some secretary that does not know you and tell her the emergency situation and ask if she would do the honors since you do not have any more time to get screwed around by the switchboard - you are calling long distance.

When you go back to the meeting, the results, when the turkey gets the message should be quite predictable - he cannot ignore it, he will not be able to figure it out and it will bother him for quite awhile.

DECOY: MAYBE SOMEONE ELSE IN THE SPOTLIGHT

The decoy method attempts to destroy meeting focus. This can be done in many ways but the main objective is to shift focus to some other person or topic. One method involves the Prod. The Prod involves supporting someone's ideas by suddenly being enthusiastic about it.

"Hank, that was an incredible idea you just mentioned, would you expand on it for us."

"Now why didn't we think of that idea, Slim, tell us more."

"About ten minutes ago Olga mentioned some other areas which are important. Let us discuss those first."

The Prod gets someone else to speak about something else - putting this person into the spotlight. This can create a good diversion.

Another method involves **the Suck**. The Suck is similar to the Prod with the exception that one will spotlight the person rather than the idea.

"I just learned that Dr. Dork here was involved in a space research project. Tell us about your project doctor."

"Why Mr. Dingleberry, we didn't realize you were educated at Harvard. Tell us about your background."

"When did you become an expert in that area, Spurt? How did you have time?"

Basically encourage someone to talk about himself - suck him into the spotlight. Hopefully this will waste time and allow a good diversion to take place.

A third method could be appropriate if one is not the chairman. This is called **the Hassle**. The hassle is designed to provoke the chairman, thereby diverting the focus and attention of any topic. This is done using 8 steps:

1. **you can make him skim ideas or insist on stretching others out.**
2. **influence the choice of speakers or topics.**
3. **urge him to interrupt some or encourage others.**
4. **criticize the way he handles something.**
5. **complain loudly about wasting time.**
6. **point out trivial matters.**
7. **keep reminding him about time and topic.**
8. **get him to take notes.**

These eight items are guaranteed to piss off most chairmen. The results can quite easily force new focus.

Another method is **the Switch**. The switch differs from the others by using a new issue as a decoy. The hope is to provoke some action that causes a diversion. One can introduce a passionate issue that was discussed before. One can switch to someone else's argument that was brought up before. One can force a confrontation on a minor issue and then give in for a cheap victory.

The four main decoys are meant to shift things around for a while so that certain critical things can dilute or even be missed altogether.

DODGE: ANSWER THE WRONG QUESTION

The dodge is used to fuzz an argument, but at the same time creating an absolutely irrelevant answer that appears to be right on target. Politicians are experts in this area. Here is an example of Dodge Duets:

QUESTION: *"Slapper, what is your opinion on the rising costs?"*
ANSWERS: *"Rising costs is not the decisive factor. It is the decreasing specifications of systems."*

"Costs, costs, that's all I ever hear about. What about all your labor problems?"

"That's a real good question Flash, I can't think of a more pressing problem looking for a solution. It certainly deserves high priority."
"What's wrong with the costs?"

"It deserves serious study. It's like our inflation rate. What do you think of the inflation rate?"

"Opinions are of little use. We need facts not fiction. What are the facts of the matter?"

"I am suspicious of rising costs."

It will be noticed that the idea is to pick upon some little thing in the question, no matter how small. Grab it and discuss it as if it were the main focus. Make vigorous objection - it may start an argument. This way can easily cause a diversion. Be sure to be neutral on the main issue.

CIRCLE TALK: CATCH THEM IN A LOOP OF WORDS

Circle talk is used to screw up the discussion to the point where no one except you knows where the conversation is going or has gone. The idea is to trap the others in an endless circle of flip talk to exasperate the opponent. Let us assume that you have been asked a very pointed question by Dick Hotseater. You just stare at him for some seconds until he feels he has you in his grip and demands:

Dick *"You still have not answered the question."*

You   *"Just what was the question?"*

Dick *"In simple terms it is this ...."*

You   *"That's not the same question you asked before."*

Dick *"Please answer the question."*

You   *"Which one? The first or last one?"*

Dick *"The last one please."*

You   *"Can you repeat it please?"*

Dick *"It is this ...."*

You   *"I don't really understand the question."*

Dick *"Christ, are you demented?"*

You   *"Is this the way you behave at all meetings?"*

You can see by the example how you can circle around frustrating the guy until he says something more specific that you can grab to pull a real diversion on - or another Dodge for example. Here is another example:

Sam   *"How did you arrive at that decision?"*

Stick *"Because I used logic."*

Sam   *"How do you know it was logical?"*

Stick *"Because I took logic."*

Sam   *"But how can you prove that it was logical?"*

Stick *"Because I made the decision."*

Sam   *"How does that make it logical?"*

Stick *"It works doesn't it?"*

This rather simple minded exchange can frustrate some rather cool people because they get trapped into the circle quite easily. As they get caught into it they just get more and more exasperated. The more it continues, the more likely is some emotional outburst that can be used against them.

DRONE: BORE THEM TO DISTRACTION

The drone method comes quite easy to most boring people. To someone not quite boring it is fairly difficult to execute because it means that you must speak in a dull constant monotone - rambling on and on to force distraction. The drone is quite hard to stop unless someone tells him to shut up. Consider this : *"Well if you read the tables - you know the tables - then that would be it. That's what I mean and I don't mind saying that the tables were hard to get. Well, you know what I mean. It's quite a lot of effort to get a table. I heard that a table was once a guys undoing - hope that it don't happen to me. Anyway, it's a case in point, you know, for appreciation and I don't mind telling anybody. You know. Actually I found one of the numbers was really tough, you know, it took five days to balance it, you get the picture, hey. Or do you get the picture? I don't mind telling you just in case. Its like this..."*

Can you just imagine how long it would take this guy to get through a complete report, never mind just one little table! If one can turn on the drone at the right time, it can quite easily bore people to distraction and even create a diversion because one can ramble on to various topics at leisure.

PRETENCE: PRETEND TO HAVE WHAT YOU HAVE NOT

Pretense is exactly as it suggests - pretending. If an executive can see some trouble coming, he may want to use pretense. The best way is to pretend that he has power, support, authority, approval, more education, etc., etc., so as to put the opponent at a disadvantage - particularly if he has inferred that one does not have something. Consider the following statements:

"I was given authority from the top well before you came."

"There is no way that I will support that."

"The Vice President has given me all the support I need."

"I don't agree with that, you have not convinced me."

"My support comes right from the top."

"You can ask the president if you don't agree."

You can see the pretense that is being attempted in each case. If the pretence were stated with a forceful assertiveness, what would your reaction be? The attacker may well leave well enough alone.

THE DEFLECTION: DEFLECT THEM IF YOU CAN

The Deflection is required when your opponent has realized that one may be hiding something and he decides to come in for a closer look. In other words our little birdie has failed to foil the intruder who is heading straight for the nest. Now what can the birdie do except try to deflect the intruder in some way. At this point, deflections can take some fairly dramatic forms depending upon how desperate the bird is - even to the point of using itself as bait. It may even try some direct attacks. This may seem hopeless, but many a tiny birdie has thwarted some rather awesome intruders - right?

THE DEFLECTION

Let us, for example, carry on with old Grizz Buzzard, the V.P. of Finance, who is pecking away at his calculator, adding up the numbers which you know are wrong. As his beady eyes shine with glee at his findings Slick Smoothy knows four things. First, the numbers are not relevant to the main conclusions, second, the rotten shit will discredit the whole report if he finds it, third, he is is close to an agreement, and fourth, he better do something fast! But as Slick is thinking, Grizz puts his calculator down and speaks with a sardonic grin: *"Mr. Smoothy"* he crackles, *"I hope that the quality of your report is not reflected in these simplistic calculations which I detect in error."* Well, what would Slick's answer be? How about this: *"Yes, Mr. Buzzard, I noticed this just this morning but it was to late to change it. Fortunately, this section, which was specially checked by your Assistant Vice President Mr. Wimpledork is not relevant to our conclusions. The rest I have double checked myself."* What do you suppose Grizz would counter with? In fact, Wimpledork didn't check anything. But he is not there and how would old Grizz know? Grizz is not likely to attack because he may injure himself. This is a successful deflection. Mr. Smoothy just pulled a Bluff with some Bullshit thrown in to a Buck Pass, three deflection weapons. And even if Grizz finds the truth later, by taking the senile old Wimpledork to task, it would be too late. Anyway, Mr. Smoothy could use some other weapons like Play Dumb or Delegate. These are certainly not my favorites but nevertheless they are used all the time. Let us take a closer look at these commonly used weapons.

BLUFF: ABSENCE IS CAUSE FOR GUILT

The Bluff was performed by Mr. Smoothy in the above example. The process suggests that you are gambling - by inferring that you have something that you do not really have. The key to a bluff is to present it in such a way that the opponent is not able to call the bluff easily and even if he does he may still not win. In the example above the bluff was that Grizz's man Mr. Wimpledork had checked the results. If this was true then he couldn't do very much about discrediting the work. If this was not true, there was no way of proving this easily and anyway, getting Wimpledork on the carpet at this time was not exactly a relevant move. So the best thing to do would be to back off and not lose more by calling the bluff. So the bluff involves the creation of a ploy that suggests whatever alternatives are taken, it would be a no win situation and to call the bluff would possibly result in greater agony.

BULLSHIT: LIE AND DECEIVE CAREFULLY

Bullshiting is what Mr. Smoothy included in his bluff. The Bullshit was that old Wimpledork checked the numbers. Although this could have been true, it didn't really matter to the Bluff because it would have been assumed as true - simply because it was tabled so gracefully. But in fact it was just a lie which would probably not be uncovered until later. If you noticed, however, Mr. Smoothy did not say that he got Wimpledork to check the numbers, he said that the numbers were checked by Wimpledork. This means if Grizz finds out the truth, then Smoothy could say that he had delegated the job.

At any rate bullshit is just bullshit - there is no other way to describe it. It is a purposeful lie or deceit. But it must also be done carefully, for if you get caught you may regret the consequences.

CON: REVEAL LITTLE BUT HINT A LOT

The con is for those not strong enough at heart to try straight Bullshit. It is a lighter version of the Bluff and Bullshit. The idea is to move the focus to some information that has some bearing on a failing case, but in such a way that access to it may not be immediate:

"I heard something the other day but can't remember the source."
"I never believe rumors but ..."
"Well, I happen to know from confident sources."
"I have seen a confidential document."

"Are you sure that you were told everything?"

"I spoke to some of the people in your department."

"It was before you took your position."

"I'd love to be able to tell but I can't destroy confidences."

"My reliable sources indicate the contrary."

"I wish I had your confidence."

The method simply introduces doubt on anything that may have been stated against you. The beauty is that you have taken your proof outside and it cannot be revealed easily - particularly if you are to maintain your integrity. So if someone has attacked you and you do not have the stomach to bullshit or pull a bluff, then try a con.

LAUGH: DISARM WITH LAUGHTER

Sometimes you can completely disarm someone by bursting out in laughter - in their face. Laughter can do two things. The first is that it can increase your likeability so that you are more able to get your way. Laughter and humor have a natural tendency for decreasing anxiety, tension and hostility. A little joke or some laughter, if well placed can do wonders for a thick atmosphere. On the other hand, if everybody has the personality of a torn boot and the atmosphere is as dry as a popcorn fart, a well-placed joke may have little effect.

The second aspect is that a burst of laughter, if directed at a serious attack, makes the attack look potentially ridiculous. Just consider how you would feel when the guy you were making look silly just stared right in your face, stood up and started to roar with laughter - when you were expecting him to cry for mercy. Your first thoughts would be to wonder what was said and why it was so funny. And if he keeps laughing, saying "*Goddam Flip that's really funny! Ho Ho Ho...*", how would you react to him? And how would you continue your attack? If you are a vulture or buzzard you might not be side tracked but in many cases you could be disarmed before you know it. So when in trouble, laugh in his face - and keep laughing. Anyway if things are really bad, you might need the relief.

SIDEBALL: LOOK TO YOUR LEFT OR YOUR RIGHT

Sideballing is short for *"side wise eye balling"*. In other words shift a look to someone else. I love to see this one in action. Executives use this method constantly without even knowing it. Here is the scenario: A meeting is being held where you and five other people in your department are discussing costs. It is basically an inter-active meeting as talk moves around freely. Feelo Bigbum, the manager then asks about the high costs of pencils: "*I see we have spent $35000.00 on pencils last quarter. What has anyone to say about that?*" Since you are in charge of pencils, Fello Bigbum does a sideball on you - he stares at you for an answer. As he sideballs you, you immediately sideball Barf Spickens on your left. Everyone then eyeballs Barf, expecting him to respond. If Barf is not smart enough to pull a new sideball or say to you "*Your question, you are in charge*", in which case it would be a backball, he will be stuck with giving an answer. Now if you pull a sideball on a junior, you have just given him the queue to speak so it is not likely that he will backball you. The great thing about sideballing is that you can escape a hotseat or some attack simply by looking at the right person - without saying a word.

Sometimes in meetings where few know what they are talking about, a sideball can go 4 or 5 times before someone is stupid enough to speak.

BUCKPASS: PASS THE HOT POTATO

The buckpass is like the sideball except that something is stated. The buckpass is a combination of Hotseat and Sideball. Let us consider the same situation as we had before with Feelo Bigbum. When Feelo eyeballed you, it was time for you to respond. Since you didn't know about pencils but you knew that Barf Spickens had used pencils last week, you sideball him. At the time that everyone's eyes are searching for either you or Barf to focus on, you pull a Hotseat. *"Barf Spickens here has been using many pencils so he is best qualified to answer the question."* That would be a Buckpass - just pass a hot potato on to someone else before you burn yourself.

The buckpass, therefore, is used when you are stumped or caught on something. Pass it on to someone else so you don't look stupid. If nothing else, it may give you a bit of time to think up an answer or get a clue from someone else.

HANDOFF: MAKE SOMEONE ELSE RESPONSIBLE

As we carry on the scenario we had the Sideball and the Buckpass, now we have the Handoff. Handoffs mean that you are simply delegating the trouble area to someone specifically. It goes the next step from the buckpass in that you are not only suggesting that someone other than you answer, you are suggesting that he be held responsible for an answer. If we get back to our situation with Feelo Bigbum, you may have *said "Barf Spickens here has been using many pencils so he is best qualified. If you gentlemen agree we should have Barf give a complete report to us at the next meeting."* You are attempting to delegate the answer and commit some other poor turkey. Why? Because if you answered the question you would look stupid - and it was really your responsibility so you could be caught at outright negligence. You need time to get those costs, so why not pull a handoff? The handoff is required when you want to make sure that the buck is not passed on any further. And you want everyone to know who is responsible for the answers - those answers that you cannot provide yourself. It is, of course, much easier to execute the Handoff to one of your own staff.

BOOMERANG: REVERSE THE ATTACK

Sometimes, before any of the other Deflective techniques are used, you may want to execute the Boomerang. This technique may allow you to get a better idea of the state of your attacker's health. So you Boomerang his attack. The boomerang uses reversal methods to answer questions with questions, reverse arguments, shift responsibility, and do just about anything possible to see your attacker's state of health. If you find that, indeed, he is in exceptional health, then you may have to back up or "suck back to re-load" so to speak, thereby trying a new maneuver. Consider the following examples:

"Dinkly, you stated just five minutes ago that you did not agree with Sam's comment. Why can you not make up your mind?"

"Mr. Growler, it is difficult for me to understand why you are becoming so emotional about such trivia. Surely we do not have to put up with this?"

"Mr. Pester, provoking people as you are doing is hardly conducive to progress. Maybe we should deal with this later."

"So what is your idea on the issue Mr. Scumbag?"

"Is that all you have to offer? Where is your support?"

"I have listened to your points. They make little sense. Explain them to us."

"You said we need more data. Five minutes ago you didn't need more data. Which is it Mr. Waffle?"

"You're right, Bark, the benefits are nebulous but is that more important than the bottom line?"

"Your argument is not logical. Have you any logic to add?"

"The answer is No. What else do you want?"

"Your comments are destructive Mr. Boomchang. Is this the way all your meetings are run?"

"How is it possible to reach constructive directions for the company when you shit upon ideas like indiscriminant vultures."

"Mr. Hollowhead, let me first correct your grammar so you can try your point again."

"That was ridiculous Mr. Pickle - anything else?"

It will be noticed that virtually anything goes to execute the boomerang. Hopefully it will hit your opponent in the mouth and shut him up. If not you may at least get a better idea on how formidable he is and how many buddies he has. If we relate back to Feelo Bigbum's situation, he may have countered your sideball or your buckpass, and even your handoff by saying *"I am sorry to inform you that the cost of pencils is your responsibility unless you feel it too much Mr. Buckpass. Should I repeat the question for you?"*

What would you do here? Can you execute a Boomerang? How about this:

Buckpass *"Mr. Bigbum, why are you suggesting that the responsibility is too much?"*

Bigbum *"I am suggesting that it is your responsibility."*

Buckpass *"Then why is it too much? You obviously have some problems with competence."*

Bigbum *"Competence is not the issue, the cost of pencils is."*

Buckpass *"You specifically referred to responsibility and competence - everybody heard you. What are your concerns?"*

Bigbum *"I did not specifically mention competence."*

Buckpass *"Then why would it be too much?"*

Bigbum *"I meant it only as a little joke. We are concerned with costs."*

Buckpass *"Such matters can hardly be considered a joke, as you put it. I have just asked Barf to provide us with a thorough report and at the same time he can get valuable experience. Do you also consider that a joke?"*

Bigbum *"No."*

Buckpass *"Mr. Spickens will have a detailed report next week."*

Bigbum *"Thank you Mr. Buckpass."*

Bigbum was no dummy, but his focus, aggression and power began to diminish quite rapidly as Buckpass picked up on some silly little thing and hung on like a horny bulldog. His boomerangs just kept knocking more and more of Bigbum's teeth out - until he couldn't say too much more. Bigbum was had. He couldn't really continue or Buckpass would end up making everybody look stupid - so he backed off. The point is, however, that Buckpass never could answer the cost questions but nobody found that out.

BLAME: PUT IT ON SOMEONE ELSE

When an executive gets into trouble at some point and there appears to be little left to do, then they use a method that shifts the responsibility. The handoff was used to shift the hot potato to someone else. At the time that the handoff was executed, however, no one really knew that it was a hot potato. At some point it could well be the case that the issue is recognized as a hot potato so it is not likely that you will be able to hand it off. That is where you need to use the Blame. Let us return to Mr. Bigbum and Mr. Buckpass. Suppose Buckpass did not Boomerang Bigbum into submission and that he was waiting for a reply. *"I am sorry, Mr. Bigbum, but I do not have the details of those costs at this time"* could be the most graceful answer. *"But Buckpass, you are responsible for those costs. Are you not in charge of pencils?"* could have been the next question. Well, guess who is on the hotseat? How does poor old Bill Buckpass get out of this one? How about this:

"Yes, I am sir, and I meant to tell you yesterday, but Mr. Craggledorf who was assigned to the task has been away and was unable to complete the tabulations."

Fortunately, Buckpass had someone to blame - a fairly easy escape for him. Here are some other examples:

"Why I gave that assignment to Mr. Wissle. He will be held responsible for the error."

"The numbers were derived from Accounting. It is they that need reprimand."

"It seems the committee failed to inform us of their requirements."

"My assistant obviously underestimated the importance."

"It was done by an outside consultant."

"He did not have my authority to do that."

"The computer made a mistake."

"We did not have enough money to complete it."

Blame can be placed upon various things, the most effective being some non-person since a defense is not necessary. Here are a few possibilities:

WORKERS	Your staff, other staff
OUTSIDERS	Consultants, Services, Government
GROUPS	Accounting, Administration, Engineer
MANAGEMENT	Upper, Mid, Lower
OBJECTS	Money, Manpower, Equipment
PROCESSES	Budgets, Systems, Sales
FORCES	Economy, Prices, Circumstances

As a last resort the experts use Bullshit and blame anything they like. Just make sure that you don't get caught in your own shit if you do this.

EXTERNAL HELP: CALL IN SOME HELP

The external help ploy is used to attempt a recovery when all else looks rather dim. The idea is to suggest that external help be solicited for one of the following reasons:

- A second opinion on the matter.
- Clarification of some issue.
- Verification of some statement.
- A new analysis of the matter.

- Breaking a deadlock.
- Getting some approval or higher authority.
- New expertise.

If one is to go for external help, then one must clearly identify the reason :

"We do not and will not agree on the issue. My suggestion is to have the information assessed by an outside consultant."

"This is a complete waste of time. We must have clarification on the issue before we continue. Then we can continue the meeting next week."

And there is nothing wrong with doing this but if it is a conflict that is to be resolved by an outsider, then first one must create the conflict. Second, one must be at least hopeful that you can bring in new information to help you through the time period you just bought yourself.

THE RECOUP: RECOUP TO MINIMIZE LOSSES

The Recoup is the name given to a group of weapons used to minimize wounds to ego and power. It must be assumed that someone has not only ignored diversions, also broken through some deflections and someone is on the spot. On the other hand, someone may have just caught another off guard and he is on the spot. Either way the recipient is up shit creek to put it mildly. Like the bird, your enemy has found the nest and direct attacks are not effective - a wing is broken and one must get away before being eaten alive. The Recoup weapons are used when there is little left to do but minimize losses. Remember the old adage of "*he who turns and runs away lives to fight another day*"? The Recoup is the same idea.

Let us return to old Grizz Buzzard who found the little errors in addition on Page 353 of Flick Smoothy's proposal. Let us assume that Flick did not have a deflection ready and that Grizz made the whole report look like a joke. In addition he made Flick look like fly shit on a swatter. So what does a demoralized, beaten Mr. Smoothy do? He executes a Recoup: *"You are absolutely correct Mr. Buzzard, the figures are incorrect. I only wish you to understand that I and three of my staff have worked 18 hours a day for the last week in order to prepare the report for the meeting. Two are suffering from fatigue because they were so dedicated - the stress undoubtedly caused the errors. I find it hard to understand, when the error is trivial in respect to the main purpose, why you should shit so prodigiously upon all those dedicated company employees."*

SO HOW WOULD WE KNOW THAT MR. GRUNT WAS AN ASSHOLE ?

THE RECOUP

How does Grizz eat that one? As it looks now, both are at a standoff since they both have made each other look stupid. Flick did not recover completely, but he did manage to regain some dignity and a little bit of territory - by executing a Recoup. In this case he executed two recoups, the Pressure and a Sting. Let us look at these weapons.

PRESSURE: BUT WE WORKED SO HARD

The Pressure technique is an attempt to dissolve the effects of getting caught by inferring that pressure was the culprit. The pressure in turn caused the stress or strain that caused the real problem. If one can get away with this, then the errors might be quite excusable and not so devastating a failure. The pressure method must be used with company dedication in mind to be the most effective. We just saw how Flick Smoothy used it on Grizz Buzzard:

"We were understaffed for the job so we took it upon ourselves to work nights."

"There was not sufficient time in a day to do a thorough job so we had to cut corners."

"The strain of the overall responsibility was too much for the staff. It caused tension and anxiety which affected the results."

"The equipment was overtaxed. It just couldn't handle the throughput so we had to get outside help to try maintaining accuracy."

"We tried to keep costs at a minimum so we took shortcuts.".

No matter how bad things are, somehow when it is realized that people have busted their asses to get the results out - and made some error in the process - the wrath diminishes. If these people tried to help the company in so doing then the blow is even less harsh.

SPRINT: GET OUT WHILE YOU CAN

The Sprint is for those who don't like battles or the sight of blood. Quite simply, you just bugger off as quickly as you can when you smell a foul wind coming. All you have to do is look at your watch and say *"Look I am terribly sorry gentlemen but I am already 2 minutes late for a very important engagement which cannot be delayed. We will have to continue this later".* Then leave before any other questions are asked. Now bear in mind that it may be even more dangerous to leave than to stay because nobody may be left to defend your case. When you come back your situation could well be unrecoverable. Nevertheless, leaving can have several useful and varied purposes:

- It can cause complete chaos.

- You can withdraw without losing your temper.
- It can delay an issue and buy you some time.
- It allows you to escape without blood.
- It keeps you from being a participant.
- You do not go through the pain of losing.
- It may precipitate a quick conclusion (even victory).
- It spares you the boredom of staying.
- It stops you from wasting time if ideas are not accepted.
- It allows you to avoid someone.

On the other hand, you may be pleased to find out that while you are absent, the problems sorted themselves out and the situation healed itself.

Another favorite method is to make your cell phone beep as if it was a beeper. Of course this would be an emergency situation to vacate the place!

REFERRAL: GET SOMEONE ELSE TO JUDGE

The referral works much like the External Help tact. The difference is that you make some rather poignant accusations that the group members are not qualified to make a judgment or a decision on. You would say, for example:

"It is obvious that no one here has the authority to approve the proposal. It must be presented to someone who can."

"I do not agree with your conclusions on this matter. An outside consultant will settle the issue."

"There is no point to the attack when we do not know the conditions whereby the costs were created. We must get a report from the Accounting Department."

"Horfle, you are an asshole of supreme proportions for blowing this out of context. I would withdraw my proposal completely to present it to one more capable and objective."

"What is the point of continuing when all that transpires is destructive nit-picking? Let us bring the president in to listen."

"We don't know what we are talking about. We need a consultant."

The idea is always the same - bring in a new face, subcommittee, consultant, or whatever to give it a second chance.

PLAY DUMB: BUT HOW WOULD WE KNOW

Playing dumb comes quite natural for many. All they have to do is just be themselves at a meeting. The only problem is that they are not playing and being dumb is just a natural process. When you play dumb you are effectively admitting that you did not know something that was crucial. Somewhere, there was a communication breakdown and it was not your fault. Consider the following examples:

"But that is the way we have always done it."

"How was I to know you were in a hurry."

"But that is not my department.."

"No one told me to go ahead."

"But I am still waiting for an OK."

"No one told us that it was so important"

"How would we have known the difference?"

"That is his job not mine."

"But I wasn't hired to do that.."

"No one showed us the way to do it.."

"We weren't told about the request."

"But we were waiting for the boss to tell us."

So when the truth is finally revealed, you play dumb. How can you be held responsible when someone (and you don't know who) didn't tell you something. You cannot be expected to just know what is in other people's minds. In order to then give the excuse some zip, you should follow it with one of the following:

"How is this possible?"
"How did this happen?"
"Why did this occur?"
"Is this not correct?"
"Where is the problem area?"

It may be quite possible to cause some upheaval and a potential deflection if someone is not able to answer the question.

SORRY: BUT WE DID OUR BEST

Sometimes, when there appears to be little escape, you may want to execute the Sorry technique. A humble apology and an admittance of guilt can generate a very sympathetic reaction. Sympathy, in turn, can easily stimulate generosity. It is quite common to see an apology for wrong doing dissolve aggression fairly rapidly. A boardroom is not an exception. Once the opponents have trapped their victims, no matter how fierce they have been, they must then figure out what to do with him. A Sorry will give them an immediate escape and at the same time give everyone a chance to bring the adrenalin levels down. The Sorry method does not always guarantee that wrath is minimized. And after all, it does admit guilt, so there is always the possibility that the wrath that befalls you may be considerable. If the fury seems to be upon you, try something like:

"It was my fault, I am sorry but what would you have done if you were me?"

"I cannot offer a humble enough apology for the error. But what would you do now?"

"To say that I am sorry is probably not sufficient but how can we fix the situation?"

"I have been humiliated and I offer my apology for the wrongdoing. What can I do to rectify the situation?"

"You are correct in your criticism. What now?"

We see a combination of an apology with an appeal of what to do reconstruction so to speak.

STING: SORRY BUT WHY BE AN ASSHOLE!

We saw the Sting in action when Grizz Buzzard caught Flick Smoothy. Flick used pressure as his excuse. After everyone offered freely to work overtime with no complaints, the pressure created fatigue that then caused the errors. The sting came when Flip said: "*I find it hard to understand, when the error is so trivial in respect to the main purpose, why you should shit so prodigiously upon all those dedicated company employees.*" He could have added some more poison to the sting by saying "*Do I take this as your directive to reprimand these people immediately?*" If Grizz says no then he must explain why not - particularly when the smell of shit is still in the air - and look stupid. If he says yes to be consistent then he is solely responsible for reprimanding dedicated and loyal employees.

The Sting is therefore a duet of opposites. It starts by an admission, gives the reason but attempts to pick out some bad tact taken to reveal the problem. Here are some examples:

"Yes there undoubtedly is an error as you have pointed out over and over. These people did their very best to serve the company. It is unfortunate that you cannot recognize this."

"You are correct but why do you insist on being an asshole about it?"

"I am sorry, the best job possible was done in those circumstances but why is it necessary to crucify the efforts?"

We have a Sorry along with some excuse and a Shot at the attackers to make the sting. Like a dying wasp, the final sting is still available even though it can't fly. So the idea is to use that sting before you croak.

MINUTES: BEND THE MINUTES - A BIT

Sometimes if you can see a foul wind brewing, you may want to make what would normally be a silly offer. That is, to take minutes or summarize the proceedings. If you offer to summarize the meeting activities - formally - then it is quite likely that everyone will be relieved because nobody likes to summarize meeting proceedings - it is clearly a pain in the ass. By making this offer, you are effectively in control of what is to be published and it is in this way that you can conveniently omit certain details which are unwanted. If you wait awhile, say 2 to 3 weeks after the meeting to publish these minutes, then usually the attendees will not remember all the explicit details, so it is not likely that they will question certain omissions. The document so produced can have your own summary and conclusions that will become the official record. This could be quite useful for future referencing.

LET'S VOTE: MAKE THEM TAKE SIDES

There are times where it may be a wise idea to precipitate a vote. Typically if it can be seen that you may be losing ground but you still have a majority of consensus, then force a vote. Simply suggest or coax the chairman to hold a vote. On the other hand it may be possible to force the outcome in a negative direction if that is what is required.

Holding a vote can do one of three things for you. First, it can polarize a group so that suddenly there is a clear indication of the two sides. There may be some static when each individual is forced to take a side. Second, the vote can force action when the outcome is uncertain. In this way there may actually be a solution when there appears to be none. Thirdly, as mentioned, one can take advantage of a majority (or minority) when such can be detected.

GROUPY: IT WASN'T JUST ME ALONE

The Groupy method is used to take the focus of the wrath and to disperse the blame. The best way is to distribute the blame on others as well as yourself. We saw this process in action when we looked at Flick Smoothy's response to Grizz Buzzard's final attack. That was the Pressure combined with the Sorry. In many cases it is quite legitimate to spread the blame and it must be so stated - particularly if you can spread some of that smelly shit on some higher up types as well as yourself. In other cases it may not be entirely truthful to blame others but still just as much fun so you may have to use more general statements:

"This was thoroughly discussed with the experts. They all said it would work."

"It has been proven over and over and it is standard procedure in other areas of the company."

"We were all involved in the decision to proceed so why are you all negative at this time?"

"Did you not approve the idea first?"

"The complete support staff was involved in compiling that segment."

"I tried as best I could with virtually no cooperation from your group."

"The best consultants were chosen for the job. .

PROMISES: MAKE A PROMISE - A VAGUE ONE

A promise can potentially dilute the wrath that may result from your inability to perform in a specific situation. All you do is to make a promise to do better or to correct the situation. The trick is to make the promise in such a way that it means nothing specific but it is enough to satisfy those vultures that are picking away at your hide:

"I will make every possible endeavor to correct the situation."

"I promise to reduce costs as best we can."

"We will expend every effort to meet the deadline."

"We promise to dedicate ourselves as much as is possible."

Notice, if you will, the qualifications that make the promise meaningless. "*Every possible endeavor*", or "*as best we can*" or "*every effort*" or "*as much as possible*" means that you have an escape route, simply because every endeavor or every effort may still not be the right ones needed to satisfy the promise. Similarly reducing costs as best we can means that should you fail, you have at least tried the best you can - even though you are an imbecile - and you have fulfilled your promise.

STROKE: NICE DOGGY

Sometimes flattery can go a long way to maneuver yourself out of some encroaching wrath. Some subtle verbal stroking that strengthens an attackers reassurance can establish an instant softening. If you pour the bullshit on too obviously or too thick it will not work - in fact it may even aggravate the situation. Like two dogs fighting, once one is down, any efforts to recover could easily result in the fatal kill by the dominant dog. If the downed one lies still and accepts his position he could quite possibly live to tell about it. The stroke is like lying down:

"You have a good point there. I had not looked at it that way."

"There is a lot to what you say. What should we do?"

"I must respect the way you did that. That was very clever."

"You have certainly proven me wrong. What would you suggest we do to correct the problem?"

"You are absolutely correct. I cannot counter argue that point."

The stroke in no way allows you to be the winner - it is not meant to. It does allow you to possibly be a live loser.

SHOWDOWN: TELL IT LIKE IT IS

The showdown is for those quite courageous at heart or for those who just don't give a shit anymore. Opposite to Stroke, the Showdown simply tells it exactly the way you feel it. And you tell it in such a way that you really don't give a fiddler's fart what the consequences are. The showdown is what each and every one of us has upon some occasion wanted to say but have never had the guts to say it.

"We have pissed away four hours arguing about nothing! You are without a shadow of doubt the most incompetent narrow minded assholes I have ever encountered."

"Grizz, you are a sick vulture crawling around looking for dead meat. It is difficult for me to understand how this company allows such disgusting, unconstructive parasites to hold top positions."

"My greatest pleasure at this time would be to stick the proposal cross-wise up your assholes."

"Mr. Wafflecrap, you have clearly proven yourself to be a fucking obnoxious and incompetent idiot who is not capable of judging anything. I refuse to waste any more time with you."

"Fuck each and every one of you! I will take my proposal to more deserving people."

So there you have a multitude of defensive techniques to use like the executives. As we have learned when an AQ is too low for the position, these tools bring it up quickly. If an AQ is too low, these can be used to impress line management. They may elevate position faster. Better still, try not to engage and keep a smile! But if you have to, do it politely!

3

AO TOOLS IN THE AVERSIVE ARSENAL

THE IF YOU DARE TOOLS

Admittedly, some of the previous stuff got a bit serious. Yet I have encountered countless examples of these tools. But the funniest one I left for last. You will read these in total disbelief but nevertheless there are those repulsive creatures in a company who dare to use certain measures that are in a class of their own. These special weapons although not popular, are classed as **Aversions**. Nevertheless, they are boardroom brawler techniques and deserve special attention. The **"If You Dare "** aversions are of three main varieties, all of which affect the sensory organs of the opponents. If used effectively, they are sure to undermine any serious opponent or even neutralize any stoical boardroom atmosphere. These are the art of emitting gaseous materials, commonly referred to as **Farting**; the art of exhaling gaseous material, known as **Cigar Smoking**; and the art of expounding with colloquial injectors, known as **Cursing**.

Although there are many other techniques, these are by far the more important ones. Believe it not, I once met an Executive (Murk Mudler the lawyer) who did this simply because he could!

AVERSION IN ACTION

The use of these, however, can be a very delicate matter so it is recommended that one treat these techniques seriously since if applied poorly they could cause irreparable harm to an executive! Let us recall Murk Muddler, for example. Not only had Murk built up the confidence and stupidity to use these tools, but he had also developed the ability to sometimes use them to his advantage. Here we go... bite your tongue when you read these.

THE FART: GAS AND SMELL TO SET THE SPELL

Since our hypothesis suggests that by the time one reaches the executive level, the majority of people look upon you as an asshole, it may not be out of place to behave like one and fart. In fact, if you have ever sat in on a meeting and listened, sometimes it seems that all these assholes are just farting profusely at each other to get each others attention and to see who can make the biggest smell.

All the groaning, grunting, wheezing and huffing are just preludes to the vast varieties of sounds and smells which fill the room. The real fact of the matter is that a well-placed, controlled fart can work to one's advantage.

- It can startle others to bring down their guards.
- They commonly have a tendency to distract people from serious issues.
- They can totally destroy a serious situation.
- They can dull an opponents brain so that you can take advantage of him.
- They can accelerate progress.
- They can temporarily knock an opponent off guard.

Just imagine the situation where someone is being hot seated. There has been dead silence for 45 seconds. The guy has gone beyond a time period where he can recover. Do you think that a loud resounding Fart would break the tension? How about the situation where three guys are in a small room and after three hours of trying to get a contract signed, the guy wanting the signature just keeps farting quietly. After a mere 20 minutes, a lack of breathing air, watering eyes and a dulled brain, could cause the other guy to sign and leave quickly? And what would happen at a long presentation where someone was just pouring out obvious bullshit and dribble, and no one knew how to stop the guy politely? Do you think a high frequency "Hisser" would break up the meeting? You better believe it!

Now suppose you are in a deadly argument at a meeting - every fraction of a second is crucial to maintaining good counter attacks. If you let out a squeaker after purposely crossing your eyes, and the squeaker slowly rumbled into a brap brap brap, do you not think you would destroy your opponent's advantage? What if you totally ignored the fact of what you had done? All this may seem a bit silly but there really are some silly people in Corporations. Just imagine, if you will, just how effective farting could be if it was treated as an integral part of the Arsenal. Imagine the ability to vary pitch, frequency, duration and smell as well as control timing. Would this not give effectiveness to farting as a brawling tool. Suppose experts in this field began to associate rather unique and effective smells with the ingestion of certain body chemistry catalysts like prunes, beer, pepperoni, eggs, sausage, pizza, exotic fruits and so on. These, in combination with various liquids could get one a considerable variation in caustic penetrating odors. The control of audio aspects could also be quite a science and depend somewhat on ones posture as well as how one positions the cheeks of his ass. The effects could not only be notable, but varied in purpose. For example:

- **RESOUNDING** (Braaaap) This one would have a tendency to startle people, particularly if loud enough.
- **LOW FREQUENCY** (Burruurruupp) This would be an awesome variety since it carried the suggestion of forthcoming gas of incredible volume.
- **SQUEEKY** (Peeeweeeww) Usually would need to tighten the cheeks for true squeaking. It would usually be non scary but if coupled with a wicked smell, it could really upset the balance of a group.
- **HISSER** (Sissssississ) Hissers would be excellent for shifting blame. It would be hard to detect where they came from unless they were too long in duration. You could easily make the guy beside you look pretty bad if you blamed him shortly after emission.
- **WHISTLER** (Pheeeeeep) Whistlers would be fairly harmless but good for breaking tension immediately, the smell being fairly mild. But they would be good warning of what's to come.
- **WET PLOP** (Phhoooploop) Wet ones would be extremely difficult to execute without shitting oneself. This is why they would have very serious effects on opponents. The possibility of forcing the more serious act of shitting ones

pants would always have enough awesome connotations to curtail everyone's activities for at least one minute.

- **ROLLER** (Rrbop rop rop rop) Rollers could be sustained for considerable duration. They would be effective by absolutely destroying opponents thought processes, particularly if one could continue the Rop Rop without any notice to the activity.
- **SILENT** The silent ones, with smell, would be most effective in destroying the atmosphere of a staunch boardroom, particularly if one could keep the activity going for a while. When the air was watering everyone's eyes and they were breathing loudly for air, you could be sure that their brains are dull. That would be the time you could get agreement on an issue quickly.

On the other side of the coin, one would take care not to fall victim to an expert farter. One would not only develop his own special control, but he would develop immunity to others. The ability to immunize would be critical.

THE CURSE: A FEW VULGARITIES AMONG GENERALITIES

Yet another method is the **Colloquial Injection** technique. Once again we have Murk Muddler as an example of an expert. Angus Steadfast also started to gain some expertise in this area. Colloquial Injection simply means that you inject foul four letter words into your normal sentences. But another note of caution - you must use the principle of **Grammatical Polarity**. This idea is based on the fact that at the one end of the grammar spectrum are the well structured, precisely worded and educated literary "flowery" type words which make up a sentence. The other end is made up of unstructured vague imbecilic word conglomerations that are mostly meaningless and gross swear words. As an example of the first type we could say: *"With clear perception, we now understand the set of unprecedented and paradoxical conditions which have* *led to our disagreement on this issue. Perhaps it is only now that we may undertake a more constructive approach to a clearer cooperative venture."*

At the other end, we have "*Ya fuckers ought to know what ya fucked up - hey - now that youse all gots shit in your goddam pants youse all smellers. Now all youse fuckin cockwalapers gots da fuckin goods to giver shit - hey?"* We have here two attempts at grammatical poles, to say the same thing. Now let us combine them through the Grammatical Polarity and Colloquial Injection: *"With clear perception, we now understand the set of unprecedented and paradoxical fuckups which have led to our disagreement on this issue. Perhaps it is only now that you imbecilic, ignorant cockwalapers may undertake a more constructive approach to a clearer cooperative venture."* The polarity principle simply merges the two extremes for effect.

One may ask what is the effect? First, it goes without saying that the better formed the sentence and its content, the more clearly it communicates its purpose and brings connotations of knowledge and education. Secondly, there is nothing like a strong, disgusting colloquial expression to project anger and disgust - unfortunately it may also project ignorance and stupidity. Thirdly, a well-constructed combination creates clear communication with superior knowledge but with a projected intensity of anger or total disgust. In the example above, if such was stated in a corporate boardroom, in the first instance the speaker would be classed as an educated wimp, while in the second case just a dumb klutz. The last one could well be an angry executive asshole. So what do these injections do for the arsenal? Let us list some:

- **AMPLIFICATION** It goes without saying that "Fuck Off" is a much stronger emphatic expression than "Go Away".
- **FEAR** There may be some significance to the use of a colloquial to inject fear. This is probably because the use of a colloquial is usually associated with people that have more muscle than brains and are creatures living under

physical laws. "*I'm goin to kick your fuckin head to shit pulp*" is an expression which would inject more fear *than "I am going to kick your head* " - it sounds like it has more adrenalin and force behind it.

- **EFFECT** There are certain words which are just better suited to saying things more effectively. You can look through the dictionary quite a while to find a word equivalent to "fuckup" in intensity of meaning.
- **SURPRISE** There is the element of surprise, which if dealt properly always leaves a feeling of one upmanship. This may be purely psychological but every little bit helps.

Essentially, however, the whole idea behind the Injection Method is to play the "Big Tough Guy", since all big tough guys use swearing as their means of communication. If you are to be tough then you must make sure that you use the expressions wisely, otherwise you could be reduced to a "muscle brain" and defeat your purpose. Consider someone who says:

"What reasons do you have for being late?"

"What ya late for, ya shit the bed?"

"You are late. What excuses do you have for being so fucking irresponsible?"

Which one has the most energy and effect behind his question?

THE PUFF: SMOKE AND HUFF TO DULL THEIR STUFF

There are always those who like to smoke cigars. Cigar smoking, being a much more moderate form of aversive weapon, is less common now depending on what country you are in but I can certainly recall many episodes that used to make me giggle and snort quietly. If you have ever sat in a closed room with a heavy cloud of smoke surrounding you and the smell of burning camel dung mixed with mint leaves and hair permeating your senses, you know exactly what this weapon is. And there is no way of escaping this if you are in a meeting, so keep this in mind as a good weapon. If you have the courage to smoke in a meeting, (if it is legal) the effects can be quite dramatic - to non-smokers - within a fairly short period of time. As the meeting participants gag for air, show watery eyeballs, take pills for headaches and fidget and squirm, you will find that you can get rid of them quickly or dull their senses enough to take advantage of them. If you are a connoisseur of cigar smoking then you may consider special mixtures for special purposes. Although, many brands are sufficient, without alteration, to cause some rather severe effects in closed areas, it is more difficult to control your foul environment with cigars than it is to do so with a cigarette. A pipe however can be stoked with virtually any combination of devastating materials.

Another key factor is that cigar smokers and pipe smokers are "cool". Right? Cigars, especially the enormous variety from which you can send billowy smoke signals for 50 miles are, of course, status symbols of power, success and class. Well perhaps they used to be! So if you want to be a big cool powerful dude, you smoke a big powerfully obnoxious cigar. This will immediately place you on the superior list of other members, treading fear as you huff and puff, right?

Pipe smokers are not quite as tough but some surely think they are "cool beings". The pipe, being symbolic of superior intellect, will surely show the others that you are not a mere mortal to be intellectually jockeyed with. As mentioned, the pipe brings some advantages over cigars since you can pick a mixture to get the desired effect. Here are some key effects and recommended mixtures:

HEADACHES Just any brand of tobacco from Havana with some dried dog shit mixed in at a ratio of 1 part dog shit to 5 parts tobacco. Throw in a snip of horseradish powder.

NAUSEA Ten parts aromatic pipe tobacco with 1 part chopped cat fur and 1 part brown sugar with a sprinkling of chopped anchovies.

AESTHMA Five parts dried chopped deciduous leaves, 5 parts regular pipe tobacco, 2 parts dried horse turds, sprinkle of peat moss.

POOR SIGHT Three parts aromatic tobacco, sprinkle of paprika with ground cloves. Soak in vinegar and dry. Add a few hemlock needles.

FAINTING Two parts tobacco, 2 parts marijuana, sprinkle mono sodium glutamate.

It must be remembered that one should not inhale this mixture since the results may be fairly dramatic. Cigarette smokers are not given the same status as those who smoke cigars and pipes. In fact, cigarette smoking being a more acceptable habit is less noticeable. To cause an impact you must roll your own, thereby putting your own mixture in.

Now one word of advice. You must try to avoid the effects yourself, unless you are used to such smells. A nice way is to light up and excuse yourself while the fumes take their toll. Leave it burning in the ashtray. Now for something a bit more serious.

THE OUT: OUT OF SIGHT TO HELP YOUR FIGHT

There are times when it is just not a good idea to attend a meeting. This may be simply because you are unprepared or you just know that you are going to get hurt or you have a feeling that you may be put on the carpet on some rather sensitive issues. The problem is that you cannot just stay away to see a dentist, take the cat to the vet, or be sick. Another problem is that it could well prove to be more dangerous to be absent than to go to the meeting. The decision to avoid a meeting can be a fairly big one.

If you decide to be absent then do it gracefully. First, arrange to have another 'important meeting' with someone else at about the same time on the same day. Do it with outsiders, since it is always more difficult to cancel outside commitments, and certainly less proper. If possible, try to involve someone else in the meeting so that he can represent you. At that time you can say "*Excuse me gentlemen, but we have a very pressing issue to solve which we can not delay. I am really disappointed that I cannot attend this meeting, I really wanted to be involved. We hope to be finished before you so that I can catch some of it.*"

Of course you will not finish. The effect is that you look fairly dedicated and certainly interested, but unable to attend. There will therefore be a normal tendency to have the others leave certain things alone that required your presence. They may even ask you later, without all the corporate vultures attacking you or they may have even decided certain things graciously on your behalf - because you definitely could not avoid your absence.

In closing this section on the Arsenals and AQ Tools, you need to keep in mind that even though I have used "you' as the one deploying the tools, they are simply meant to exemplify what so many "successful" executives have learned to be effective in maintaining order, power, and focus on the bottom line of profit. Many of these are not nice; heartless, crass, and ruthless but they do work... and what they do most of all is support AQ'ISM and the AQ virus.

There is a nice way of doing the same things without destroying others credibility and pride. But alas, this is a satire, right?

Let us continue...

4

WHEN THERE ARE TROUBLES

THE ARSENALS & THE GREAT TRANSITION

Earlier we discussed the executive arsenal in depth. We looked at the Great Transition. This was a time of corporate menopause where a need for boardroom brawling weapons would outweigh the need for specialized technical expertise. It was a time when new tools were required to fill the void created by the ever-increasing lack of knowledge on the detailed workings of the company.

The Great Transition was the time where staying on the corporate playground meant using executive arsenals to keep AQ's in line with positions. These were the necessary weapons required to survive on the battleground found primarily in the boardroom. Those who learned the rules well obviously survived the best, attaining power and money.

But there were many other aspects of the Great Transition that require scrutiny. These we will deal with in due time. We have seen part of the executive weaponry designed for direct combat in the boardroom - aversive, offensive and defensive weapons. Let us now look a little deeper into the arsenal to see what other goodies the executive uses. The next section is devoted to yet a new set of weaponry used for troublemakers. These are what we call **Trouble Tactics**, as taken from the **Tactical Arsenal**.

THE TROUBLE TACTIC ARSENAL

Inevitably there are always people at a meeting who will do their very best to piss you off - possibly because of that instinctual white collar urge to help you raise your AQ. Some do this directly by design while others do it without even knowing it. Some are really good at it and some are superb. Others are mere amateurs. This part of the AQ story we devote to dealing with these people - helping them raise their AQ's equally fast.

TROUBLE TACTICS

The common way, as we shall see shortly executed by so many executives, is to quickly identify and eliminate the troublemaker type by the use one of the arsenal weapons. After all, executives need all the tools possible to keep their AQ's high.

In dealing with trouble makers at meetings, it is common to see a subtle intervention - sort of a Probe to see if someone really wants to take on an opponent or to find out if they should let the situation alone. Upon deciding positively, however, it is best to keep in mind that they will try to adhere to Groinkicker Rules for troublemakers (*Corporations Stripped Naked: Exposing the AQ Virus*). These rules are simple in principle but effective in application. Firstly, they must identify the type of victim and what the victim is doing wrong. They then quickly invade his private space by catching him off guard with a strong statement directed at him - one that embarrasses him and makes him look stupid for engaging in that which is irritating. Let us recall these rules from my previous book.

GROINKICKER RULES FOR TROUBLE MAKERS

Typically skilled executives heed the six groinkicker rules for trouble makers:

RULE 1: identify the type and folly
RULE 2: invade his space
RULE 3: catch him off guard
RULE 4: sarcastically amplify his folly
RULE 5: make him look like an asshole
RULE 6: leave him no defense

The real key of course, and the great skill, is wrapped up in Rule 4. This is obviously developed over time. You can see this all the time. Another aspect just briefly mentioned was the position from which such an attack is launched. That is, it may be a chairman, speaker or quiet participant at a meeting. If one is speaking then they have the floor so that Groinkicker Rule application is direct. If they are the Chairman, then they must first step in momentarily by asking the speaker to hold on for a few seconds while they dispense with the identified idiot.

If one is chairing the meeting then they will take the primary initiative to dispense with troublemakers, before a speaker has to, otherwise they may lose control. If one is a quiet participant and no one is taking any action against such a turkey then others may, like the chairman, first ask for a momentary pause so that they can apply the Groinkicker Rule themselves to look "good"..

The statement must sarcastically amplify his violation to leave him looking like an asshole. Troublemakers are a special breed of meeting people since they are usually breaking meeting rules. Many of these rules are just simply acknowledged as universal unwritten protocol. For example, sleeping, being late, wearing jeans, or clowning around are just not readily accepted habits at executive meetings. For this reason, it is usually quite easy to use sarcasm in making the guy look like a real turkey. In applying the Groinkicker rules, the experts keep in mind that there are two different levels from which they are applied - either as a chairperson/presenter or as a meeting member. But it really doesn't matter whether it is in a private office or any meeting, the effectiveness is the same. And it seems that the use of these tools that make one look like an asshole, or, at the same time, be an asshole, are the norm. As one loses control and fears a loss of position, money and ego, one seems to gravitate to this more aversive side of the way they think, infer, call, tell, and treat others... to ultimately improve their AQ's.

Some people just clearly jerks and troublemakers and again, the executives are skilled at dealing with them in a way that improves everyone's AQ. Many executives can destroy a troublemaker in an instant, completely humiliating them and reducing them to idiots. In many cases, these people are not real troublemakers at all, they just have irritating habits contrary to what the executive sees as relevant. Here are some common trouble makers:

THE WHISPERER

The whisper is always the stupid jerk that is carrying on some secondary conversation while someone is talking. The whisperer and his neighbor make it difficult to concentrate as they giggle, smurk and whisper. Needless to say, even if you are just in the area of these problem people, you can become irritated or distracted. If one is doing the talking, the best way is to stop talking and stare at the whisperers. The longer they continue, the more likely it is that other attendees will join the stare - to embarrass them when they realize what is going on - usually 30 seconds is sufficient enough time, after which the speaker can choose his shot:

"Is it possible to keep one speaker at a time, Mr. Whisp?"

"Would you like to share your important conversation with the rest?"

"Wimply, you should sit over there away from Grimly so we can continue without your distracting conversations."

"Before you leave would you like to share with us your conclusions on this matter?"

"You, Mr. Whisp, and your girlfriend Mr. Gigglepuss make it impossible for us to focus on the topic - or is the topic of trivial interest in comparison to your love affair?"

Most effective is to see the speaker, if standing, to walk over to the pair and then stare at them. If one is simply a meeting attendee whose patience is being tested, just before they choose their shot time, they say to the speaker or chairman: *"Excuse me Mr. Waffle, would you hold on just a minute...?"* Then they turn to the guilty pair and give it to them!

THE GOSSIPER

The gossiper likes to bring outside gossip, hearsay or just plain unsubstantiated garbage into a meeting. He is the asshole who is heard to say "*It was just the other day that I heard someone talking about ...*" or "*I remember the report mentioning something about ....*". These gossip items are typically introduced with vague crap that is difficult to prove or disprove without external clarification. For this reason it is easy to waste valuable meeting time arguing over whether something is true or not. It is difficult to catch a clever gossiper at his game. The first thing typically done by the experts is to settle it quickly for a temporary focus

"Fartly, that is pure conjecture. Can you substantiate this for us?"

"Can anyone here verify that comment?"

"And how do you suggest we find the answer to that question Mr. Gossip?"

"Your statement is not relevant unless you can back it up Mr. Gossip."

"Can anyone give a reason why such horseshit has any bearing to our topic?"

"Fartly, this is not the ladies luncheon where gossip prevails."

What they do is fire it back to the gossiper or check the gossip out quickly. If this is not possible then they take a break to see where or how they can get the information. Some, to make a point, invite an expert in temporarily in order to proving their case, then use the Attack to get rid of the person and the gossip.

THE INTERRUPTER

The interrupter always has a bad habit of talking before others have completed their sentences. There are various types of interrupters that range from loud-mouthed creeps to excited attempts to help the speaker. How the executive decides to shoot the interrupter will depend on the amount of assistance or detriment he offers by the interruption. Remember, however, that the more the interrupter gets away with, the more the meeting will lose control or focus.

"Hold on Bark, let Mr. Gink finish his statement."

"Not a bad idea Bark, but just wait your turn."

"Your interruptions are in poor taste Mr. Interrupt. Is it possible that you can control yourself?"

"Bark, we all acknowledge your graduation from the College of Interrupters, please give us a break."

The interrupter at the extreme end is a loud-mouth that simply tries to dominate the meeting - he just loves the sound of his voice. The tone and sarcasm typically used on this type will undoubtedly be directly proportional to the loudness of his voice.

THE LATECOMER

There are many types of latecomers. At one extreme there are those painful puff brains who come in late, make a big commotion, and continue to bother everyone - even stopping the proceedings - so that they can be brought up to date. At the other extreme, you have the silent creeper, who slinks in quietly to sit down, hoping not to be observed. In either case, the magnitude of the embarrassment can be high depending on one's tenacity to embarrass. The executive like to use satire:

"Let us welcome Mr. Goofoff who has decided to give us his company."

"Gentlemen, I propose that at the end of the meeting we take a collection to buy Mr. Goofoff a watch."

"We would love to bring you up to date, Smurdly but we have an agenda to maintain."

"Smurdly, perhaps you should be at your own meeting."

"Hi Smurd, glad you could come."

"Obviously the meeting wasn't important enough for you to be on time."

"Look Mr. Smurdly Goofoff, either report on time or don't bother to attend."

.

If the chair really does not like this fellow then they will Hotseat him to further embarrass him.

THE EARLY LEAVER

The leaver is the opposite of the latecomer. Clearly he doesn't feel the meeting important, he is hiding something or he has another commitment. The greatest effect is when he is caught just before the door. Then a focus on the attack follows.

"Goodbye Mr. Flitter, we have enjoyed your silence."

"Slink, do you think we can cope without your presence or should we have another session at your convenience?"

"What is it that you consider more important?"

"Slink, before you leave, could you sum up your observations for us."

"If we have somehow bored you Mr. Flitter we sincerely seek your forgiveness."

Again, Hotseating and Shots are effective to get this type. There is nothing worse than to have people wandering around entering or leaving a meeting while others are attempting to seriously focus on some issues.

THE REPEATER

A broken record is the best way to describe the twerp who just can't resist bringing up the same point over and over and over again. In some cases, the guy is just an imbecile. In other cases the guy is using repetition to get his point across. In most cases, he is just a pain in the ass that attempts to treat the others like imbeciles. Skilled executives make a note, firstly, as to what is being repeated before they drive a spike into this asshole.

"Do you have any idea how many times you have said that?"

"This we acknowledge is important to you, Warfle, we have written it down twelve times."

"Is there something else you want to add or do you think we are all deaf?"

"Warfle, you are the closest thing to a broken record I have seen. Would you mind getting yourself unstuck."

"Is there some point to your repetition Mr. Lipp or are you finished now?"

Whatever the reason for the repetition, it becomes more and more aggravating to listen to this type of attendee. If, however, the person is genuinely trying to help and someone feels sorry for him, they will suggest that a few minutes be taken to hear him out - to get it off his chest.

THE DOUBTER

The doubter is another painful schmuck who just does not believe anything. His sole purpose, it seems, is to exude negative expressions like: *"There is no way"*, *"I don't believe it"*, *"It won't work"*, *"I'm not convinced"*. The biggest problem here is that others are always wrong until they can prove otherwise. If you remember the Offensive Arsenal, this was a Counter technique to find the state of health. On the other hand, the doubter could just be a stupid asshole. The best way to deal with a doubter is to either reverse the scenario or shut him up through a delay:

"Why is there no way Grimly? Explain yourself!"

"Whether you believe it or not is irrelevant - it is not our purpose to convince you as a junior."

"We are seeking constructive criticism, not vague negative opinions, Mr. Doubtfull."

"Would you give us the pleasure of telling us your solutions?"

"This is not the time to offer subjective evaluations - we will deal with everybody's concerns later."

"If you have no positive input - just subjective feelings - then shut up and listen."

"I think most will agree with me that we should deal with concerns in a more formal manner."

"Hold on Grimly, you will get your chance later."

The better approach, however, is the Reversal. The skilled executive will answer with a question that extracts something from him that he can attack. The simple tack of asking "why" will usually start the ball rolling. If one can extract something from the doubter, one will usually have something to counter on or attack.

THE SNOOZER

The Snoozer is always fun to deal with since it is so easy to literally scare the shit out of him - taking him by complete surprise. His position is so indefensible that the embarrassment can serve him to be everlasting. Executives who do this well will remain on his AQ list forever. Snoozers are bored, lazy, tired or just stupid to be attempting such things at meetings. Although they offer no direct threat to meeting attendees, it is fairly distracting - and certainly distasteful - to see someone slumped over or snoring quietly in his chair. If the guy is a hard sleeper, the executive will walk over and shake him - then hotseat him after remembering the last guy's statement.

"Jerk, now that you have had a good rest, perhaps you could comment on Philip's last suggestion."

"What would you do, Jerk, if someone was snoring at your meeting?"

"Welcome back to the meeting Mr. Snoozer we are honored that you have decided to listen."

"Jerk, I am beginning to wonder whether you really passed your lessons on meeting etiquette."

"Jerk, you said before that this issue is outrageous. What do you have to say about it now?"

"We now call upon Mr. Snoozer here to chair the session for ten minutes while I make a phone call."

"Do you agree with the report recommendations Mr. Snoozer?"

"Lets here from Jerk Snoozer who is now all rested."

Some Snoozers are light sleepers so that he may awake quickly at any movement or silence. He may even be partially aware of what is going on. The skilled executive in such cases will simply switch the focus to him from wherever they are to make sure that everyone's eyes have moved to the appropriate culprit before they Hotseat him.

THE HEADSHAKER

The headshaker is much like the doubter except that he likes to display disagreement without saying anything. He just loves to disrupt a meeting by clearing his throat loudly, shaking his head, rolling his eyes, slamming books shut, pushing his chair back noisily and so on. It becomes very easy to become angry at the insidious little creep who is too gutless to say anything directly. Sometimes the asshole will sigh in disdain at someone's suggestions or he will suddenly appear to write notes frantically as if to appear like there is incredible force behind his disagreement. Needless to say, any continued performance of this kind will lead to a need of putting a boot to the headshaker - in even the most respectable and cool attendee.

Usually the execution entails that this turkey always be stopped dead in his tracks by hotseating. Hotseating is best because this type of individual is usually gutless and doesn't wish to say anything that would commit him.

"Spazmo, I see you shaking your head - what is the problem?"

"If your little display means that you disagree, then let us share your reason for the reaction."

"Spazmo, you are interrupting the meeting. What is bothering you so badly?" "Your little habits, Mr. Headshaker, are disrupting, distasteful and immature. Either tell us what your problem is or get out!"

"Let us now hear from Spazmo Headshaker who has taken some notes on the issue."

Sometimes, people do these routines without even knowing that they are doing them. Regardless of the reason, the end result is the same - annoying. The severnes of the hotseating may be somewhat reduced in such cases.

THE INTERPRETER

The interpreter cannot resist speaking for other people. It is as if he and only he is the gifted one who not only understands everything better, but also can explain everything better. You can always hear the interpreter saying *"What Grunt is trying to say to you is..."* These incredible mouthpieces like to either interrupt or quickly attach their mouths to the end of someone else's sentences. If they are interrupters then the executive will treat them as such in combination with some of the following:

"Hold on a minute, Garble, let Mealy tell us what he means."

"Mr. Voicebox, you have an extremely annoying habit of speaking for others when they have not asked you to."

"Why do you persist, Mr. Voicebox, in persisting to act as a mouthpiece?"

"Mr. Voicebox, when and if anyone decides that you should make the presentation, they will so inform you."

"We all know what Dino means. Are you sure that you know what you mean?"

Whatever tact is used, the norm is to convey that this mouthpiece activity is both recognized and unwanted by all.

THE SLACKER

The slacker likes to be as inconspicuous as possible. He sits at the back of the room, says nothing and pretends to be involved in his own important space. Hoping that no one will bother him, he will be quiet, pretend to read or write or he may even doodle. These deadbeats will even yawn while others are talking or read magazines. The more senior the slacker is, the more brash - and the more disturbing - is his behavior. There is always an irresistible urge to catch this person in such a way as to make him squirm and embarrass him. This is precisely a skilled arsenal user will do, as with the Snoozer. A bad slacker can quite easily, in fact, become a Snoozer. So the tactics are similar:

"What do you think about that, Scruff?"

"And what is your idea on this, Scruff?"

"Now that you have had all that time to think Mr. Slackass, perhaps you can give us your interpretation."

"We wish to thank you for all your ideas, Scruff, do you have anything else?"

"Scruff, are you sure that you are at the right meeting?"

These deadbeats, dropouts or slackers are particularly disturbing at meetings which are meant to be energetic and creative. Sometimes, unfortunately, these people are an indication that the meeting is boring or not being conducted well. Whatever the reason however, no one wants deadbeats.

THE YAPPER

The yapper loves to hear his own voice. He is typically loud, talks too much and likes to dominate the meeting. At the worse extreme, he cannot resist being a smartass. These people are very opposite to the slackers in that they are sometimes impossible to shut up – particularly when the yapper is a senior.

The approach entails moving up to them, constantly staring at them maintaining a piercing eye-to-eye contact. As he speaks, the deplorer's physical position will unnerve him or even make him realize what an ass he is - enough to shut him up. Some will even sit beside him to further highlight his folly. If he is standing then the skilled executive will walk over to him and stare at him until he stops, then cut into him to make him realize his folly.

"Are you really finished or do we have the privilege of your voice for another half hour, Mr. Yapper?"

"Now that you dominated the conversation do you think we can get on with the meeting?"

"Here is a pad and some pencils, Yip, maybe you can summarize your soliloquy for us."

"You are preventing others from participating Mr. Yapper, would you kindly shut up now?"

"Of what relevance is your little speech?"

"Horfle, why don't you speak for a while and give us a break from Mr. Yapper."

The more senior is the Yapper, the more difficult it is to shut him up. Typically the skilled executive will take care to take action only when it is quite obvious to all that he is indeed yapping. If he attacks, then the speaker then he will look like an even greater asshole.

THE ATTACKER

Quite often the attacker is seen launching various types of attacks at other members of the meeting. Some attacks may even develop into personal arguments that can get fairly hot and heavy. It should be noted that these attacks, being unlike those discussed in the offensive arsenal section, are more personal in character. The key here is that some personal attack has been launched or an argument has developed. Before such behaviors embroil the meeting participants, it is best to stop the attacker or argument as quickly as possible. The skilled arsenal users will physically and verbally interrupt a fight. Then, unless they feel some compassion, they will attack them to make them look foolish.

"What the hell is this all about? What is the problem?"

"This is not a meeting place for emotional children. Would you gentlemen try to focus on the real issues."

"Dorkfield, is there any reason that we should allow you to launch these personal attacks?"

"I suggest you both get out and settle your differences elsewhere."

"What is the purpose of this subjective outburst? How is it of any relevance to our topic?"

"Mr. Badmouth, you are clearly out of order. Either cool down or get out."

"I think you gentlemen will agree that we do not have time nor patience to listen to Mr. Badmouth and his attacks."

"Gentlemen do we allow Prokfield Badmouth here to attack members?"

If the attack is aimed at the speaker, the best tactic has been to remain silent and cool. Then typically thank the attacker for the criticism (sarcastically if possible) then boomerang the attack back with a question for solution or a question as to relevancy or objectivity. Then hit him with one of the above examples.

THE ADVISER

The adviser's main objective in life is to tell others what they should be doing. Advisers always think that they know better or can do better than someone else. It is usually rare that he can, however, since most are just blowhard bluffers. Typically, they use the "If I were you..." scenario: *"If I were you, I would tell him to get out", "If I were you I would shift the meeting", "If I were you I would move to*

111

the next item", "If I were you I would take a break", "If I were you I would show more aggression". These are all painful examples of Adviser statements. Unfortunately, the advice given usually has very little meat to it so that it is difficult to commit him. The adviser may sometimes suggest something that one may act on - through the others. The skilled executive will simply say: "That's fine if the others agree". If they do, then they act immediately. If they don't then the Adviser's issue is not relevant an can be dissolved. with you. Here are more direct ways:

"Bear with us for a while, we may try it later."

"You are not me so I suggest you keep your advise to yourself, Mr. Knowitall."

"Do you wish to take over or will you do us the courtesy of holding your criticisms?"

"If I were you I would not backseat drive, Mr. Knowitall."

"Why don't we take Honk up on his advice and see if it works."

To say that an adviser can be an annoying pain in the ass is perhaps an understatement. On the other hand the advice could be useful to others, so one may want to take advantage of this indirectly. If it turns out good, then all may win. If it turns out bad, the adviser loses.

THE BRAGGER

The bragger is the intolerable asshole that must tell everyone of his accomplishments, credentials and other things, which are supposed to receive immediate respect, admiration and superior status. Thus credentials, professional status, age, length of service, affiliations and old projects are all used to create "superior" input or assessment. The bragger can be heard saying: "I've been in the business 20 years so how does this whippersnapper think he knows more?"; "I have a PhD. in Geology so I know the interpretation is horseshit", "I produced research papers on the *topic 15 years ago and I know damn well it won't work"; "Who do you think taught the little squirt all he knows?".* These little comments are typical of some "has-been" whose power and prestige is lost somewhere in the past. There is nothing more irritating than some senile fart who demands superior technical know-how because he has worked forty times as long as everyone else or because he got a PhD. in 1893. On the other hand, one may just be close to some detailed stuff that the old crotch may know a bit about.

"Dr. Highhorse, we appreciate your expertise but we must make a group decision."

"We know that you consider yourself an expert Herfle, but that does not make everyone else ignorant."

"We have noted that as your opinion, now grant others their own."

"What does age have to do with technical know-how Herman?"

"What factual evidence do you have to support your statement?"

"Your degree is also older than we are so we will weight your statement accordingly."

"Why do you make such conclusions Dr. Highhorse? Please explain to all of us."

"Of what significance are your 20 year old papers?"

"Your affiliations are about as useful as crotch crickets so shut up until we ask your opinion."

Braggers are typically obnoxious in their presumed importance and it is a treat to see them reduced to their deserved stature. The skilled executive finds it best, therefore, to hotseat them by forcing them to firstly explain the relevance of the stated background and then secondly making him clarify the details behind the conclusion. The statement *"My degree is from Hotshit University so I say it won't work"* serves to show the two areas of potential hotseating.

THE BUSTLER

The bustler is the guy who is always running in and out of a meeting. Some are so bad they purposely have their secretaries interrupt so they can look really important and busy. They are always whipping out of a meeting to take an important phone call or deal with some crisis that cannot wait. Often this turkey is fairly senior, which is why he thinks he can scurry back and forth at his convenience and not anyone else's. So he leaves - thus interrupting and he comes back to be re-briefed. Each time, continuity, focus and time is wasted. If the person is key to the meeting it becomes an impossible situation. In such a case it is best to postpone the topic or meeting. If this cannot be done then some choice words need uttering. The other creep who never seems to get the message is the cell phone fanatic. He is the one that can never resist taking it with him and can never ever not answer it.

"I would suggest that we deal with the topic when Mr. Bustle has settled in."

"Whip, you are a key to the meeting, it is senseless to continue while you run back and forth."

"We are in deep appreciation of your required importance but do you understand that good management infers that someone else can handle the crisis?"

"Either give us your attention or get out. We have had 24 interruptions."

"What type of call or crisis is it that cannot wait for one hour Mr. Bustle?"

"Look Oink, you are proving to be a very painful disturbance. You are wasting everybody's time."

If for some reason, you are sympathetic or the person is too senior, then the tactics deployed will try to delay the meeting (or topic) until the bustler settles down. Otherwise, the best tactic appears to be to point out how absurd the individual looks.

THE SLURPER

The Slurper we all know about from an earlier chapter. This was the unbearable suckhole who slurped his way upwards. These people constantly seek out and focus on anyone higher up who they try to impress. They look for approval, credit or whatever from any senior - whether it is at the expense of others. In addition, slurpers are typically wimpy little shits who couldn't make a decision if they had to. They are particularly painful and obvious at meetings, almost to the point of precipitating physical anger - to strangle the awful insipid creep. Slurpers are best at agreeing with seniors, either to cover their ass or to try to gain approval. They are typically saying *"Why I agree with what Mr. Supershit said. He was so thorough that I could add little"*. The fact is that the little shit couldn't add anything if his life depended on it. *"I am equally concerned about what Mr. Sidewinder is worried about"* or *"Golly gee, shouldn't we check with Mr. Highness first"* are slurper tactical expressions.

Contributing virtually nothing except to take up space these crawly vermin have good instincts towards survival, by plagiarism or taking the same stance of someone who is in power. Difficult to dethrone them it is, but not impossible:

"We are seeking original ideas and thoughts on the issue, not an echo chamber Mr. Slobberslurp."

"Agreement or disagreement will be voiced at the end of the meeting when we vote openly. Restrict your comments to your own ideas."

"Look Wimply, we are all worried. That is why we are here - if that is all you can contribute then don't bother."

"And what is it that Mr. Sidewinder is really worried about?"

"What precisely is it that you are worried about and why, Mr. Slobberslurp?"

"Yes, you go and check with him, then report back."

"You have agreed so many times with others, Mr. Slobberslurp, that, if the others agree, you should write up a formal summary."

"You, Wimply Slobberslurp are in a position where you must make a stand on your own - what is it?"

It is, of course hard to trap him or make him look stupid because he is quick to attach himself to someone else's idea. The frontal attack is therefore a potential attack of someone else as well. The skilled executive will therefore take care in not discrediting the one with the original idea - unless of course it is absurd. Remember that slurpers retain their positions by suckholing, plagiarizing, leaching and applying well-placed liplocks on lofty corporate members. Willy Liplock and Barf Chapstick were good examples of slurpers.

THE PECKER

The Pecker we have also dealt with before. He was the one, like the slurper who just got to be a humungous asshole using similar tactics to the slurper but with a new dimension. The pecker has a good memory to peck at someone with. Usually, therefore, it is even harder to catch this vermin because he remembers details that he can use against another who attacks him. Peckers can also apply liplocks with great accuracy and strength. *"I agree with Mr. Almighty on the issue, why did you disagree with this very issue yesterday, Flick?"* is a typical example of how the pecker adds new dimensions and why he is a more dangerous cockroach. *"I think Mr. Greatgruffer has brought up a very important aspect of the issue. So why is your staff, Mr. Greaser, violating this?"* or *"Grunt, you said 7 years ago that you would follow this principle. Why are you now going against the Presidents mandate?"* or *"You, Mr. Blastoff are over budget, not us. I concur with Charlie Costcrotch here that we need more control - because of people like you"*, are other examples of how a pecker, under the wing of some lofty flyer, uses a Shot to Hotseat someone.

Although we now encroach on Boardroom Brawling more than problem people, we must still admit that this type of creep is a problem at a meeting. He so obviously is a scab who attempts to start trouble and to make others look bad. Such unconstructive stuff is therefore a real problem - and difficult to deal with because he is perhaps adding some information (albeit conflictive) to the meeting. What needs stopping, however, is the potential emotional turmoil or subjective fight that can result.

So we have here a form of Attacker, which we have already dealt with - but some extra tenacity must be added to the recipe.

"Mr. Peckerface would you be more specific on your accusation?"

"If you gentlemen agree, we must have Mr. Peckerface explain what he means."

"Of what relevance is that to the topic of our discussion Mr. Peckerface?"

"Mr. Peckerface, if you are deliberately attempting to provoke a confrontation we must ask you to leave."

"What facts do you have to substantiate your statement Peckerface?"

"We cannot tolerate vague attempts here which attack credibility and reputation of the members."

"That is very interesting Peckerface, we are indeed pleased to see your concern, but do you have anything constructive to say about the issue?"

"Either give us your accusation and its evidence Peckerface or shut up."

"This meeting has been held to create constructive solutions not destructive finger pointing Mr. Peckerface."

"If you have some problem, Mr. Peckerface, formalize it in a memo."

Now there is the possibility that what the pecker is doing is Hotseating someone. If that is the case, typically the skilled ones would amplify the situation to get the response - then shit on the pecker. That way two birds can look stupid.

THE BLUFFER

The Bluffer is another goon who can destroy the meeting by bringing in some unsubstantiated crap from outside. The bluffer is heard to say: *"I just saw some details the other day that don't support that"* or *"I overheard some evidence suggesting the contrary"* or *"I happen to know from confidential sources that..."* are bluffer tactics (Dancing in the Defensive Arsenal) which introduce doubt into a discussion - thus diverting a conversation. Before a Bluffer succeeds in forcing the meeting on a tangent, one must call his bluff immediately:

"Mr. Windbag has introduced some external information - do we allow it or not?"

"Bluff, we suggest that you substantiate your statement or be silent."

"If you gentlemen agree, I suggest Bluff Windbag here, be excused for ten minutes to get the backup papers."

"Anything that is relevant here is not confidential and must be brought out Mr. Windbag, so give us your complete explanation now."

"We want facts, Windbag, facts - no more, no less."

"Until you qualify your statement, Windbag, we can only consider your statement as bullshit which we do not and will not tolerate."

The bluffers counter is typically that he cannot reveal anything without destroying confidences or confidentiality. He may even suggest that it is not possible to back it up with facts. An executive must not let such crap infiltrate a meeting so it is key that statement includes the clear options of either providing evidence or dismissal.

THE DETAILER

The detailer is also a meeting problem type if he wastes too much meeting time. The detailer will typically spend ten minutes answering a question that requires a simple yes or no. He is also the one who cannot resist bringing out reams of technical crap when not required. So the detailer's main impact is that he wastes time. In addition, the more unnecessary information he brings in, the more likely he is to cause little diversions as others may query or get embroiled in stupid irrelevant details. The solution is to be quick, therefore, to bring a detailer back on track and into the focus of a meeting:

"I think Mr. Hyperdetail, that we now have sufficient information to carry on with."

"Sorry to interrupt you Blab, but would you get to the point."

"Blab, we require a simple answer not a speech."

"Mr. Hyperdetail, we are dealing with a simple monetary problem not a lesson in Micro Economics."

"I am sure that everyone is impressed with your knowledge of the details Blab, but can we get on with our topic?"

Most detailers are just trying to help so it may not be necessary to destroy them. On the other hand some detailers just can't quit for fear they may not be able to hear themselves. Those are the candidates for destruction.

We have identified some twenty different troublemakers at a meeting. Most of them can be dealt with by simply identifying what type of problem they are - then voicing a statement that makes them look foolish for the folly. Can one do this diplomatically? Of course one can but remember that the executive is always trying to look superior to his underlings and strong to his overlings. As we earlier stated, most of the problems are based upon *"meeting etiquette"* rather than corporate laws. As such you can make people look fairly stupid for violating those unwritten rules.

But these people are, as I have describe them, plainly irritating, and it is difficult not to treat them like assholes. And remember that if you want to climb in the company, you will spend more and more time in meetings where you will work on your AQ in conjunction with the AQ Phases and meet these trouble types who cause issues for all. So typically one resorts to these sarcastic, negative tools to become an asshole with a strong emotionless dedication.

So can you be polite and elegant using these tools?

5

THE EXECUTIVE CULTURE

THE FIVE C'S OF EXECUTIVE CULTURE

In looking a little deeper into the executive Echelon, and even beyond the Arsenals, we can identify some cultural characteristics of these executives. This can be summed up by the statement that: *"It is difficult to soar with eagles when you walk with turkeys"*. Clearly, if you are to keep within the company of Eagles (or Condors, depending upon the case) then you must at least appear to be of the same species. So although your strength and skills may vary, your appearance and habits are less likely to deviate from a general norm. This *"general norm"*, in a Corporation, is equivalent to the various appearance and habits of our executives. Similar to those birds, there are cultural norms that must be acquired or developed by the executives. In the case of executives, however, the process may not be quite as instinctually developed as with birds. So whereas the Eagle can attain great heights, the executive attains great position. Whereas the Eagle has nice shiny feathers, the executive wears well-tailored suits. While the Eagle has great strength, the executive has great corporate power. Whereas the Eagle can attack and kill swiftly, the executive has his Arsenal to do likewise, and so on. But what is it that allows executives to share the company of other executives? It is the **Five**

C's Of Executive Corporate Culture, more hidden rules beneath the power and posh.

Executives often develop a secret culture that the other peons must learn the hard way. If we peer closely at the hidden rules prevalent in this culture, we could categorize most of them under five groups. These five groups would be **credentials, class, communication, compatibility** and **cultivation** - the Five C's of executive culture. The five c's identify those key requirements that are picked up along the climb upward to power and posh.

The Five C's are the glue that keeps the flock together. Although it is not absolutely an essential item for an executive, one may find that those who abide by the 'C' rules the best are the ones most likely to *"soar with the Eagles"*. In addition, they are the most likely to stay with the flock. Those who do not follow the rules eventually are cast out or just fall out. And yet, the Five C's, like all the other aspects of the Arsenal, are for the most part unwritten laws of corporations. No one will ever tell you that you have to have a university degree, or that you must wear three piece suits to board meetings, or that you must play squash with the executive Vice President, or that you must entertain visitors occasionally, or that you should learn to give speeches at clubs. Heaven forbid that this be true. Least of all, will anyone tell you that to be with assholes, you must be an asshole?

Once again, the Five C's are Credentials, Communication, Class, Compatibility and Cultivation. These proceed from something fairly concrete (credentials), towards something quite vague (cultivation). Moreover, they also require more and more *"off working hours"* dedication and time to be effective since the C's become more and more personal in practice. The executive community has its own clique with its own cultural rules and to pay little attention to these rules is probably not a good idea - unless you have lots of money and just don't give a shit. Let us now delve into this **Cultural Arsenal**.

THE CULTURAL ARSENAL

CREDENTIALS: IT'S WHAT YOU TAKE THAT MAKES YOU

We understand that in more cases than not, a formal education and an executive position was synonymous. If we can recall Franklin Hardass from the first book, he had many credentials which he liked to display on his office wall - to show any young wiper-snapper that he could not be fooled or foiled easily. The fact that Franklin did not even remember how to spell "Differential Calculus" did not have any relevance to his Engineering abilities - it was enough that he was an Engineer and therefore it was to be assumed that he knew how to spell it.

Although many credentials are indeed useful, most serve as a requirement for entry to the clique or as a means of *"warding off evil spirits"*, just as a dog pisses on a tree to warn other dogs that it is his territory. The executive likes to collect credentials to warn others that he has his own territory that not so endowed intruders should avoid for fear of death. In fact some of these old dogs can't even lift their leg to piss on the tree, but never mind - it is a game that must be played.

If you have ever heard some young technologists discussing their new found hierarchy information, you will understand the meaning of education: *"Christ, did you know that old Fric Quantum, the VP has a PhD in Physics? Wow! Golly gee whiz!"*. You will not hear someone say the same about a graduate of the 10th grade from Schmuuk High, will you? The level of formal education will obviously command respect, regardless of how old it is. The fact that old Fric got his PhD in 1902 has no significance to most. The 10th grade type, however, will be talked about in a different way: *"Christ, did you know that the VP didn't get through High School. How does such a dumb old shit get to be a VP?"* If we look at the executives at Steadfast we see them to hold formal degrees, their passes to the echelon. The rest must work harder to achieve similar heights.

COMMUNICATION: SPEECH AND PEN FOR FORCEFUL MEN

The second item in the list is communication. The ability to communicate cannot be under-rated since it is the primary means by which an executive operates. If he cannot speak, write and present well, either publicly or on a one to one basis, the eagle quickly becomes a turkey and even a penguin. Whereas the technical inabilities can be disguised, communication inabilities cannot be.

If you cannot speak well then you will not be able to discuss things intelligently. *"Well you know what I mean... the guy sucks, you know, hey? What you gonna do man... juice the creep for playin with da broads?"* is hardly a well communicated idea. *"The situation is that he prefers to pat the secretaries on their posteriors and this has caused an uproar. We must decide what our action will be"* is on the other hand a more literary sentence. *"His patting the girls asses infuriates them so we must act"* is concise and direct. Similarly, the ability to write is also an important aspect of communication, for sooner or later, your ideas and thoughts need to be formalized on paper. A bunch of incoherent dribble on paper, if this is your style, is sure to create some obstacles in your climb upwards. Memos and reports are the formal communication means of any company so it is difficult to avoid them if you wish to climb the pyramid.

Another aspect of communication is presentation. Being able to present material well is mandatory if one is to be able to convey information rapidly in meetings. Putting together a forceful presentation aimed at getting approval for something or presenting new ideas is as necessary as is the ability to speak. Being able to give a speech at a luncheon, or a talk at the club or a slide show in the boardroom are all necessary duties of the executive. This is all part of the little rules behind the scenes and it is a significant requirement.

Have you ever heard: *"George is just a technical whiz, but he can't write anything but a formula?"* Needless to say, baring special isolated circumstances, George is unlikely to get promoted to a management position. And Filbert, the new supervisor won't move upwards because, as his boss puts it: *"Filbert stutters badly whenever he has to talk to more than one person - how can we give him a position where he must deal with meetings?"* How about: *"Finklestein is really a good shit and quite able but can anyone understand what he says?"*

As you climb the ladder, your need for better and better communication becomes more and more obvious. As a technologist hiding in some cranny of the company, it matters not whether you speak, write or fart. But as an executive, it is not likely that you can remain silent or keep from committing yourself on paper for any length of time and still maintain your level. In fact, the use of the offensive, defense, tactical, manipulation and cultural arsenals are highly reliant on ones communication ability. Without good communication the arsenals are useless.

CLASS: SHINY AND CLEAN WITH LOOK SUPREME

Class is the funny part of the game that makes them all ironically look like penguins. If you ever ask a certified accountant why he wears 3 piece pin stripe suits he will look at you bewildered and stunned and respond with *"What's wrong with 3 piece suits?"* Somewhere along the line, Accountants and Lawyers grow these suits on themselves just like a monkey grows fur. They will never admit that they were told to wear them or that they read it in the CA rules. They just wear three-piece suits - probably because other successful CA's wear 3 piece suits - who knows?

Corporate executives have similar growth characteristics. As they rise in the pyramid they move more and more to the predictable plastic penguin image of the corporate executive. He is the one with the dark three-piece suit, the white teeth, clean face, coordinated shirt and tie with glossy shoes. Just walk into a boardroom and check out how many guys are wearing sneakers if this is hard to believe. Executives have leather briefcases or attaches with shiny gold letters and they have highly important papers inside. And no one tells the other how he should dress - they just mimic each other like plastic assholes because of some cultural protocol that it represents business success. People who worked for IBM in the earlier days learned this well for down the tree you can spot an IBM'er in a crowd easily. He was the young dark three-piece plastic blue penguin trying to get high altitude air, just waiting to say "*Why, how do you do, my name is Flick Feerless, I am with IBM...*"

COMPATIBILITY: SMILES AND FLIRTS EVEN WHEN IT HURTS

Another cultural "C" is compatibility. If we think back a bit and consider Angus Steadfast we will recall that he was not chosen as President, even though he was a member of the family. Angus was not "*compatible*" because he had a funny habit of leaving his fly at half-mast to tease the girls. This little habit was not "*boardroom etiquette*" and certainly not executive behavior. Murk Muddler was an even grosser example of some odd incompatibilities. Murk may have thought that his vulgarities and farting made him tough and great but there weren't too many other people who thought so - especially the executives. Who wanted to associate with this big fat bilge rat?

Compatibility covers four main areas, mainly manners, etiquette, diplomacy and dedication. Manners and etiquette are needed in meeting wives of executives, other friends, clients, professional associates and so on at parties, functions meetings, dinners etc. etc. If this is hard to believe then think about Murk Muddler being invited to speak at a special wine and cheese party for executive wives. Do you think anyone, even Angus the old piss tank, would want to be held responsible for setting such an occasion up? Not on your life - Murk is not compatible enough with the corporate culture.

Diplomacy is another requirement of the Cultural Arsenal, which is not always mentioned. If you lack it, however, it will surely be mentioned: *"Flash, why did you tell the people from IBM that their proposal was horseshit? And why did you make them so uncomfortable by not introducing them? Is this the way you think we executives behave?"* What about this: *"Suffering hemorrhoids, Angus, where the hell do you get the gall to tell my wife that her ass is wider that a jeep? We invited you to the party in good faith and fun"*. Diplomacy is the skill of handling affairs without causing hostility. If one does not have it then it is surely quite noticeable.

Dedication is another form of compatibility that requires mention. Dedication means loyalty to the company and its people. It is important that an executive shows his dedication strongly and visibly. Thus, dedication becomes more of a compatibility with the company and company affairs. For example, you cannot have a Vice President walking around a shareholders' meeting, with his brain pickled in martinis and his fly open, saying: *"Those figures are absolute turkey turds, the Vice President of Finance doesn't know how to count the number of peckers in his crotch."* Instead, he should be walking around in a well-pressed suit, spiffy and trim, smiling coolly and saying *"We of course feel that those figures are quite conservative. As our Vice President of Finance points out, the next quarter's earnings will show our company in the true light of excellence. He is especially competent in his area"*. Dedication requires that you and the company are one, and that you are compatible with it - even if it hurts to admit it.

Compatibility also means that all time is company time - you are available 25 hours a day, without question. You rise to the call of the company with a smile and your briefcase. Somewhere along the cultural climb, your attitude must change from giving the company your time to taking some time from the company.

CULTIVATION: GROOM THE BRANCHES TO INCREASE CHANCES

WHY DORK AND I BOTH FLASH IN THE PARK. HE'S AN EXCELLENT MAN FOR THE VICE PRESIDENCY!

CULTIVATION

Cultivation refers to the process of aiding your growth up the corporate tree by providing bits of fertilizer in special places - better known as horseshit. Effectively, you cultivate your superiors with bits of horseshit to help your growth. Very simply, it is difficult for anyone to give you a promotion if they do not know who you are, what you have done and how you fit in. So the best way to seek paths and promotion is to let people know - influential people that is - who you are. Consider the example of finding a new job as a Mining Engineer out of the country. Where do you start? If you had maintained a friendly correspondence with 3 or 4 guys who had themselves moved to international locations, then you would know exactly where to start and your odds for success would be much higher than if you fired off four resumes to international companies. Whether there is a genuine friendship or not is insignificant, the fact of the matter is that you have used fertilizer (correspondence) to cultivate your growth (new position) up the tree.

So cultivation refers to a personal process usually conducted away from the office - otherwise it does not get personal. And it may work in reverse as well. Consider the Chief Engineer working at a mine in South Africa - he is looking for or knows someone who needs a good engineer. Now, since he just had a letter from you - an old buddy - guess whom he recommends as a good engineer? You may in fact be an incompetent slob but you are good because he knows you.

Well the same idea works in a company. If you go to the club and slurp scotch with the executives, these fellows will know you the same way and when something comes up, your name is right there as a candidate without even applying. In the meantime the silent competent fellow who goes home doesn't have a chance in hell.

Cultivation is like the business of sprinkling manure all over the place. This way you could get some nice growth occurring. For those who have a natural tendency to socialize, the task is easy. For those not so inclined, socializing with those on your AQ list may not be so easy. In any case, procedures involve getting personal with those who may somehow assist your growth and this requires after hours frolicking. Clubs, socializing, partying and just general entertaining are means whereby the horseshit can be spread around. Playing golf with the VP's, going to wine tasting parties with the Chairman, drinking cocktails at the Exclusive Arseholes Club of America, or having the VP's over for a good piss up are all good cultivation scenarios. Here you can bullshit them to death on how good you are - or they are - and how great the company is, embedding in their minds you as a good candidate for joining their ranks.

Many a promotion has been acquired this way, by simply placing yourself in the conscious part of someone's brain. Here you can be "pulled out" whenever a position occurs - as first choice. Some slurpers make their way to great heights this way. *"It's whom you know and how you blow"*, they will tell you with a straight face, and mean every word of it.

A good example of this principle in action is our friend Willy Liplock the Assistant Vice President of Operations. Willy started by going to University just like anybody else. He was a personable enough guy, but with a gusto for bullshit. Willy was a bit different in that he knew how to cheat on exams and plagiarize with the best of scabs. So many of Willy's school friends just considered him a cheating blowhard with few engineering abilities. But Willy was developing something that would become particularly useful when he finally went to work for a corporation. He was developing abilities in the Cultural Arsenal. Willy cheated his way through Engineering and spent a lot of time at the Faculty Club "*mingling*" with University professors. He also joined B.F.O.A (Bullshitters Federation of America) where he received honorary recognition within two years. This is how Willy got his first job - at a bullshitting free-for-all at BFOA Convention - where he met some fellow bullshitters who were looking for new engineers.

It didn't take Willy long to join local golf and squash clubs as well as the Amiable Asshole Association (Triple A it was called), knowing where the managers hung out. Here Willy would bullshit and play with his boss and other managers, telling them how great he was. It was here that Willy met Scooter Blastoff from Steadfast Meats. It didn't take long for Scooter to offer Willy a job at one of the plants as an engineer. Willy went on to play with top people at the plant, moving in as Chief Engineer because the plant manager liked Willy.

He, Scooter and Willy got pissed out of shape and had great fun every time Scooter came up for a visit. When an opportunity came up for a plant manager position it was almost automatic that Scooter choose Willy. *"He's a goddam good engineer"*, Scoot would say, *"He's going to go a long way in this company"*. The truth was that Scooter and Willy got caught in an old whorehouse near one of the plants and Willy quite faithfully never told anyone so it was not difficult to understand why Willy was such a "good engineer".

As plant manager, Willy now had new games to play and new players to rub arseholes with - not surprising to see him move to head office as Assistant Vice President. Willy, in just five short years moved up the ladder very quickly - getting into positions where his ability as an Engineer meant nothing - his credentials, his cultural attitude, and his bullshitting ability were more important. In the mean time, all the poor drips who were technical marvels at school with Willy and were still struggling away at junior to intermediate engineering levels, could only wimp and wine at Willy's progress - absolutely bewildered at how such an asshole made it so fast. But Willy was hardly a big dummy. He used the Cultural Arsenal to move swiftly.

The cultural arsenal as you can see, is a set of conditions rather than rules. These are mostly requirements rather than methods, reflecting behavior. Nevertheless, the Five C's are the basic foundation of the executive's move through the Great Transition. If we could summarize the Five C's into rules we would have the following:

RULE 1: It's what you take that makes you great
RULE 2: Speech and pen for forceful men
RULE 3: Shiny and clean with a look supreme
RULE 4: Smiles and flirts even when it hurts
RULE 5: Cultivate the branches to increase chances

MEETINGS-THE MEDIUM OF PROGRESS?

Another great "culture in corporations is the meeting. Before I identified three levels as typically represented by the executive, the middle management and the workers. These three groups, I said, represent the corporate functions of Decision Making, Doing and Working. Although each group holds meetings that have the fundamental purpose of exchanging information quickly, we find that the individual style, format and content differ within each group. The working class has a tendency to provide, gather and process information. Middle management (the doers) have meetings to coordinate, analyze and report information. And at the top, the executives (Decisions Makers) have meetings to direct, evaluate and decide upon information. So we have three types of meetings

STAFF OR DEPARTMENTAL (Workers) This includes the working force, relating to individual isolated groups, departments or functions. These meetings are oriented towards providing, gathering and processing information.

PROJECT OR INTERDEPARTMENTAL (Middle) This includes middle management people who attempt to organize, analyze and report information on sub-projects or functions for which they are responsible. They consolidate and report progress, findings, etc. in accordance with some executive guidelines.

COMMITTEE OR EXECUTIVE (Upper) These meetings are made up of senior management and executive members who review and evaluate the information or results provided to them. Their function is to make decisions on this information - having the power to reject or accept proposals.

It should be noted that there are two sides to each meeting. That is, although the executives can decide upon the results presented, they must also be able to present, direct or execute the procedures necessary to get the results. While middle management meetings are to provide, analyze and consolidate information, the participants must be able to supervise, manage and present the activities that will provide the results. Finally, worker meetings that are to provide the basic information, must also have the mechanism to present it. So the presentation and the evaluation of the information are the key ingredients to any meeting.

It is in this aspect that meetings bare their prime purposes, for they show everyone who matters how any individual can handle both presentation and evaluation aspects to the "good of the company". That is, how does he evaluate, manage or do what he is responsible for? In any company, therefore, it is wise to pay attention to this aspect. Thus we have the LAWS OF PROGRESS:

LAW 1: You will progress only when you "do your job well".
LAW 2: Your "job competency" will be judged by someone above you.

LAW 3: You must "convince" someone above you that you are doing well.

Well, if you dare to venture into this arena, the meeting is the quickest way to progress. This is where you can "show off" to those above you. This is called exposure.

You can show that you do your job well and you can convince others besides your boss that you have great potential. On the other hand, it could be a quick way of proving to those above you that you are a real twit.

Meetings, it seems, always have "judges" in attendance. They will attempt to evaluate presentations and performance. Since the meeting's function is to deal with information, it will also be judged. The quick way to stardom is to get these judges together and put on a performance. A couple of good performances can even put pressure to bear on your own boss - if you so desire.

It should be noted that certain items in the LAWS OF PROGRESS are in quotes. These deal with your "competency" and the act of "convincing" someone of your competency. When one considers that, according to the PETER PRINCIPLE, each has a tendency to rise to his own level of incompetence, it makes a mockery of the competence judging process. Secondly, how one convinces these incompetent people is also quite a joke, particularly if one tries to relate this to his technical ability. In conjunction with the LAWS OF AQ'ISM, we find that because corporate people constantly seek profit, power and prestige, meetings become great gatherings of corporate assholes that meet to "jockey" for position.

Everyone attempts to impress someone else, regardless of whether someone else is an asshole. And, because companies exist to produce and make profits, it follows that the best way of impressing superiors is to convince them that you can get things done in a better or more efficient way - convince them that they can affect the bottom line of time and money. When you consider that the three types of meetings provided, analyzed, then evaluated information successively, and each group became less concerned with details because they were closer to their levels of incompetence, you begin to seriously question how companies survive. But this is the game you must play. Let us sum up with a new law:

Meetings bring together a group of incompetent assholes who attempt to exchange and present ever-deteriorating information in such a way as to impress each other so they can become bigger assholes and affect company profits.

THE BOTTOM LINE MENTALITY

Whatever management group one is in, whatever the meeting is, a corporate culture will always include being tuned to a "bottom line" That bottom has to do with profit and efficiency - making things better. If one does not tune into this in their climb, one will quickly fall off the AQ productivity slide. Of note are different levels of special knowing that gets less and less defined.

In our examples, we see that the climb into middle management was aided by some special service, accomplishment or luck in the lower depths of the company, but not one of them seems to be an exceptional hero. What is really relevant here? They seem to have a formal education but do you really think they remember their training? Not on your life! That is what I call **the first level** of training... useless and forgotten except for papers (degrees) on the walls and a bit of has-been bullshit now and again to scare the troops into believing they are smart. I have yet to meet an executive who had a clue about the things he learned to get a degree. Believe me, executives do not maintain their status by being technically competent! This was abandoned years ago.

There is a **second level** to note. If we should look back into the profiles, we see that in addition to being educated formally, certain business courses or degrees (business administration, commerce, finance, economics) were earned. Franklin, for example earned a degree in business administration. Scab, already somewhat trained as an accountant, supplemented his arsenal with commerce. Both Slink and Scooter added business administration to their lists. The backbone of a company... and the backbone of the second level of training is... you guessed it... PROFIT and THE BOTTOM LINE! Not exactly a surprising conclusion, is it? I have yet to meet a successful executive (I said successful) that did not know about profit and the bottom line. In a high level meeting, did you notice that good executives were always focused on finance – the bottom line – as it is commonly referred to (budgets, profits, revenues, etc.), and those things that affect it (efficiency, cost benefits)? This is the new "technology" for the executive.

But now comes a new clue. I call this the **third level** of training. It is even less obvious than the second level. The more prominent executives added some very interesting courses or outside specialties to their credentials. These were a mixture of interesting techniques revealed by the course titles. If you cannot recall the details, here is a short list of examples:

- Exclusive Executive Manipulators
- National Groinkickers
- Boardroom Brawlers of America
- Hedging
- Dress to Kill
- Super Scabbing
- Sidestepping to Fame
- Choosing your Corporate Victim
- Tough Kookie Tactics

- Brotherhood of Loudmouths
- Belligerent Tactics
- Shabby Business Practices
- Direction by Misdirection
- Business Facades
- Narrow Outlooks

Sounds silly doesn't it? But these courses provided certain valuable skills *not* acquired at school. The reality is that these are really not taught in school at all... guess you knew that all the time! The reality is that these executives did learn some tricks from somewhere. They are picked up as extra "tactics" that were needed to deal with and to move through the **"Time of the great transition"**. What is particularly interesting about this process is that I have observed these same tactics in boardrooms around the world, whether it is in government, Fortune 500 companies or even the smallest company. If we look closer, in fact, we would see that the ones who have progressed the fastest (Franklin and Scab) have taken the most courses... or perhaps learned the most effective tricks.

There is a time in every executive's life where he is groomed, or grooms himself for the title of executive. The ones who get here and stay here appear to have learned a very effective set of tools that I call weapons... through that third level of training. If you have ever been in a room with some of these experts, they can cut you to ribbons and make a fool out of you or your presentation in an instant. For this reason, I call this weaponry the **Executive Arsenal**. You may wonder why I choose to call these an arsenal. Two reasons: They truly are weapons used to disarm, immobilize or injure and I guess we may as well keep focused on that human posterior again... the arse as it is commonly referred to. When you get through this chapter, you can judge for yourself how appropriate this is.

THE GREAT TRANSITION

At some point in one's corporate life, if one is to climb upwards into the upper echelon, fly with eagles, sit high up in the tree; one must go through the Great Transition - sort of like a corporate menopause. This happens somewhere in the middle management phase when one has to start letting go of that which he has learned and been trained for - to become immersed more in the methods of business and management. Towards the end of this period, he must also develop his arsenal in preparation for the move into the upper management and executive echelon. If he fails, then the process will be difficult and perhaps even disastrous. The Great Transition involves getting your degree in the second and third levels of training.

If I could possibly summarize the Great Transition, it would probably be that period of time where there is an urgent need to understand and adapt to dealing well with "Boardroom Brawling" and the "Bottom line". I say this because executives spend more and more time in meetings… the boardroom… that is where they jockey for position, power and recognition. If you were to spend most of your time in meetings, it would make sense to gather up a new expertise in performing well at meetings. Clearly, some must be weapons that allow one to survive in the boardroom - that place where executives spend the majority of time. Clearly you can't use your technical skills any more so what can you do when AQ Disequilibrium knocks on your door? My contention is that the majority of the Executive Arsenal is therefore made up of weapons used in boardroom brawling so as to adjust that AQ because more often than not, these tactics are mercilessly deployed to protect power, money, ego and position. we have already learned about the six arsenals executives use.

These are the secret tools that keep AQ's high. Putting people down, in their places, keeping tuned to the bottom line seems to work effectively when one become heartless and emotionless maintaining the cold tact of: "it is just business". Why, consider this profile of so many executives:

- They usually have forgotten the discipline they used to get the position.
- They have picked some business related education or experience.
- They have developed boardroom brawling techniques.
- They have picked up "bottom line" savvy.
- They have learned to treat people like assholes.
- They are not shy about successfully telling people they are assholes!
- They made it through the Big Transition into management.
- They have somehow successfully come through the Great Transition.
- They have a very high AQ.

Because an executive has moved into a world where boardroom brawling and the use of this arsenal takes up a majority of his time, this distinguishes them from the pyramid below. But they have usually elevated the AQ through the AQ phases of calling, treating and telling so they are good at it. This means that they can treat others like assholes and get away with it as part of normal function. It is this aspect that one must pay attention to. The executive arsenals are just the tools that allow the executive to stay in AQ Equilibrium.

And this little aspect is one of the most significant secrets that executives learn... the art of AQ Equilibrium using the arsenals. How do they do it? Well these tools are very effective in creating assholes so if you need to get the AQ higher to maintain your position, use the tools. If, on the other hand, you find your AQ is too high and you need to elevate your position, try using tools to make yourself look good... at the expense of creating or maintaining assholes. And where is this best accomplished? In the boardroom or in meetings of course!

BOARDROOM BRAWLING

One final word about this most popular AQ training ground... the meeting or the boardroom. It is pretty clear that the executive spends a lot of time in meetings. Estimates vary but this time can be around 60%. That is why the meeting is the true place of performance for an executive. This is the prime battlefield. I can also tell you that there are many executives appearing on this battlefield who do not know how to align their AQ's... and have not learned the arsenals very well. In reality, things don't always happen smoothly in meetings and many are quite a joke, but if there is an executive present who is skilled in AQ Arsenals, he will surely be the one to watch. Some executives are quite aggressive, and in many cases, self-centered individuals with appetites for power and an insatiable appetite for ego food. Others are just plain stupid. It is not uncommon to see some fairly volatile performances occur when there is a possibility of others threatening a position.

It must be remembered that the vast majority of executives did not get to their position in the tree by just sitting there and doing nothing. And it must be also remembered that these people are constantly being threatened by newer executives lower down who are themselves similar in aggression and needs... and with their own arsenals. They had to replace someone or they had to be better than someone else. So these boardroom meeting places are truly places where great performances (funny or sad) take place.

It has been suggested that meetings are a means of accomplishing critical things fast. We listed several main purposes. It has also been stated that executives are decision makers. This means that they must get to the heart of things fast and make effective decisions on spending money, resolving problems and making profit for the company.

Well, if it worked this way all the time, it would indeed be an efficient corporate world. The truth of the matter is, however, that many executives are not well trained and meetings do not work efficiently all the time. As I said before, the reality is that they do not have much of a clue about technology... or the area of expertise in which they may have started. That makes it a new scene for all. What's the substitute "technology"? Why the "bottom line", "cost benefits", "budgets", "efficiency", "revenues", "commitments", right? It is this that forms the basis of meetings and if you don't believe this, then my advice is to keep away from this group. But I have noted another interesting phenomenon at these meetings that makes it easy to apply AQ tools effectively. I call this the Laws of Executive Regression.

THE LAWS OF EXECUTIVE REGRESSION

It is not hard to understand how many executives become outdated and helpless in a family of "eagles" or "condors". Most have forgotten their chosen technology... called a *has-been*. They also require a new area of expertise, called finance... that makes them *dummies*. This means that has-been dummies are running companies. Think back to the big meeting we had at Steadfast Meats. Is it surprising, in view of this to understand why the following laws are in force at an executive meeting?

LAW 1   Information deteriorates as it moves upwards in a pyramid.

LAW 2   Meetings bring together a group of incompetent assholes who attempt to exchange and present ever deteriorating information in such a way as to impress each other so they can become bigger assholes and affect company profit.

LAW 3   The more general or simple the topic is, the more likely it is that it will get blown out of proportion.

LAW 4   Authorization is quickly given when the authorizers cannot be held responsible should the project fail and when all of them can claim credit should it succeed.

LAW 5   The greater the cost of putting a plan into operation the less the chance there is of abandoning the plan - even if it becomes irrelevant.

LAW 6   The higher the level of prestige accorded the people behind the plan, the lesser the chance of abandoning it.

LAW 7   Rationality will prevail only when all other possibilities have been exhausted.

LAW 8   The more distant the participants are from the facts the more likely they are to believe what they hear.

LAW 9   The amount of time spent on detailed discussions can be inversely proportional to the financial commitment.

LAW 10   If a majority of the attendees are responsible for a miscalculation no one will be at fault.

LAW 11   Justification procedures will become more difficult as the cost decreases.

Can you better understand why so many meetings are such a joke? Yet things do get done. These are the laws commonly working against progress and these are the laws that help AQ's rise quickly. It is this mixture of idealistic approaches and regressive obstacles with which we see executives functioning. This is the corporate playground where the rules are learned and executed by has-been dummies.

But, when this does get out of hand, the AQ Virus sets in and everybody thinks everybody else is an asshole, guess what?

Insolvency! Bankruptcy!

Of course, one can always work for the government or be a politician where even the asshole saturation can be the norm!

6

AQ TOOLS TO GET YOUR WAY

MANIPULATOR METHODOLOGY

There is yet another important aspect of the Great Transition that an executive needs to add to the AQ Arsenal - Manipulation. So far we have looked at Boardroom Brawling and Trouble Tactics. We then looked at the importance of the Corporate Culture. What we have missed, however, are those special tools needed to create the insidious little ploys and deceptions required to get your way - to suck your opponents in, so to speak. To suck people in properly, a ploy is needed whereby a chronological set of planned steps is executed so as to lead someone towards an inevitable conclusion - the one that is sought. If we should look back at the Defensive Arsenal, we would see that the method of Fast Forward and Flash were methodical ploys to hide vulnerability. Clearly these methods were designed to control the material being presented so as to avoid entrapment and potentially bad issues.

Manipulator Methodology attempts to go one step further - to force a required decision or conclusion. This is a particularly useful segment of the arsenal should you be negotiating, selling something or just seeking approval on some proposal. As an executive, it is not likely that negotiating situations can be avoided. Whether it is a new deal, a contract negotiation, convincing superiors, or just a plain con job the need for **Manipulator Methods** will be inevitable. As the executive moves through the Great Transition, these methods must be learned, used and tucked away in the Arsenal. Once again, we take lessons from the experts; the executives.

THE MANIPULATOR'S ARSENAL

The manipulators' methodology involves the creation of a pre-meditated ploy to lead others towards your own planned conclusion. As ones skill increases in the use of such techniques they will be executed in an almost automatic manner. One must invent his own little facades that surround the ploy. Following is a list of the more popular methodologies:

EXHAUSTION: WANT TO GO THROUGH IT AGAIN?

Exhaustion depends upon the perseverance of the manipulator.

WANT TO GO THROUGH A FEW RESEARCH PAPERS OR SIGN NOW?

EXHAUSTION

Clearly the principle used is to exhaust the opponents into submission. You can insist upon going through your pitch over and over until they are sick of hearing it. You can hold a sequence of meetings. By the sixth meeting on the same issue, they may be quite happy to agree to your proposal - anything to avoid another performance!

TYRANT: DO YOU WANT THE MEANIE BACK?

The tyrant method requires a dual play. Typically, negotiations can start with some mean uncompromising son of a bitch who can get everyone riled up. It may even be the case that some trivial issues are blown out of proportion - all a ploy to make this guy look like a mean cookie. The second player is the one who gets things approved, after the first leaves. The key here is to subtly threaten to bring the tyrant in to take over should there be the slightest suggestion of deadlock. Once the initial image is imbedded in their heads, the threat of having this asshole in again could scare them into accepting.

LESSER EVIL: LOSE A LITTLE OR LOSE A LOT

This method sets up some choices that clearly reflect losing situations. The ploy is to create alternatives that are loses greater than the one desired by the manipulator. The statement "*sell now at half price or wait and go broke*" illustrates the idea. Needless to say, the idea of going broke is the greater evil so that the lesser evil will be chosen. If done properly, the choices may even look superb in comparison to the other evils. In many cases the ploy may not involve bad situations, just undesirable ones - in comparison to the one desired.

HUMBLE PIE: I TOO HAVE BEEN SUCH A TWIT

Humble pie uses a ploy that breaks down barriers and potentially disarms opponents. *"I too have made those same errors but I learned to live with them"* may have a tendency to relax the environment, especially if the manipulator is known to be highly successful. Opposite of a know it all or braggart, a humble admission is done in such a way as to break down barriers but at the same time serve as a reminder of the power that one may have. A self-made millionaire who says "*I too lost my shirt seven times before I learned*" somehow does not seem as awesome an opponent as if he just sat quietly waiting for your mistakes. And "*Yes, I too have been such an asshole*" may for a few moments make you feel sorry for him and be vulnerable as a result. It does not really take away from the fact that he is a plagiarizing anus.

PAPER PILES: SEE ENOUGH TO GIVE UP NOW

Paper piles are used more as a bluff than anything. The method relies on volumes of files, memos, reports, etc. which could be totally unrelated to the topic. The real papers are just on top of an awesome pile of material that may have to be addressed one by one - a fearful alternative of wasting time.

Continued bluffing references to more detail could tread fear in their bones, particularly when you say "*Well it appears that I left that portion in my office - should I go get it?*" Anyway, who is to know that you just picked up some silly stuff at the library - just before the meeting?

LEAD-IN: I KNOW I SHOULDN'T BUT

The lead-in is less of a ploy and more of a tact. It is used to get at touchy, sensitive matters that normally cannot be dealt with directly. "*I know that this may have been a sensitive issue with you before Quigley, but...*" or "*This may be personal Flash, but would you mind if we addressed it again*" are lead-ins which acknowledge the sensitivity of an issue and therefore, theoretically, give the manipulator the right to pry a little further. "*I know that you are sensitive about this Dr. Dork, but could you explain why you screw sheepdogs?*" may well soften Dr. Dork's reaction and at the same time cause an admittance that could severely destroy his credibility.

DEADLINE: WE MUST LEAVE IN 5 MINUTES

Consider yourself having flown to Dallas for the day to negotiate a price on a shipment of Whiffits. Upon arrival you are met by two executives who know that you are leaving for New York at 5:00 pm. After a leisurely breakfast, they insist that they show you some breathtaking scenery, and finally after cocktails and lunch, head for the office to talk turkey. After a few delays in finding legal people and odds and sods, the meeting starts at 4:00 pm. But the two executives insist that they can discuss the deal in the car on the way to the airport since "your plane leaves in one hour". Knowing that you need to make a deal or possibly look stupid for wasting a day - guess who is likely to settle for a stupid price? Deadlines can be used to precipitate settlements - after carefully wasting the majority of time.

INVESTMENT: JUST A BIT MORE OF YOUR TIME

The investment method is a good ploy against salesmen. The idea being that if you should walk in to a store, look at a stove marked $599.00 and offer $399.00, the salesman could easily tell you to stick it where you don't need it. On the other hand, if you come in repeatedly each day for four days and kept asking Mr. Wizzbanger, the salesman, for more and more details, for half an hour each time, you have forced Wizzbanger to invest considerable time in you - with no sale. If on the fifth day you tell him that you can only afford $350.00 and you have it with you, what is the possibility of getting that stove for $399 - much better isn't it? Wizzbanger, who has spent all this time with you and has little to show for it may well settle for considerably less.

FINALE: AND NOW WE PRESENT

The finale simply keeps all the critical stuff for last - sort of like the key witness in a legal case. The idea is to parcel up favorable facts in little bundles to spread them out over the length of the meeting and then when the time is right - whammo - you hit with all the key stuff. Alternatively, you may prefer to offer little until that last crucial moment when others have spent their efforts. Just imagine trying to convince a group of investors on a new computerized trading method, spending hours of technical discussions on how the system works. Then table the receipts of a clients transactions with a 60% return on investment.

FAKE FIGHT: OK YOU WIN NOW LET'S MOVE ON

The fake fight relies on the creation and losing of little trivial battles to make it look like the opponent is winning. But all the time, you are moving him closer to the big kill (the real fight). By giving him ground, he may gain over-confidence and increase his vulnerability. This is the same idea as luring an animal into a trap. You must, however, be prepared to pounce upon your victim at the right moment.

SAMARITAN: I ALREADY HAVE SEVERAL OFFERS

The Samaritan is the one who is always saving the deal for you. No matter how many others are clamoring for it. So you bear this in mind when you yourself are attempting to sell something or negotiate a deal. Without looking like a complete bullshitter, you create the pretense that you have other alternatives available but as yet you have not closed the deal. Or you may have other offers but you prefer dealing with more reputable and competent people. Consider yourself walking around a furniture store and after 15 minutes you stop by a couch that you like. The salesman, who has kept an eagle eye on you from a distance, notices that you, his prey, are ready. *"What is the price of this couch?"* you ask. *"I am sorry, sir, but I believe this one has been sold and it is the last one. Do you want me to check for you?"*. If you like it you will say yes with a hope that perhaps it may be available. You have just become emotional about it and increased your vulnerability to price - without even knowing the price. In fact the "sold" was pure fabricated bullshit but how do you know? When he returns he says: *"They are checking , is there anything else that interests you?"* If you say you will wait, then he has you by the short hairs. *"There seems to be a problem with the other guys credit. Would you pay cash?"* Guess who just got sucked in by the Samaritan? These same little ploys can be used in the boardroom.

AMPLIFIER: AND NOW FOR THE GOOD NEWS

In this ploy, the idea is to start with bad news, negative items, etc, and then relieve the disappointment with good news. There is a time of transition where the continuance of bad has a tendency to gear one's mind towards expectation and therefore an emotional vulnerability. The immediate break of such an anticipated trend has a tendency to amplify how great the good news is.

We saw this starting with the sale of the couch in the last ploy. This could have gone on quite a bit further as the salesman built up your emotional need for the couch, and also the distance between you and the possible acquisition. Then the good news would have seemed an incredible opportunity - despite a ridiculous price. The same effect is caused by going through numerous trivial disadvantages of a proposal first, then canceling them all by bringing in a few great advantages. Not only are they amplified, but also the others are lost in time.

SWITCHO: LET'S LOOK AT IT THIS WAY

The switcho can be used to present a new look at something. In many negotiation cases it becomes easy to become bogged down in a rut and get nowhere. It is at this time that you must switch to a different approach because obviously the first is a dead end. For example say you have been trying to convince your superior that you need to subscribe to the Wall Street Journal to get some statistics for your project. Your boss just can't see the justification so you say *"Lets look at it this way. Mr. Hotshit, the President mentioned that the journal is the most comprehensive and informative paper around. Maybe, he would share the cost?"* Your boss would obviously understand this a bit better since his decision on getting the journal, especially if he mentions it to Hotshit, would possibly receive recognition from the President. The non-support very rapidly switched to support.

ONE MORE: JUST ONE MORE TO GO

The one more ploy is much like patting a dog on the head for being a good boy. The pat suggests that what was done before can be done again. Consider a case, where multiple items need resolution, and one sticky one is left. The pat is thusly "*We have done such a great job of resolving all those issues. It would surely be a shame to stop now. I am sure we can resolve this last issue*". Although it is sort of an insipid little appeal, sometimes it relieves tension to highlight positive aspects - and to in fact attempt a solution.

TRIGGER: AND AT THAT TIME...

The trigger is used to create a fear in someone. An anticipated fear or the realization of a potential loss can cause a trigger effect that precipitates action. Salesmen love to use this one by telling you that in 3 months, the price will go up by 30%. That is a trigger ploy to get you to buy now - in fear of the 30% increase. Consider this statement: "*Rolly, we see that you are late on your budget preparation. After September 1st. we will get three engineers to help you.*" Rolly, who is a true blue bean counter and has the hair on his neck straightened out at the thought of engineers helping him will surely get his budget done before September!

GEARSHIFT: ONE, TWO THREE AND SIGN

The gearshift ploy, much like the "*Wham bam thank you Man*" requires clear control. Here you must shift to the right topic at the right time, increasing the speed of information transfer and keeping all others on the defensive. When you are going at a good speed, much faster than they can assimilate, they become further removed from a true understanding and are less likely to stop the proceedings for fear of looking like stupid assholes. It is at that time that you want agreement and, if you are dealing with turkeys and simps, this is the time that agreement could come quickly. Gear shifting requires a careful control of material. In this way, one can control what it is that the others can see, avoid details, skip stuff, scan and so on.

THE MANIPULATOR'S MENTALITY

The 16 odd Manipulator Methods discussed are only some of the many methods that tenacious negotiators use. They do, however, serve to illustrate the main ideas. It goes without saying that a Manipulator must have a certain cold mentality, without any fear of being an asshole... by treating people like assholes. In general, a good manipulator will show the following characteristics:

- He is well prepared and knowledgeable on his topic.
- He is not easily ruffled.
- He does not delegate since it dilutes authority, knowledge and control.
- He does not make snap decisions.
- He has a clear course of action, concessions and ploys.
- He uses language and grammar wisely - without confusion.
- He has a strong instinct in detecting weakness.
- He is a diplomatic asshole.

So the mentality of being a cool, narrow-minded asshole is a very important aspect of being a good manipulator - and a good executive! Does it make you wonder about the MBA and how useful it is?

THE EXECUTIVE LESSONS

Well, we now come to the end of the executive secrets. The previous chapters have attempted to reveal key ingredients that executives seem to develop in order to maintain AQ Equilibrium. These we revealed as the essential tools of the executive "trade", making it possible for the executive to truly be the asshole that he tries to aspire to.

We looked at the executive meeting. Here we saw the executives in action, using their tools as best they could. Although the meeting seemed funny and even absurd, it contained many of the brawling and tactical techniques also discussed - they just may not have been obvious.

After looking at these tools, one will recognize them clearly ad in many cases one can come to understand how an executive can so effectively how the executive operates to hide his deficiencies. The AQ tools - known as the Executive Arsenals are used to maintain power, execute control and to make decisions. They are a direct substitute for any technical details that executives lack. More important, these tools can be used to maintain AQ Equilibrium. The six arsenals, mainly the Offensive, Defensive, Aversive, Tactical, Manipulator and Cultural were AQ tools developed through the Great Transition. We have looked at all sides in the use of the Arsenals - to illustrate more clearly how to deal with them as well as how to use them.

But here is the crux of the matter. The AQ allows you to measure your relationship to others in the company. But the AQ level is directly related to your position. If these are out of line you are in AQ Dis-equilibrium, in which case you have four choices:

1. Raise your AQ to be in line with your position
2. Raise your position to be in line with your AQ
3. Leave and zero it out
4. Refuse to engage in its viral tendency

All these arsenals are used to make 1. and 2. happen as quickly as possible. And the executive, who spends so much time in meetings, has become expert in the application of these methods in this forum.

So ends our satire on this part of corporate life. Hopefully you have gained a new perspective on corporations and those pillars of strength at the top. Yes, they were all stripped naked for a while to give you a new look at them. Yes, this was presented as a satire but in reality there have been many people and situations that may be more real than we care to admit. I reading all this, you may have wondered what was real and what was fiction. But from now on, at the end of each working day, after all those dealings with your co-workers, just think about a simple question: *"How's your AQ today?"*

There is, however, one other important aspect about the executive that we have neglected to discuss. This relates to the fact that they have come through the earlier phases of the AQ progression - through Middle Management and successfully navigated the **Great Transition.** It is in the travels through Middle Management that he has picked up other AQ tricks and tools that were needed for AQ Equilibrium - the ones picked up through the **Big Transition**. These tools helped him move through Middle Management. Obviously these are known as the Manager's Arsenal.

7

WHAT ABOUT MIDDLE MANAGEMENT?

Should one study the career path of many individuals, it would be easy to see that they start somewhere in some junior position in the company. This is the first level we call WORKERS. After they have spent time they would attain more responsibilities and possibly become a manager of people and processes.. We call this level the DOERS This would be the second level. To simplify things we have the third level of Executives we call the DECISION MAKERS. It is time to see what this second level has evolved as their secret arsenals to climb in the Corporation.

WHAT DOES MIDDLE MANAGEMENT USE?

THE NEXT LEVEL - MIDDLE MANAGEMENT

As we step down into the next level of the corporation we encounter the group known as Middle Managers. Technically, these are the ones who maintain AQ's between 40 and 80 and are the guys *"caught in the middle"*. They do not do the real work and they do not make the big decisions. They are, however, the group we call the DOERS and are an important part of corporate structures. If one could summarize their purpose in a sentence it may look like this:

MIDDLE MANAGEMENT ATTEMPTS TO IMPROVE PRODUCTIVITY OR CAPTURE A LARGER SHARE OF THE MARKET PLACE WITHOUT CREATING A PROPORTIONATE RISE IN COSTS.

To continue on this noble cause, there are a limited number of ways that this may be accomplished :

- Method of production or quality of service improves.
- Production or service costs decrease.
- Market place quantity or demand increases.

And these must be done without causing a proportionate rise in costs! Hence we have more profit! Once again, there must be certain tools required to do this. Just as the Executive had his own tools refined through the GREAT TRANSITION, the Manager must develop his tools through the BIG TRANSITION.

As we look back, we will recall that in order to move into and through the Middle Management group, a person had to go through the AQ phases of **calling** others Assholes and **telling** them that they were Assholes, and finally **treating** them thusly so as to qualify for the next level. This gave them the *"moxy"* and the *"balls"* to *"get things done"*. The qualification was that this had to be done in a step by step fashion in line with AQ levels and Corporate position otherwise a productivity slide would ensue. But unlike the more direct methodology behind the Executive Arsenals which dealt with treating others as Assholes, the Management Arsenal is less direct, dealing with the process of calling and telling - a more subtle approach to AQ'ISM.

And these are needed so as to allow a graceful move into the GREAT TRANSITION. But just like the AQ Phases, the BIG TRANSITION is a primer, and necessary stepping stone to the GREAT TRANSITION. For those who fail the process, productivity slides threaten the climb upwards, offering ample opportunities for precipitous slides downwards.

This section of the book is devoted to the Manager's Arsenals. The tools within it are used to move in AQ Equilibrium, maintaining a nice steady growth to the AQ process. Like the "successful" executive who has evolved some AQ oriented aversive survival tools to maintain order, focus, and power, so has the Manager.

THE BIG TRANSITION & MANAGEMENT ETHIC

During the Big Transition, a worker moves his corporate orientation towards **managing** rather than **working.** Managing becomes the new work load. In this state, there are new concerns and objectives that were previously of little concern. When Franklin Hardass moved into a Supervisory role, it was because he had accomplished a few things at a technical level. The just reward was to make him a supervisor over the area which he had excelled in. His entry to supervision brought the need for new tools to deal with people and processes in general because he knew nothing about managing people. Consequently, the technical level would have to be left behind. He would trade technologies for techniques - The Big Transition. Here Franklin would have to learn how to *deal with people and processes from a new platform* - with a strong urgency to use methods not learned at University.

So Dealing with, Evaluating and Improving People or Processes would become part of the Management Arsenal. The application of Power to People who effect Processes then effect Profit (or loss).

In a nutshell, we have the Middle Management Process, which we call the MANAGEMENT ETHIC:

THE APPLICATION OF POWER TO PEOPLE WHO EFFECT
PROCESSES SO AS TO INCREASE PROFIT

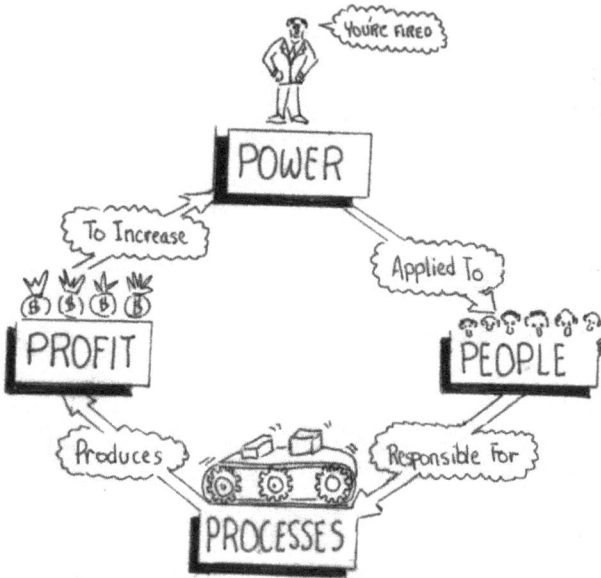

Looking back once again, in the discussion of the Great Transition, it was noted that from an educational point of view there were three distinct groupings. Let us dwell on this a bit :

PRIMARY EDUCATION.
Primary education refers to the main university or college degree attained. In the case of Franklin Hardass, he attained a degree in Mechanical Engineering. Murk Muddler, on the other hand, got his Law degree as his Primary mechanism. This, was the initial ticket to the professional world, starting out in the worker levels.

SECONDARY EDUCATION.

The secondary education refers to the college or other formal courses which brings one into the Economic or Financial Realm of Corporations. Here one learns about Finance, Accounting and Economics - the fundamental backbone to Corporations. This secondary process, in the case of Franklin Hardass was supplementary education in Business and Commerce. For those who have this type of primary education as their main profession, the secondary area will become related to the company specialty (i.e. mining, manufacturing, etc.). This secondary education facilitates the ticket to, and hence travel within, the middle management empire.

TERTIARY EDUCATION.

The tertiary education refers to those tools and techniques which are learned the hard way, or through extra curricular courses. The area of application, is of course, the Arsenals which we have spoken of. In the case of Franklin Hardass, he had taken Boardroom Brawling and Groinkicker courses to help in his tertiary education. This education, depending upon ones ability, gives one the ticket to proceed into the third executive empire.

As one proceeds up the pyramid and into the BIG TRANSITION, he moves further away from the primary education and begins to rely more and more on the techniques learned and developed in the secondary area. Similarly, progression upwards into the GREAT TRANSITION will move even further away from the primary education, and rely heavily on the tertiary education. It is hardly surprising, given this situation, to see Executives as stupid, incompetent, cold and influential assholes if viewed from a lower platform - since they rely less and less upon knowing anything about the details, people and processes (except from a general viewpoint). They rely more upon their Executive Arsenals. The same can be stated about a worker's view of Middle Management.

So what are these new weapons acquired through the BIG TRANSITION? Let us move on and find out.

THE MIDDLE MANAGERS – WHAT MAKES THEM SO GREAT?

We come now to the serious question of determining what makes a good manager. Have you ever heard Executives make statements about a good middle manager?

- *"Penelope Pennypinch always comes in under budget."*
- *"Phil Feeler really knows how to motivate people."*
- *"Slip Solvo knows instinctively how to get to the bottom of a*
- *problem."*
- *"Bill Bigstick never takes any shit from anybody."*
- *"Carl Crasher can be trusted to get the job 'organized'".*
- *"Suzy Smooth sure makes that process hum."*
- *"Sam Sleeze sure knows his area."*

And have you ever heard any of the following statements about middle managers coming from the lower reaches?

- *"Penelope Pennypinch, the rotten bitch, just cuts indiscriminately."*
- *"Phil Feeler has to be the biggest two-faced egocentric son of a bitch around."*
- *"Slip Solvo's biggest problem is himself."*
- *"Bill Bigstick, the loud mouth scum sucker, really thinks he is tough."*
- *"Carl Crasher the stupid twirp, would never do anything if it wasn't for us organizing ourselves."*
- *"Suzy Smooth, the goddam prima donna, doesn't even know what is going on."*
- *"Sam Sleeze plagiarizes so much he could make a leech run for cover."*

This, as you may have guessed, constitutes the delicate line between the Worker and the Executive as walked upon by the middle managers. But perhaps you may have heard different comments coming from those workers?"

- "*Penelope Pennypinch knows how to cut costs in the right area.*"
- "*Phil Feeler can really make you see how great the company is.*"
- "*Slip Solvo puts all the pieces together to solve a problem.*"
- "*Bill Bigstick is always firm and fair.*"
- "*Carl Crasher is a wizard at organizing jobs.*"
- "*Suzy Smooth gets into the swamps to help things move well.*"
- "*Sam Sleeze puts people's ideas together to make things gel and makes us look great.*"

Whenever the executives note that an improvement has been made it will undoubtedly be at some expense somewhere down the line. It is more likely, therefore, that the second set of statements will be the result of the first set. Isn't that the way things usually go? There seems to be some perverted Corporate Law at work here which states :

FOR ANY POSITIVE EXECUTIVE ACTION UPON A MIDDLE MANAGER THERE IS AN OPPOSITE AND NEGATIVE REACTION ON THE PART OF THE WORKER

This is the **MANAGEMENT DILEMMA.**

So managers are great when they can cut costs, motivate people, solve problems, get tough, organize, make things efficient, show job knowledge and be trusted. But there is typically an effect down the line. The Law is quite a mouthful isn't it? If we look closer at this we will see that fundamentally, Managers must be able to deal with four major areas. These we already noted as the components of the MANAGEMENT ETHIC, mainly POWER, PEOPLE, PROCESS and PROFIT. These were the areas where a new arsenal of weapons are required. It is here that we find the stuff that makes "good managers". They may not be very likeable chaps but they are good managers. It's just business, right?

Before we forge ahead to inspect some of the evolved techniques, a few comments need to be made. The so called good managers must also start phasing into the EXECUTIVE ARSENALS and the use of these, particularly as they become involved in more and more meetings and negotiations, this becomes essential. Since there is more emphasis on meetings at the executive level, we have simply included those arsenals under the Executive. But just as the Executive developed, and must still use Management Arsenals, the Manager must start the development and use of the Executive Arsenal.

THE MANAGER'S DILEMMA

First, look at the picture on the next page. This is the Management Dilemma. As you move into Middle Management you must learn to deal with these conflicts. Whereas you were responsible for what you did as a worker, now you are responsible for what they did. If they screw up, then you get the flack. If your process screws up then you get shit. If you spend too much or produce too little, you get shit. If you push people too hard, you get flack - and so it goes - the Managers Dilemma! Middle Managers are truly in the middle and there are many, many ways of screwing up and getting shit. It is just like the Executive who is caught between the board or shareholders and the Middle Management who are there to replace them if they fail.

If you are one of these lucky ones, where everything always runs smooth, on time, on quota, within costs - good for you - but this is not the way things work normally. Sooner or later something will go wrong or you will have to deal with a problem. How you deal with it will then give your superiors the means of evaluating your performance. It is when things are going astray that you need weapons - not when they are going well. And of course, good weapons are necessary to keep AQ Equilibrium. Well, as our hypothesis goes, a manager must develop new ways of being an Asshole and must also create new "Assholes" to keep position and AQ Equilibrium balanced.

And, as we will see, some of the most aversive tools have evolved as being the norm.

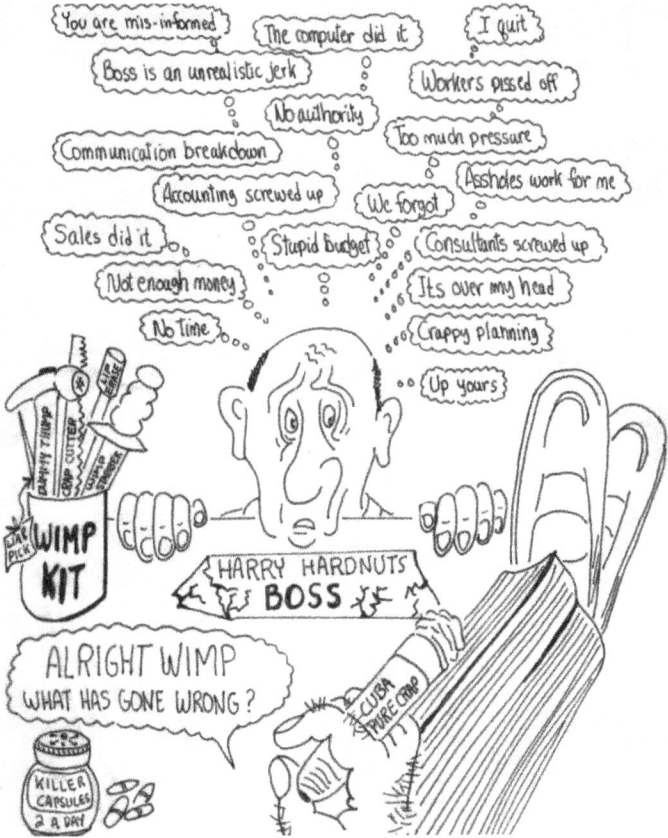

8

THE MANAGER'S POWER SYSTEMS

CORPORATE POWER
WHAT IS IT?

Let us recap some old AQ Theory. As you climb your way upwards on AQ Mountain, your AQ and your position within the Corporation

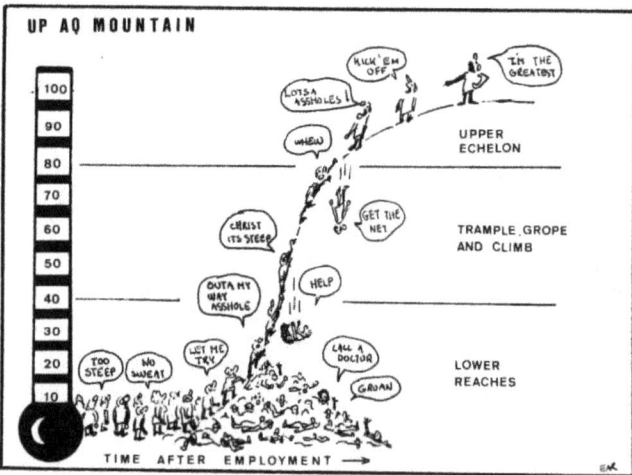

supposedly increase. With this increase comes a phenomenon

known as POWER; power over money, people, and resources. Without power, you have no control, no influence and therefore questionable leadership. Clearly, power is the ability to cause an event to occur or not to occur. It is the ability to influence or control events and people, so it equals control. And control equals fewer surprises and greater predictability - those sought after aspects of good management.

But power is not simply attained through a Corporate position. It can be assumed by attaining a position where it can immediately evoke fear and respect - up to a certain point. But position is not enough. Something else is required. If, for example, you do not use your power, then people will quickly assume that you have none. If you are a senile old fuddy duddy, it will not take long for you to lose any power that a position would have given you. You may be powerless and loved or powerful and feared. If you cannot stand behind your orders because you do not want to hurt someone's feelings, you will lose power very quickly indeed. That is when one

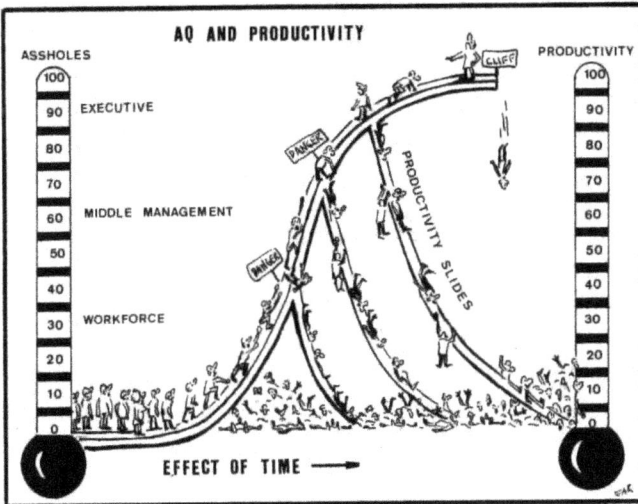

AQ AND PRODUCTIVITY

faces the prospect of the AQ out of whack and a productivity slide. On the other hand, the assistant or secretary who knows more than the boss actually has more power than the boss - they just don't have the position or title. In the case where "powerful" people do not have the position, they make up for it by having influence. They can exert indirect power through influence. The result is still the same. So how is it that one gains and retains that illusive portion of power known as influence? This is the stuff that a position may give, but not retain.

It is here that we have the first clue about the group that we have classified as Mid-management. As a mid-manager you are given power by assuming a position where you can control and influence events and people. You are granted a formal authority from those somewhere above you. So the position symbolizes a certain amount of power, but it is up to you to cultivate and keep the power of influence - the stuff we call informal power.

There are two types of power systems in any corporation - formal and informal. Formal power is defined by position, responsibility and can be specified on paper. It is the process by which owners or top management delegate responsibilities. It is also the means by which power is given to meet those responsibilities. Informal power, on the other hand, is not so clearly defined. It cannot be controlled or defined or accounted for. It crosses the formal power channels. Let us look more closely at some of the characteristics of these two power systems.

FORMAL POWER: Defined Structured Positions and Responsibilities.

This power is typically:

- Defined by the organization chart and position description.
- Warns of territorial boundaries and emphasis is on job designation.
- Exists to provide a sense of direction and security of a

structure.

- Assures outsiders and insiders that a clear organization exists.
- Reflects top managements values.
- Represents the formal means by which an organization is structured and functions.
- :It is the formal set of rules within which everyone is to work .

Despite the importance of formal power systems in any corporation, there are some problems with it. These are as follows :

- The formal system cannot be changed quickly since it can only be changed formally - sometimes a long and tedious process.
- The process by which it functions can be cumbersome and politically inclined since many players must all protect their positions, rights and interests.
- It can not force cooperation. People still decide in their own way who will work well together.
- When a breakdown in cooperation occurs, the system looks back to the rules of the formal system. This may not be the most effective way to get a job done.

INFORMAL POWER: Undefined Cooperative Organizational Lines & Functions.

This type of power is different:

- Uses a face to face principle and is not formally written.
- Everybody can function as an equal.
- Nobody does anything for nothing.
- Relationships are negotiated and deliberately created.
- Position is not relevant - only the ability to perform dictates respect.

- Ethics are rigid. Excuses are not acceptable since there are no ways to enforce informal agreements. There are no reprisals.
- System operates like a society and if someone ignores it he is denied membership. There are no dues except reciprocity.
- The system can never be publically acknowledged.
- The quickest way to lose power is to not perform a promise.

If we compare the two systems we find that one of the key things about the informal system is its ability to get things done by ignoring organizational lines and position descriptions. It also cuts red tape. In a nutshell the key advantages are as below.

Ultimately the informal system makes the company work. People need extraordinary, not formal cooperation to get work out. If people do only as there job descriptions say, then the result - when complications arise - is to say *"It is not my job."*

Business is conducted by an attempt to adapt the formal system to fit crisis situations. The informal system is commonly used to solve a crisis and to resolve political problems.

As one reaches higher up the ladder the informal system becomes harder to penetrate. It becomes more and more invisible but it becomes more and more important. Position descriptions become more and more scarce. An Executive's effectiveness is measured by his abilities to penetrate the informal barriers and to use the system.

The informal system carries with it an informal system of communication and information. It is, like the informal power system, a fast means of moving uncensored news.

In order to gather a better grasp of Formal and Informal systems, consider the following example:

It has become necessary to fire Mervin Mealymouth. It seems that Mervin, for some time now, has not gotten along too well with his boss Herb Finkle. Herb finally brings him in to the office and gives him the informal ultimatum: *"Mervin, you have two options; resign or get fired."* A while later, Mervin the unhappy employee hands in his resignation. The formal system then receives the appropriate termination documentation on the resignation. If he would have chosen being fired, the formal system would have been tediously demanding for documentation and it would have been cumbersomely ineffective. The informal system was much more effective probably for both Herb and Mervin. The clincher, however, is that the informal communication system knew that Mervin was really indirectly fired - and it probably knew why!

Here is another case :

Herk and Jerk are two engineers, working in different departments. Herk gets into a panic situation where he must get a job out in four days. According to all calculations, there is a need for four days. On the second day the shit hits the fan because a miscalculation in one segment requires a two day set back. After work, a depressed Herk tells his buddy Jerk, over a few drinks, about the big problem. Jerk tells Herk that he knows what went wrong - there could be a short cut to the design calculations. If they went back to the office, he could have a look.

At the office, through the night they worked. The next day, a short beer with the boys verified an assumption that Jerk wasn't sure of. Once again they worked away. So what happened? The job was done on time - through the informal system crossing structural barriers and responsibilities - through informal cooperation. If the formal system would have been used Herk would probably not have met the deadline and the job would have failed - for both Herk and the Company. And Herk's boss would not have been pleased. In this case, Herk's boss never knew how it was accomplished. But the informal system knew how the job got done - it started in the pub through bullshitting with the boys.

What we see here is the means through which power manifests itself. Remember that Power applied to people who control processes creates profit. But to make things happen so that these people produce profit you need three critical items. You need the information or knowledge to put the plan together; You need some resources such as people, money, materials, and so on to use; You need to build and maintain critical relationships that will execute the plan. Now theoretically these are the items that you get along with the position, but as we have seen in the example the information, relationship and even resources are not always available through the formal system - they are gotten through the informal system. If the job had not been done both Herk and his boss would have lost some power (and influence). As it was, they both probably gained a little power and respect. Now Herk owed one to Jerk. Thus one of the key ways of maintaining power is to deliver information, relationships and resources so as to get things done.

INFORMATION CHANNELS: GOSSIP OR FACT?

We have seen that within the Formal and Informal power systems, there exist formal and informal communication channels along which information flows. Delegation, reporting, correspondence and formal communication functions flow along the formalized organizational solid and dotted lines. But through these Informal communication channels flows different information - and in different paths if necessary. Typically known as gossip, the information that flows here can carry factual uncensored news, impressions, reactions and speculations on what may happen. And it is usually much more current. Through the use of these channels you can gather consensus, test ideas, kill bad ideas and move your own manipulative information if so desired. Just like the situation when Mervin's "*resignation*" was known by the informal system, many other such little "*goodies*" are known well in advance of the formal system. And this information can be used to your advantage. Here is an example:

The Director of Personnel, Turd Gruntly, is fabricating a great new policy which he thinks will get him some hero medals from upper management. His foggy brain tells him that if he forces everybody to have their phone bills reviewed by the next two people above the guy making the calls, that this will save piles of money. This will stop all the personal calls immediately - or most of them. But his secretary, Lila Whisper, hangs around with a few of the Executives' Secretaries, so she knows all about those personal long distance calls the boys make - fringe benefits of sorts.

As she types a draft of the new policy, Turd Gruntly, her boss, asks her what she thinks. Fortunately for Turd, Lila told him. "*But Mr. Gruntly*" she said, "*the Executives won't like this, they are always making private calls*". Guess what Turd did with the new policy? And who is running who in this matter? Lila, a mere secretary just killed a policy with one piece of information from the informal system - indirect power and influence - even though she didn't do it purposely or even knowingly. The point of the matter is, however, that she could have done it purposely if she wanted to. It is here in these gossip channels that the illusive part of the power lurks. It is this process and the tapping of it that helps one retain some of the power one gets. If you don't believe this, think about the next time Turd Gruntly wants some clues about the boys upstairs - he may even buy Lila lunch. And if Lila has information aplenty about such matters - guess who really has the influence?

Although the informal system of information and the informal power system are always at work in an organization, there are few who will admit that it is significant and powerful. It would be sheer heresy to have the inmates running the asylum, wouldn't it? But in reality, it would be sheer heresy to ignore this informal system. What Turd and Herk used to their advantage was an information system called the "SOCIAL INFO CLUSTER" Network. This system, better known as the SIC Network also knew about Mervin

Mealymouth and his resignation. SIC Networks could well carry a lot of gossip, but they also carry a lot of facts.

THE SOCIAL INFO CLUSTER SYSTEM – THE SIC NETWORK

The SIC NETWORK is what it infers. It is a "social" system mostly operational during social times such as coffee breaks, lunch, functions, and so on. It takes place at parties, in bars and even in the office, if possible. Info, short for information, is what the whole system exchanges, the root of this information being the Corporation. Cluster refers to the little `cliques` that form throughout the corporation. These little clusters are where the information is exchanged - between the cluster members. Network refers to the fact that these clusters are inter-connected through the Informal Power System.

The Informal power system, we have already seen, is quite an effective one, even though the Formal power system will not acknowledge it. The informal power system's life blood is the SIC network. So to get a tap into the Informal power system, you need to get hooked into the SIC network. People may like to sleep alone but they do not like to eat and drink alone - they prefer to get together and exchange lies, ideas, gossip and even facts. These little get-togethers (or clusters) become little reservoirs of information.

Every time you and the boys or girls go out for a drink after work, at lunch or at play, you form a social info cluster. It is difficult to not talk about work since usually work is the common element between you. As the cluster ages, the information exchanged can indeed be interesting as confidential barriers disappear and any corporate information is exchanged freely. Each cluster has a tendency to think in like terms and to agree with each other. For this reason the information, after a while, has a tendency to look more and more like gossip and catty social dribble exchanged by nosey schmucks and busybodies.

Who is screwing who, who is having an affair, who is the world's biggest asshole, who has no balls, who just got demoted or who just went bankrupt hardly seems like useful information. And what someone got for a raise or what their impression is of the new VP may be useful. But a potential new boss, new project or new policy is certainly useful. News of the company going bankrupt is most definitely useful information. All this type of stuff collects in these clusters where there are no secrets.

In every nook and cranny of the company, people are working away on confidential matters, personal things, projects, reports, memos, deals, policies, etc., etc. It is not often that the formal system attempts to suppress in police like fashion all this secret stuff. And this is what people share - as friends. Let us get to know some SIC's - with a fellow named Piles Bumrubber.

Mila Meatseeker is the executive secretary of the VP of Finance. She *"hangs out"* with Olga Titwopper, Tina Tinkle and Torn Member. On Fridays, after work, this little cluster trades juicy news at the bar next door. Sometimes Karen Klutz and Hump Pussywip join the team. Together this group covers Finance, Legal, Engineering, Personnel and Marketing. Sometimes they get quite pissed and get into some fierce discussions about philosophy and other non-company matters, but it is not before they exhaust all the company business.

At the other corner of the bar is the favorite table of another cluster from other areas of the company. This is where Buff Windbag and Blam Featherfash from Marketing bullshit with Piles Bumrubber and

Sleeze Huffer from Engineering. This cluster does not meet quite as frequently as Mila's cluster, but nevertheless they vent their daily frustration out at this watering hole quite often. Here they solve all the Corporate problems and trade opinions and impressions until they get so pissed nothing makes sense.

So here we have two Social Info Clusters, one at each corner of the local watering hole - Mila's and Buff's clusters. Mila's group is discussing the big meeting that the Executives just had about budget cuts and freezes. Mila knows because she had to type the minutes of the meeting for Scab Dancer, the VP of Finance. Of greatest concern is whether the secretaries will still get their new printers for their word processors, or whether it was just Engineering that would be frozen.

At the other end of the room Piles is rancid with rage about the stupid asshole boss, Clone Mimicker who figured they could wait another six months before they would need new CAD workstations. *"What a stupid son of a bitch he is. He wants to look great by not spending the money now. The asshole can't see the turmoil that goes on in the group. That old station doesn't work worth a shit and it won't last another month."*

Now upstairs in the lounge there exists another cluster - Switcho Maggotbrain's. Having a few more liberties with the expense accounts, Switcho, Willy Liplock, Marcus Mule and Fred Fantasy are knocking back a few cool ones before heading home. Switcho has heard a rumor about the Columbia deal and the new plant design in Ontario. They are discussing the incompetence of those mindless executives who just figure they can get everybody to produce at the snap of a finger. *"Those goddam turkeys, the clueless crotch vermin"* Switcho snorts, *"will expect immediate results when we have scheduled 3 other critical jobs through the next months. They don't warn us and they never heard of planning!"*

If you look closely at this situation a lot of people could be up shit creek when the dust settles. Karen Klutz may not get her printer in engineering - typing backlog and poor quality. Piles will be run ragged and possibly not get the job out because of poor, inadequate equipment and Clone, Pile's boss, will be shitting on everybody with royal zeal. Even Switcho ,the newest manager, himself could get into deep trouble - why? Because Clone is trying to look good by delaying a capital purchase. But none of this information that these three clusters possess is formal news. Yet it is clearly part of the informal communication system. Each Social Info Cluster has its own time and place to discuss and trade the news.

No doubt you can see how such news, if traded between the three SIC's could quite possibly spare many people considerable chaos. Let us just suppose that Piles happened to stop at Mila's table and he sat down for a few drinks. Piles would then have found out about the potential budget freeze. At this point Piles could tell his boss Clone about the news so that he could get those workstations. This would maybe force some action that would help Piles and his coworkers work under less turmoil. But it would also help that asshole Clone, his boss, avoid a possible pickle, so why would Piles want to save him? Suppose, however that he decided to talk to Clone's boss Switcho.

He could tell him about the budget and tell him that Clone is trying to be a hero. This could be tricky through the formal system since he would have to *"go around"* his boss. Such action might be quite risky business.

But let us suppose that Piles has, upon occasion, tipped back a few with Switcho and his cluster. Being just a mere designer, socializing with mid-management at the office would not work, but after hours, it is more likely that such socializing is OK. Upon joining the Switcho cluster in the bar, Piles learns also the news about all the potential work that could overload the system. Now Piles is in possession of two key pieces of information - one about budgets, the other about all the potential crisis work coming up. Piles also has information from his own SIC.

This information is that Clone's stupidity will result in a work overload situation where everybody is going to look stupid - even him. But something else comes up quite unexpectedly as Piles trades bullshit and company information with the Switcho SIC. He learns that Switcho never did like Clone because he farts in his office constantly and he never uses deodorant. *"The guy is a big scumbag but he's been here so long he's a permanent fixture",* Switcho slobbers in his drunken stupor. Now Piles could quite easily tell Switcho about the situation here because there are no formal lines of communication. Then Switcho could order the equipment promptly before the budget freeze. The problem would be, however, that Clone would come out looking like a winner. But something must be done now since there is no way that one could escape a two month delivery on equipment. *"How are we going to pour all that work through?"* probes Piles. *"No sweat, Piles, we have the extra equipment budgeted. Clone better have it all under control or his ass is history".* At this point Piles can inform Switcho of the news or keep quiet. He decides to do a bit of homework. The next day after considerable digging, he finds out that there are two new sources for the CAD workstation.

One is a company in Texas that will be trying to sell their workstations in a few months and another that rents them (with 10 in stock and low turnover). So Piles, at his next SIC meeting insists that Clone will not be able to handle the pressure because he can't plan ahead. When the news finally hit - no more capital expenditures - the news of all the work caused Clone to panic. Switcho was not happy when Clone told him of the 2-3 month wait for equipment - and no alternate sources. The meeting was a beauty as Piles had difficulty in holding his giggles back. *"It's your fuckin' fault Maggotbrain"* Clone cried, *"This would never happen if you had any clues about planning!"* The best part was when Clone called Switcho an incompetent pisstank.

When Piles joined the cluster that evening, it was as if they didn't want him there - to hear what Switcho was going to do to Clone. So Piles broke the ice. *"Look Switcho, I can't believe that the A should get away with that kind of lip, he's the one who screwed up. Why don't you let me see if I can do something about this workload business".* Now Switcho wouldn't have known where to even start so an offer like this couldn't be refused. *"Just give me four guys, say Moon, Spasmo, Bite and Nose and I think I can do it by finding some rental gear."* By this time Piles had invaded another SIC made up of Sam Le Slam, Irk Guffer and Dink Primrose from Accounting. Dink always knew what went on in Accounting so it was easy for Piles to extract information on whether rentals fell under the big freeze. *"Shit no!"* Dink guffawed. *"Rentals is rentals, it ain't capital".* Well you can guess the rest of the story. Piles made the spotlight and got promoted.

In this case, Piles chose to keep the news quiet rather than use it with Switcho and Clone. He could have transmitted these little tidbits of information to gain a more subtle influence with Switcho - by becoming a powerful source of vital information - particularly if Piles picked up such information quite often. It wouldn't be long before Switcho would almost depend on Piles - this is indirect power.

What we see here is a "SIC NETWORK". Within each cluster we saw information being accumulated and it was not until Piles bridged the clusters that the information started to flow. Piles formed two bridges, mainly between Mila's and between Switcho's. In so doing he added to the whole SIC Network which in reality has many bridges. It would not be unreasonable for any person in any SIC to make a personal bridge to another SIC. These Personal Info Bridges or PIB's are the informal communication channels in a Corporation (and out of it).

And the creation and use of SIC's and PIB's is what the informal power system is all about. SIC's are everywhere. They form at coffee breaks, at lunch, at clubs, in bars, in homes and at parties.

They even form in offices on the job. There is hardly a place where SIC's don't invade with an insatiable appetite for information. And the information can be had any time you can create a PIB. We have seen how Piles was able to use the information for his own gain. As we look deeper into this SIC phenomenon, we will see how vital it is to Middle Management growth. If you can remember the Five C's in the Executives Arsenal you may now realize that they were just a post graduate course, after the Bachelors Degree in SIC networking.

THE POWER SPRINGBOARD

Piles Bumrubber, a mere and lowly Design Engineer, used the SIC network to gain power. He did this in two ways - one to get a more powerful position, the other, by influencing Switcho's decision making process. If we recall earlier discussions, it was suggested that power was mad up of three critical items, mainly information, resources and critical relationships. We have seen how Piles used the information system to get resources. In this case we are looking at two types of power, mainly POSITION and PERSONAL. There are two more, mainly GROUP and MONEY.

POSITION POWER:
Position power we have already talked about. It is the visible stuff written into position descriptions and organizational charts. It is your position in the AQ hierarchy. But we have seen that although this power may seem considerable, it may also be reduced to mere protocol - like old Boomer Steadfast versus Franklin Hardass. This visible stuff gives you the right to hire and fire. It gives you resources to use and it sets up the initial relationships. It also, supposedly, gives you formal information with which you are to work.

PERSONAL POWER:
Personal power is that invisible stuff that some people have when they are well liked. They exude that special charisma. There are

always those who see more, hear more, and even know more. These are typically cultivated by power seekers. Piles could have been cultivated by Switcho, his second line supervisor. Personal power is developed when you become tapped into many SIC's, becoming a barometer of news, expectations and moods. It is personal power that allows one to sway others - the power of influence. Garfle Greymatter the systems analyst, is a prick to many because he speaks FORTRAN instead of English. Tina Tinkle on the other hand, knows all of the new policies in personnel so she is quite different.

GROUP POWER:
Group power is that power that comes with numbers. When several unite to go against or for a common cause, the result is group power. Typically, labor unions have such power. Corporations, however, are not based on democracy so that group power is not always effective. It is nevertheless a power source built through an alliance toward common objectives.

MONEY POWER:
Money power is that which is derived from controlling the purse strings. If someone believes this to be false, he is indeed a fool. Money is power clear and simple and the one who controls it has a good portion of the power. Just think about budget time and then think about the budgeted items and how you have to suckhole to the money keeper. Try delegating the budget allocation to a subordinate and see how the power shifts.

Of these four power types, it is the second that is the least understood and perhaps the most important. It is also probably the key to building a power base. And it is usually this base that leads to the other three power types. It is the POWER SPRINGBOARD. Now there are many ways to develop a Power Springboard to catapult higher into management and one cannot deny that hard work and technical/management ability certainly helps. But hard work and technical ability are things that one goes to school to learn about. So we should be concerned more with those things that are not learned from text books - right? Building a power springboard through personal power is the stuff that is not in text books - it is part of the Management Arsenal.

POWER POLITICS – THE SIX RULES

The Executives and Managers are very cognizant of power politics and always creating a lucrative spring board to power. The key to power politics is to build yourself a power platform from where you can nurture your personal power and influence. In so doing you can accelerate your progress up AQ Mountain. There are those who simply prefer to work quietly and diligently, waiting for that promotion to be handed to them. Some are bewildered when they are forgotten. Others think that putting in time is the sole criterion. When your AQ is rising, however, it may be expedient to do as some others do - build personal power from a power platform - so that AQ Disequilibrium is avoided. Playing Power Politics can help keep that position in phase with your AQ. All you need to know are the **POWER POLITICS RULES.**

RULE 1 : DO YOUR NICHING UP FRONT
Many people get into the Corporate world to do well both financially and professionally. This should hardly be surprising when one has spent some 16 years getting educated. After one considers his capital investment, loss of income and time spent in this period of life, it should be normal to anyone to try to attain payback quickly.

Who wants to piss around wasting time and losing money by slow progress, dead ends and wrong jobs? If money and power is your game then do your niching up front.

Niching is the process of finding a niche, - your niche. This niche is best found with your own species. If you have spent four or five years at a University to become a Mining Engineer then it is unlikely that you will become the President of an Accounting firm. Your odds are much higher working for a mining company.

Similarly, an Accountant will probably find his chances for CEO better in a chartered accountant firm. The choice is whether you want to take a staff or line position. An Accountant working in a Mining company is a staff position but an accountant in a CA firm is a line position. If you do not want to reach CEO status then staff functions may be more desirable since the competition may be less intense.

A second consideration, particularly if the staff approach is your game, is to try to match your style of management with the corporation type which best suits it. If you like to deal with people and prefer making decisions through consensus then you should not work for an organization which needs fast decisive decision making. You may be better off in slower moving welfare departments or social services of governments. On the other hand, if you like to command people into action, then social services may not be so great. Since it may be difficult to decide your type before you have worked for a company it may be necessary to look at this aspect a few years into your career. For this reason we will analyze this aspect again as a subsequent rule.

RULE 2 : RESEARCH THE POWER STRUCTURES
Finding the sources of power is like taking a little archeological expedition back in time, checking out the ruins and records to uncover the secrets from the past. The difference here is that we must investigate values, styles and traditions in order to determine how the power structure has worked and does work. Of particular interest are those people and processes that have created change. This type of information is vital to building a power platform. Here are some questions that help uncover the organizational culture :

- What are some of the major changes that have occurred and how have they come about?
- Do major changes occur by changes in management (new ideas, styles), by market force changes or by influential fighter type people?

- Are there any traditional procedures, values or styles that the Company has?
- Do annual reports and public releases stress particular organizational styles like history, products, people, founders, technology, etc.?
- Can the older people tell you anything about the critical parts of the company?
- Is there an elaborate SIC NETWORK and how is it used and by whom?
- Who are the powerful people in the organization and how influential are they?
- Who is good at packaging ideas and presenting them to the company?
- What projects initiated by top management have been killed or stifled by middle management?
- Do ideas come from below or from above?
- Where is the path of greatest resistance to new ideas?
- Were there any reorganizations in the last 2-4 years and who gained or lost power?
- How powerful are the various departments and functions?
- What is the direct growth channel to the top?

What you are trying to do is to get an idea of the corporate profile.

You want to identify what people are key in the power system, what traditions or taboos are important and key tactics or events that have led to change. All this is needed to minimize wasted time in the climb upwards - the power platform from which you spring.

RULE 3 : CULTIVATE THE SIC NETWORK TO BUILD THE PLATFORM

Building the power platform is the crucial part of the procedure. It can be grueling and time consuming if you are not up to socializing. Whenever you get a new position, there are those above you who assign tasks to you and watch your performance. The performance you make forms part of your platform - the framework. So you work your ass off to do your job. Now that you have formed the framework, you can put the boards on the frame - the SIC Network is the other half that helps you attain the launching pad for your next position. Here are some ways to help build the platform.

The organization's senior secretaries are close to power sources. They always know what is going on. You want to find the SIC's that they belong to and attempt to become a member.

Power is gained through tapping into the SIC network which has no secrets, just news and gossip that you have not heard. It is essential to tap into the clusters where power sources lurk. You must identify and cultivate these people since they spread impressions, reactions, ideas and facts.

Research the kind of power or influence these people have. Your contribution is to trade information from other SICs. Building numerous PIB's (Personal Info Bridges) is therefore essential to building the platform. It is never a good idea to stay with the same SIC since it will probably consist of like minded people and ideas. It is like talking to yourself.

By forming PIB's from SIC to SIC you will trade valuable information that not only gives you an edge but it may also give you bartering power with your boss. In this way you gain influential positions within the Informal Power system.

People will begin to form a relationship chart of you, your allies and enemies. You must use the information wisely since you can easily know more or have more influence (power) than your boss. *"Look, I think I can help you solve that"* or *"Here is what I think will happen"* is deliberate personal power building - in an attempt to build a platform.

Check out the powerful people's life styles and values. Do they belong to sports clubs, jog, have sports cars, play golf, socialize, and so on. Any life style that separates you from these will reduce your power. If you don't drink for example, then you may not effectively cultivate certain SIC's. A lack of participation will keep any comradeship from developing (those critical relationships needed for getting things done). If some of your "Super Execs" drive sports cars and you drive a motorbike, it may be difficult to build on common interests.

Modify your styles professionally and personally so that you can cultivate through common denominators. If they belong to the 100 Asshole Club then you try to join that club. If they play golf at the Snotty Greens Country Club then that's where you go. You want to try to look like you have similar tastes and habits to those whom you have detected as having power and influence. If they live in HOTSHIT HEIGHTS you should consider that as well.

Now all this may sound a bit dramatic and excessive but the sooner you *"join the club"* the faster you can move. If you want to stay an eccentric, competent technologist then that is your prerogative. You may find that eventually your AQ Equilibrium (or lack of it) may affect your prerogative quite radically.

Before we pass to the next rule, one important item needs to be mentioned about SIC's. Info Bridges allow the flow of information from SIC to SIC - through you. If you are to make use of this then you must treat the information wisely. Remember that much of the information can be confidential and only a friendship or trust will release it. If you "gossip" such information freely and frequently then your sources will dry up since you will not be trusted. The result of being an outcast from the informal power/communication system can be very devastating.

Remember also that the same condition can occur if you ignore SIC's since they are the social culture and communication media of the corporation. You can be shit listed as an outcast very quickly if you do not play the SIC game. If this is hard to believe then just consider the situation where your boss has been told to cut his staff in half. You happen to be a design engineer just like your coworker, perhaps a bit more competent than him. He, however, is always playing golf and tennis with the boss and they often have hangovers on the same morning - so who do you think will get chopped? You or him? And suppose you, as a boss, have a crappy job for someone to do and you have two people to give it to. One works quietly and hard but is a loner, the other belongs to your SIC and he has exactly bugger all to do. Who do you think the boss will find it easiest to delegate the job to? Building Power Platforms is a key tactic in Power Politics. If you can adjust yourself to this way of the Corporation you will hasten your travels through the middle management jungle.

RULE 4 : CULTIVATE A STYLE - BUILD YOUR INFLUENCE
The whole process of climbing up AQ mountain towards the upper echelon is a sort of cyclic procedure. You attain a position where you work hard at accomplishing those new tasks, then you work at gaining a new position. Each cycle brings new tricks to be learned. The first half of the cycle is where a power platform is developed or earned while the second half is where power and influence is used through power politics. It is the use of these power politics that can accelerate the movement from position to position. If you look at the old AQ Meter you will recall about 20 positions from the lower reaches to the upper echelon. If you are to move through each level to get to the top you will need to spend no more than 2 years in each position. So using about 20 years as a starting age where you induct yourself into Corporate life, after graduation, you will be about 60 before you are chairman - if you spend not more than two years in each position. And why is this? Remember that after 2 years your AQ can get saturated in any one position. So after entering each position, you have one year to establish yourself and develop the power platform. That leaves one year to find the next position before your AQ works against you.

Remember the middle management dilemma - always caught in the middle? Much of the success of a Mid Manager will be measured by the ability to satisfy both upper management and the lower workers. This means dealing with people to get things done effectively. There are three types that one needs to deal with, mainly SUPERIORS, PEERS and SUBORDINATES. It is with these types that your influence and power must be developed on a daily basis. It is here that you must use the SIC to your advantage.

Dealing with people is a complete topic in itself. For this reason, we will deal with this in the PEOPLE SECTION coming up. Since this will be covered in detail later, let us just summarize some of the fundamental topics.

INFLUENCE & STYLE: This is essential in building power - you must be known for something. Even being known as a Flasher in the park may be better than not being known at all. At least people are aware of your existence. Usually this will be most effectively developed by considering your work relationships to others.

IMPRESS THOSE SUPERIORS There are ways of getting your way with your superiors. Methods to get key projects and develop your own influence are essential to good tactical manipulation of superiors.

WATCH THE PEERS Peers are potential predators and difficult to make power trades with. Certain ways of creating alliances are required.

MOVE THOSE SUBORDINATES Subordinates are the ones needed to get things done. To optimize their productivity, certain tactics are required.

YOU HELP ME GET THAT ASSHOLE FIRED AND I WILL GET YOUR BUDGETS APPROVED.

DISPENSE WITH PEOPLE PROBLEMS There are always the inevitable people problems upon which you will be judged. Effective means of dispensing with these are required.

These are the major ingredients which help in getting things done as well as assisting in the development of both style and influence. They will be dealt with later in a following section. The SIC NETWORK is the key to unlocking these ingredients - as we shall see.

RULE 5 : CHECK OUT THE POWER SPRINGBOARD

Once you have *"learned the ropes"* so to speak, and been in one place long enough to build a platform in Middle Management, you may want to take stock of your situation. Before you begin your spring boarding to new levels, you may want to check out the water. There is nothing worse than being in a job where you are out of synchronization with the Company. Suppose your AQ skyrockets but your position and power diminish. You have, unfortunately, formed your best alliances with piss-tanks, has-beens, slurpers and peckers so you are in jeopardy of falling down one of those fatal productivity slides. One of the worst things that can happen is that your power quest has been curtailed because those whom you deemed as powerful and influential have turned out to be losers. In such a situation it is easy to fall into the trap of *"being one of them"*.

It is essential, therefore, that you *"take stock"* or *"count inventory"* on regular occasions to see that you have not fallen into the trap that leads to a productivity slide. You might have to *"suck back and reload"* as the saying goes. Well, sucking back and reloading is easy to say but, sometimes it is like admitting that one is an

185

alcoholic. So how can one objectively take stock of the situation? Obviously the AQ, the AQ phases and your position are the first clues. AQ Disequilibrium is a sure sign that the warning flags should go up. Before you go jumping off your power base, you may want to make sure that you have a good base.

Typically, if you have begun to stick with one or two SIC's, then you may be close to becoming biased towards it, particularly if your SIC drinks a lot and spends most of the time muttering about what assholes everyone else is - what a sick company it is, how they know better, and how they have been hard done by. Here are some clues deployed my managers and executives that may help you determine just how much spring there is in your board.

QUERY 1 Has any one of your power idols been demoted or missed a promotion? Clearly this is a loss of power and influence in the Company and there may be good reasons for such action - reasons for you to avoid.

QUERY 2 What do the SIC's say about power changes? The SIC's are the source of informal information, not stifled by corporate rules. Pay attention to the opinions, especially if you side with those who have lost power. Siding with those falling down the slide may put you in disharmony with those more powerful.

QUERY 3 Do you spend a majority of time in a particular SIC? If you do then consider the topics and whether they are constantly involved in the "Corporate Bitch Syndrome" or "CBS". This means that there is little that each does not bitch about. Although they may be right, falling into the CBS can lead to your absolute resentment and dropping out of corporate mechanism.

QUERY 4 How do SIC members perceive your ideas and styles? As you develop ideas and styles, you want to find out just what others think about them. Typically you must do this indirectly, *"I met this guy at Jockstrap Enterprises the other day who firmly believes in the Military approach to Management, what do you guys think of that?"* is a typical indirect way of checking out a management style that you yourself may have or would like to have. In this way, as you query SIC after SIC you can assess how others may see you in a potential management style - indirectly.

QUERY 5 How has your progress been in your quest upward? Obviously the first question is based upon your AQ. If you are in Disequilibrium then is it the Line AQ that is causing the damage? If so then this is indeed precarious. Have you changed positions at 2-3 year intervals? Remember, it takes about this long to get your AQ to boil over into Disequilibrium. And what about your reviews - what do they reveal about *"required improvements"*? These are all danger signals.

QUERY 6 Have you become a Groupie or a Loner? Sometimes when you turn around and look at the situation, you realize that you just don't care to associate yourself with those assholes and roaches - never mind their pukey insipid functions. If key people on the power list are part of those insipid behaviors then your flags should go up immediately. This could well be a result of your ideas and philosophies being different from the others. On the other hand it may not be worth being in disharmony with yourself, just to be part of the group.

QUERY 7 Can you see yourself behaving as those you aspire towards? Like the dog chasing the car, who may have to face the inevitable problem of what to do should the car stop, you may also face such a dilemma by conquering your aspirations. When you look at social and corporate behaviors of those who are powerful, influential and successful in the Company, you may find that you may not be able to stomach it. So what you are striving for could end up wrong for you.

These are but a few of the more serious "*unwritten tactics and queries*" that one must face before projecting himself hell bent towards those upper reaches. Ignoring these can lead to disaster very quickly. But before you proceed, you should satisfy yourself on each issue. Then you can launch yourself towards a new height.

RULE 6 : JUMP WHILE THE SPRING IS STRONG

You may think that to jump into a new position may be quite stupid especially when your boss likes you, you like your boss, you know the job, and your people are all great, etc. etc.. This is exactly where you can fall asleep at the helm, by lulling yourself into a false sense of security. Your AQ is working against you and whether you believe it or not, any worthwhile position in management is one that will be sought - and perhaps by less scrupulous fellows than yourself! In this regard your SIC network is always useful to uncover such worms. Nevertheless, what goes up also comes down, so it is best to make your moves while the moving is good. Sooner or later you may not be able to satisfy everyone and as familiarity breeds contempt, rising AQ's breed resentment. So if you have it in your blood to head upwards, then don't waste time! Jump up from your power springboard while the spring is still in the board.

The "smart" managers and executives have learned that the cyclic process of Platforming, then Positioning, for each position sought, has its foundation in the creation of personal power. This personal power leads to position power and even group power. These in turn lead to money power. In each position, it is a good idea to pay attention to the Six Rules. The creation of Personal Power is the single most critical part of POWER. There are, however, other aspects of Power that have been referred to in Rule 4 - most of which deal with people. Whenever power is mentioned, there are connotations such as Control, Leadership, Decision Making and Delegation, as well as Influence.

188

9

THE MANAGER'S POSITIONING TOOLS

MANAGEMENT STYLING

The creation of Personal Power, after a position is taken, is a necessary step in the "*Platforming to Positioning*" scenarios. There is no doubt that this leads to position power and all the rest. If you recall Rule 4, however, it was mentioned that you had to cultivate a style, thus helping to build influence. It is this style that leads one to the control and leadership aspects of power. And these then also lead to Decision making and Delegation.

You may have noticed that many noticeable managers and executives have a certain style of personality and habit - almost like an astrological behavior (both bad and good). The most prominent are the ones that seem to be in sync with their basic personalities.

It is not hard to see that although a secretary may have incredible influence and power over her boss, she still does not have any of the other ingredients of power (i.e. leadership, control). These are developed outwardly as a style of Management.

Management styling is almost like going to the hairdresser to take on a certain style of hairdo. In this case you are choosing your style of leadership, control and decision making. Each position you take may require different styles of management - and they may not be the same. They may be different because you will be dealing with new people, new responsibilities and new demands. So you may need to change your management style just like you switch your hair style. Being a manager with a commando style approach in a Company that believes in a social consensus style of decision making could quite quickly lead to conflicts. Moreover, if your boss believes in a democratic mechanism simply because he is a simp or a wimp, it may be useful to avoid commando style supervision.

But there are many styles of hairdos just as there are also many styles of management. The styles required by various companies may be quite different depending upon their nature of business. The social worker environments will require a somewhat different approach than a manufacturing firm. When all is said and done, there are three major considerations in management styling, mainly the type of company and its traditional successful styles, the styles of those in power and the style of your boss. These will clearly dictate what tact you should consider. If you believe that you can maintain a style different than your boss likes, you may be fooling yourself.

It may be better to show a style which can compliment him. Until you can spring from your platform, to reach new plateaus, it may be expedient to just avoid direct conflicts. Still you may have a local style or you may be developing a new style for your next position. But paying attention to the traditional successful style could be beneficial. If you are lucky they are the same. The SIC Network is of course the key to figuring out what these are. Remember Rule 2?

SOME MANAGEMENT STYLES

Although Management styles are numerous in variety, there are still fundamental types which can be identified. Typically we find that many managers combine various styles into one. But in the purest unadulterated forms, here are the obvious ones. Be careful of the extremes because they can become ruthless assholes:

THE COMMANDO

This guy takes his queue from the military. Clearly all others are just mere sheep and poor assholes. Typically a strong leader, it takes a long time for this type to recognize or even acknowledge any problems even if they are stuck in front of his nose. Being potentially explosive and arrogant, this style tends to polarize people. This is the rotten son of a bitch that everyone likes to see fail because there is only one way to do things - mainly his way. As such, no one comes to the rescue of such a type when he does make a mistake. Typically such styles are dominant in the high competition industries where profit margins are always critical (like manufacturing) or in small one-owner companies. As the size of the staff grows (that the commando commands) it is typically the case that the commando's management capability is inversely proportional. He relies on being a tyrant to keep order. Danger lurks where commandos work since there is always risk associated with potential rebellion. Commandos rely mostly on the formal power system. *"Do it that way because I told you to do it that way"* is a typical commando directive. The style gets things done but also places you on the asshole list fast.

THE SYMPATHIZER
The sympathizer takes his queue from everybody. He wants to satisfy them as much as possible. He typically drives himself nuts trying to accommodate many types of people and ideas. Just the opposite of a commando the sympathizer or "symp" cannot make decisions easily and quickly unless he is sure that every last one will be happy. Clearly, this type is most useful in organizations which do not depend on efficiency and profit. Non-profit structures are the best home for this type. *"Golly, don't you think we should check with everybody before we change the ass wipe?"* is a symp's comment. If the symp is faced with giving a directive which does not make people happy, he would typically say that he is being forced to do it. The danger then lies in the inability to be decisive and forceful when needed.

Unlike the commando, he relies on the informal system to keep order.

THE POLITICIAN
The politician thinks more of the potential implications towards his goals. He swings either way in a pragmatic approach, counting up the votes before acting *"What will be the effect on me and my career if this doesn't work"* is the typical consideration that the politician considers first. He is the silver tongued devil, capable of cold decision making and cool directives without batting an eye because it is best for his career. These types will suck if they need to and will lie, cheat and inflict pain if required. Highly dangerous, because they can shift quickly and are concerned mostly with themselves, the type is mostly successful at the tops of larger corporations at the executive levels. They can cause total upheaval in playing their little games and are usually identifiable in any SIC network. They can be easily recognized as assholes.

THE MANIPULATOR

Manipulators and commandos have much in common when it comes to forcible motivation. The difference lies in the method. Manipulators will use guilt, greed, situations, emotion or whatever to get people to do what they want. This type will have a vast reserve of "suck in" methods which he can activate at any moment. "Christ, I have to meet a client tonight, how can we get this job done for tomorrow?" will undoubtedly solicit some subordinate slob into offering his help - the exact desired response. And if the first call doesn't work then you typically hear: "*Are there any ideas as to how we can avoid the wrath of not completing the project on time?*". This may inject some guilt which would potentially solicit the response. Failing that, "*Well I hope you all have a relaxing evening. I'll have to think of how to save our asses when I get home after midnight*" might cause a more dramatic response to guilt. Manipulators find it hard to believe that others have some brains or feelings. Subordinates are just subordinates who have no feelings about work decisions. The method is quite effective except when it is obvious - then the commando style prevails. There are many variations of manipulators - all varying in effect and results.

THE DECISION MAKER

This style exudes high energy profiles, with an almost incurable need to make decisions - instantly. "*Well if that didn't work, then lets try this....*" has, at least, a tendency to reassure your superiors that you can act quickly. It also has a tendency to motivate subordinates and they know that if a mistake is made, the alternative solution will be more important than the act of making the mistake. The decision maker lives to make decisions. Sometimes however, there is a tendency to make them too fast and to treat subordinates like mindless assholes who are not capable of making decisions. Typically this allows one to start something without a plan - because you can always make changes as you go. This can backfire but it takes the emotional burden off those who make the mistakes. So although it reflects a person who is in charge, we must remember also the possible consequences of "charging".

THE DELEGATOR

Skilled delegators are also a variety of decision makers with one great exception. That is that this guy does not take any of the emotional burden away from anyone. He passes it by delegation. *"Well if that didn't work then Jerk Jerkins will come up with an alternate plan by tomorrow"* means that Jerk has the hot potato. If

we can recall our leaders at Steadfast Meats, we note that Scoot Blastoff and Switcho Maggotbrain were good examples of this style. Delegators learn to hide their inabilities by appearing to *"build better subordinates by giving them more responsibilities"*. Typically these are the responsibilities that they cannot

handle themselves. Nevertheless, the delegator does give others more responsibility to the point of potentially taking away all of the delegators responsibilities. Delegators also know how to force others ideas out in the open or they can even force confrontations so that they can make decisions on material they were absolutely clueless about - the extreme plagiarist. At the extreme side, delegators are painful plagiarizing scumbags who have so few clues about anything and totally confuse people on what is to be done. On the other side, they can allow constructive growth.

THE SALESMAN

This style is exactly what it sounds like - sales. The salesman sells others on whatever needs to be done and however it needs to be done. This type will take it upon himself to discuss things to the fullest - his way - to get things done. Typically, he will not stop until the recipients agree or just give in. Quite the opposite of a Manipulator, he attempts to convince others on the benefits of helping and does not try to elicit guilt to get something done. The salesman sees a failure to comply as a failure in himself to convince others to get commitment. Sales types are deeply immersed in the pleasure or reward mechanism: *"What is in this for them if they cooperate"*. This means an involving method of constant convincing of others to get their participation as part of the team. Although an admirable style, it is not effective where strong leadership and fast decisions are required.

THE VOTER

This particular style involves blending others ideas into a general concept before action is taken. In this way everyone supports the action since it reflects a consensus of opinion. The result, as the theory goes, is that a unanimous commitment is had by all. This has its good points in a social worker environment where one may have to satisfy many ideas before action is taken. It is not effective in other cases where consensus cannot be reached or a new approach is required. There is a tendency to reject tangents, unusual ideas and odd approaches since there may not be sufficient brain power in the group to understand it. This "simple" approach is typically as average as its results. In addition in large diverse groups consensus may be impossible so that any action or directives may never come. The style, therefore, if taken too far, can drive one to drink quickly - and generate indecisive management. The voter is similar to the sympathizer except that the voter is quite capable of giving directives, once he knows which way. The sympathizer just keeps worrying about keeping everyone happy.

THE FIREFIGHTER

The firefighter style involves having a gambler's mentality. It is a decisive style but involves shooting from the hip (or lip). The great attraction must be the excitement that such tactics bring, especially when crisis decisions are made. Firefighters are either born procrastinators or they are just lazy assholes waiting for the last moment - avoiding something till the last minute. Typically, firefighting leaves many in panic and under the gun, battling time, costs or whatever obstacles you could imagine. Firefighters are typically unorganized or uninformed and, needless to say, can cause significant damage on large projects which require organization and planning. But it is not always possible to be organized so the firefighting style can be useful, particularly if the issues are minor or you want to see who can best evolve from the chaos. We saw a potential firefighter earlier where Clone Mimicker wanted to hold off on buying the CAD workstations until the last moment to save money. There is usually some stupid reason for chaos to hit and although it can infuriate the subordinates, it can sometimes get things done quickly.

THE ABDICATOR
The abdicator likes to let people do what they want to do as long as they get results. "*Let them work it out*" is a typical abdicator reaction when conflicts arise. As long as the situation does not threaten the abdicators career, the abdicator will not lead or direct. He continuously forces people to deal with the problems reducing risk inside his territory. Abdicators are like delegators in some ways - causing disastrous chaos in swiftly changing environments, but being quite effective in slow moving environments. And there are many situations where letting others work it out is the wise approach but there are also situations where such a style only embroils others and causes further problems. Similarly, letting people decide when and how to do certain things lets people feel quite good but there are many slackasses and incompetent jerks who would never accomplish anything at all if they were left alone. Obviously the abdicator is at home in a company with an informal power structure.

THE SECRETIVE
This style infers that there are always big decisions and big dealings taking place behind closed doors. The secretive type likes to make others think that they are either "in on" or "out of" some really important stuff. The closed door approach immediately makes one feel that either he is up shit creek or he is going to learn some secret. "*Hey Dork, come in and give the door a kick*" followed

by *"Keep this under your hat, Dork..."* makes you feel like the chosen one temporarily until you realize just what a facade this can be. Nevertheless, it creates the air that you are the keeper of sacred information - that you can keep people from knowing and it is all within your power to distribute this knowledge. In many cases the practice is just a bunch of dramatic horseshit covering a real vacuum underneath.

THE BY THE BOOKER
This type has a tendency to always follow policy or procedures. *"I am sorry Murtle but that is not within Corporate Policy. There is nothing anyone can do"* is a polite way of telling Murtle to piss off and not bother you - it's not your fault or your problem. By the Bookers can not be blamed for something since they are so concerned about following the rules. *"Nobody can tell us we didn't do it according to Hoyle"* is good cover regardless of whether the rules are right wrong or stupid. Needless to say, by the bookers are not too comfortable in companies or areas of a company which are not rule book oriented. Personnel, Legal, and Corporate Affairs tend to attract by the Bookers. Marketing, Business Promotion and Research & Development, on the other hand would frustrate and infuriate the same type.

What we see here are some fairly dramatic styles but all have their place and time in Mid-Management. In reality we see middle management exhibit combinations of these styles. It would not be surprising, therefore, to combine a firefighting style with a delegating style, since one can be a required style of the other. And anyone could be a "By the Booker" as a matter of convenience. But despite the combinations available, it is still possible to recognize the above prototypes.

These are both bad and good styles but the questions that you need to ask yourself are what type do you need to be for the job and can I really be that type? Just remember that certain jobs and certain styles don't mix - this is where the SIC network can help.

The other question is why is this important? Well, the "best management" pays attention to this because (depending on the style and fit):

1. they get noticed and have a reputation that others notice
2. it helps to motivate and manipulate others knowing their weaknesses
3. it helps avoid conflicts knowing the strong points

But power, we have learned, goes hand in hand with Influence and Leadership and Control. Recall the Mid Management Ethic, mainly Power applied to People responsible for Processes produces Profit. We now reach the second part of the equation - people. The application of power to people is the next key to building influence since it is the people that judge.

PEOPLE POSITIONING: WHAT IS IT ?

When you move into middle management, you must move through the Big Transition. Here you begin to lose some of that protective amour you called technology. To keep the proper protection you must acquire the new amour of middle management. The big switch that occurs through the transition is that you must deal with people - people below you, people above you and people beside

you. Everywhere you move in a corporation, you find people. But now you are not at the bottom, nor the top of this mass of corporate humanity - you are in the middle. What you must become more conscious of is your positioning within this mass. Positioning within the structure is formal power. Positioning the people around you involves informal power that leads to formal power. "People positioning" involves dealing with three corporate groups, mainly Superiors, Peers and Subordinates.

One of the secrets of the corporate culture - one which no one will tell you openly about - is the business of PEOPLE CONDITIONING. People conditioning is the process of modifying other people's behavior for position purposes. It is a very useful process that, when used with power politics, forms an awesome middle management weapon.

PEOPLE CONDITIONING - INSTRUMENTAL POSITIONING

Instrumental conditioning, in Experimental Psychology is the process whereby animal behavior becomes modified through some instrumental means. What this means is that you carefully, step by step, make an animal do something that it normally does not do. And the tools of your trade - your instruments so to speak - are reward and punishment.

As a simple example, consider having a rat in a cage. This cage is wired to get an electric jolt - nothing too devastating - just enough to make the critter jump a few inches. You have the control at your finger tips. Now this poor rat knows nothing about tricks, especially the one you must teach him - to stand on two legs in the corner of the cage. You must modify his behavior to do this so you have a little behavior modification plan. Here is how you proceed :

The rat moves around randomly within the cage until you give him a little jolt for going into the left half of the cage. His first reaction, after his four feet are back on the ground, is to run around quite frantically wondering what the hell happened to him. Another few minor jolts for going into the left half eventually leads him to the clue that this half is dangerous. So he stays in the right half. Any venture in the other direction results in a shock so that eventually his random behavior is modified to stay in half of the cage. Now you draw another imaginary line, cutting up his good space so that he is left with only one corner. It will not take too long before he realizes the same story about dangerous territory and localizes himself to that corner. Any venture outwards if stopped with a few volts yields a surprising rush to the corner - once he has learned. Spending most of his time in the corner now, the rat will have a tendency to raise up on his hind legs looking for a way out without getting a shock. It is after such a move, when he touches the floor with his front legs that a new jolt really makes him wonder. It is at this point that he may just forget about all his new education and just say piss on it - but lets assume not. If he lifts his legs up against the side of the cage he may learn the next iteration of your behavior modification - to stay on two legs in the corner.

Well what you have done, through aversive conditioning is modify the poor little guy's behavior, by a step by step iteration process which gets closer and closer to the final objective. What you did here was "instrumental conditioning" with a negative (punishment) behavior modifier of shock. This method of "aversive" treatment, psychologists will tell you, is fast in application, but less effective in the long run. A positive (reward) behavior modifier, they say, is more likely to make the modified behavior last longer. A case in point is training a dog to do a trick. Continued punishment of the dog could well instill a specific behavior in the dog through fear but if the dog had been trained to perform the same by rewarding him, his behavior would probably be more responsive (to you) and more predictable. If we applied this positive reward mechanism to the rat, we would have had a button that would have released a treat every time the rat did the right thing rather than punish him every time he did the wrong thing. The iteration process would have been different but the end result would have been the same.

Corporate people are also treated like animals and their behavior can be modified the same way. We just don't speak of the process as conditioning. We call the process training and experience. The corporate animal is even more vulnerable to rewards (promotion, raises, perks, etc.) and punishments (firing, demotion, power loss, getting shit, etc.) than the rat. Whether the executives call the process grooming, becoming a corporate citizen, taking more responsibility, or whatever, it is still behavior modification through positive or negative instrumental conditioning. Nobody likes to think, however, that he is being trained like a dog - he is much too intelligent for such things - right? Horseshit! Corporate animals couldn't be better candidates.

How many times have you seen people modify their behavior to get ahead in a company? Why? Because of money, power, position and influence? Or was it just for fun? And how many times have you seen someone instrumentally modifying another's behavior? Probably not as often. People are quite subtle about this process so it is not so obvious but have you ever considered how your boss has you in the cage? He can reward you or punish you through his power, because his power allows him to promote or demote, to fire you or to raise your wages. And if he wants to manipulate you into various positions he can do so through people conditioning.

As it turns out, many corporate mid-managers are not skilled in these aspects yet. It is this aspect that courses in "employee motivation" and "getting more from your subordinates", for example, try to address. But how is this all applied in reality you may ask. You can reward or punish a subordinate but how can you reward or punish a superior? Through this section we have discussed modifying your own behavior not others behavior. Nevertheless the idea is the same. Where you do not have formal power, you must use informal power. The SIC network is your source of information that allows you to set up your iterations for people positioning.

We proceed now to more specific discussions on the three groups upon which this instrumental positioning, mainly Superiors, Peers and Subordinates, applies. Positioning is always at work in a company as each seeks new positions, power and influence. The process of sucking others out, dethroning, demoting, promoting, jockeying, or whatever the act may be, all involve little instrumental ploys for positions.

If we should look closely at the process of conditioning the rat, we see that we have indulged in "behavior modification". We gave him a shock every time he did something wrong, thereby using a process of "reinforcement" to make him learn what was right and wrong (to us of course). Each time, we set up a new step once the previous was learned. In this way, we were able to make him eventually reach our goal. It was by no means his goal - it was something that we forced him to do. Moreover, he had no escape since he was initially bounded in the cage. In successive steps, he was bounded partially by the cage and partially by an imaginary shock line.

We were able to make him do something new because we had four key ingredients. First, we had the BOX to trap him into, second, we had a GOAL for him to accomplish. Then we had a step by step PROCESS of learning (behavior modification). Finally, we had the INSTRUMENTS OF CONDITIONING used to reinforce a negative (wrong) action until he learned what not to do. It was the fear of shock that forced him to learn each step. In this case we knew that he didn't like shock so that is what we used as an instrument. If we had attached an electrode to the pleasure centre of the rats brain, we could have given him a reward for doing the right action - known as Positive Instrumental Conditioning. And if we really wanted to become effective in modifying his behavior, we could use both positive and negative instruments.

What we have here is the PROCESS of INSTRUMENTAL CONDITIONING. This process is the purposeful modification of behavior. In corporations, we are much more subtle in the manipulative conditioning process. More subtlety put, we call it the PROCESS of INSTRUMENTAL POSITIONING. It is important to note that some of the "most successful management" are experts at this and they use the punish-reward process quite elegantly. It is here we learn how:

INGREDIENTS OF INSTRUMENTAL POSITIONING

To recap the rat's training scenarios there were four main ingredients:

BOX
This was the initial trap within which the rat would learn and from which there was no escape.

GOAL
We had a final objective to accomplish - mainly to get the little critter to stand on his hind legs in the corner.

PROCESS
We had a stepwise plan which started with a wide objective, proceeding to more specific objectives until the target was reached (i.e., half cage, quarter cage, hind legs = 3 iterations)

INSTRUMENT
We used electric shock because the rat didn't like it - so we forced him to modify his behavior. We could also have used food pellets - those which he thought tasty. He would have modified his behavior in order to get the treats. These were two instruments which were used to "reinforce" new behavior until it became permanent.

The corporate scenario is not unlike the rats. all you have to do is think back and realize how many times you have feared getting fired, or getting a demotion, and how you got screwed because of the fear. And how many times did you do something because you got rewarded?

,

10

THE MANAGER'S AQ TOOLS

So what do these Managers use as their tool box of trick and tactics that follow the AQ'ISM theory? Let us investigate this by examples of some of our Corporites at Steadfast Meats with regards to more on Instrumental Positioning because this is indeed one of the best evolved tools in their arsenals.

IMPRESS THOSE SUPERIORS OR INFERIORS?

SIR, THE CHAIRMAN SLIPPED ME THIS PROPOSAL ON BUDGET CUTS SO I COULD COMMENT ON IT. CARE TO HAVE A LOOK WITH ME

Your boss, and his boss, because they are bosses will invariably have little fears, needs, inadequacies and failings that they will attempt to cover up or hide from you. If they don't then they may look foolish, weak or stupid and lose power, influence and control. Even worse, they may appear to be mere corporate mortals. By uncovering little idiosyncrasies you have your instruments of conditioning. The fears and needs are like those shocks and pills to the rat - the trick is to find out what they are and then develop a Goal and a Process. Here are some clues :

- What style is your boss and how does it fit within the group. Can you compensate for his weaknesses?
- What unmet needs does your boss have which you can fill? Can you get him dependant on you for any special services?
- Can you help him learn the job, especially if he is new. Can you shape him in a way that is useful to your career?
- Can you anticipate his wants so you can pick the most effective and rewarding directions?
- Can you help him without making him look stupid or dependant?

How do you find these things out? Try the SIC network! Remember how Piles Bumrubber worked the information from different SIC's? Remember his PIB's? Remember also Rule 3 on cultivating the SIC network? If your superiors are not such complete assholes as to make you cringe, you may get right down to nitty gritty fears and needs by merging in with their social life. Whether you like it or not, your career will be controlled by superiors so you must somehow impress upon these people that you exist and that you can help them. This is your first step to positioning.

Let us recap how Piles Bumrubber built his new influence and power to get a new position.

- He learns about budget cutbacks from a secretarial SIC where he had formed a PIB.
- Piles is aware that Clone Mimicker, his boss is trying to look good by delaying expenditures on a critical piece of computer equipment.
- Piles knows that the existing gear is causing a bottleneck.
- Piles learns about the potential work demands coming up.
- Piles finds a place where he can rent equipment on short notice.

- When the crisis occurred, Piles reinforces Switcho and offers a solution.
- Piles checks out whether rentals were capital from another SIC.
- With no other alternatives, Switcho gives Piles control.

In this case, Piles used the tidbits of information to get rid of Clone Mimicker - his direct superior. He could also have fed Switcho the information (like little reward pills) to maneuver himself in for the kill - this is in fact what he did. Switcho would act (modify behavior) on these little bits of information - either from fear of chaos, or from a need of doing things effectively so that he would look good. So what was Piles' target? It was to move up in position and get rid of his A boss. What was Piles' instrument? It was pieces of information from the SIC Network and some relevant information (bottlenecks, rentals).

And what was his Process? He would hide or give (punish or reward) information to the two line managers (rats) so as to let them set up the disaster scenario step by step.

Now this situation is quite a complex one since Piles is dealing with several rats and both positive and negative conditioning instruments at the same time. In addition, he has set up a fairly complex process that may not be directly under his control. But let us look at a more simple scenario.

When Piles learned of the potential budget problems, knowing about the failing equipment and Clone's need to "look good" by delaying expenditures, he could have told him about the budget freeze. Clone may have thanked Piles and the equipment would have been ordered - allowing Piles to do the work and Clone to avoid the wrath. On the other hand, he could keep quiet and maybe Clone would get all the shit. Anyways, it is the second bit of information that really sets the scene, mainly the new project demands - without new equipment. Let's assume a simple target of Piles getting a promotion. What would be the Process?

Firstly, Piles checks out Clone's position on spending and reinforces his decision to save money. This helps Clone keep his direction to not activate the expenditure. Now Piles is part of Clone's team.

Secondly, Piles waits for the freeze, gathering his other information on rentals. He then tells Clone that he has heard rumors of a large workload. This alerts Clone (although too late) of the potential disaster (negative reinforcement). At the same time, Piles suggests that he has time to work on a possible solution. This gives Clone a negative jolt and a possible (positive) path out. Since the news is not fact yet, the request is still trivial.

Thirdly, when the workload is formally announced, Piles reinforces Clone by suggesting that he may be able to get around this but he needs his assistance in checking out some accounting details on rentals, capital, etc. and coming up with a list of rental companies. Now Clone is working for Piles - right! But Piles and Clone are in this together so far.

Fourthly, when Clone conveys the information already known to Piles, he rewards his boss. *"Fantastic"* he says, *"that may give us the edge we need"*. This is followed by a negative shock *"We are definitely in trouble since we cannot get a new unit. I checked with the Hardware Maintenance Group and they say the equipment needs to be replaced quickly"*. Clone at this point, is trapped; *"Holy Shit, Piles, got any ideas?"* Piles is now in control, so here comes the next iteration.

Fifthly, Piles says *"I think I could handle the load if I can get some rental equipment and I do a bit of load scheduling in the department. What do you think ?"* Piles wants authority, for which he will give Clone a solution. In typical management style, Clone says *"Ok, what's your plan?"* So Piles lays out his contacts on rentals and schedule of events. He shows how he can get away from the freeze and still show those "pricks upstairs" that together the design group can do the job. How can Clone resist this ?

Here we have five simple steps (process) to get a promotion, power or control (target), using information as the positive and negative conditioning mechanism (instrument). This was, of course, a less complex mechanism but it serves to illustrate how the SIC network provides the instruments to attain power - via instrumental positioning. Typically you will want to set up the process to get recognition, power, influence and therefore positioning relative to other corporate positions. And your exchange for this will be product or information - aimed at satisfying a need or a greed of a superior. And whether the boss has a lack of power, feels threatened, has peer pressure, is on the spot, or is just a stupid incompetent A matters not - he has some needs that you can use.

THE PHANTOM MEMO REINFORCEMENT TECHNIQUE

Recall if you will that Piles worked primarily within the informal system to accomplish his target. Sometimes we do not have the

option open to us and we must work through the formal system, simply because we do not belong to the SIC that the desired contact belongs to. A useful approach in such cases is to create the "Phantom Memo". The phantom memo is purely an indirect manipulative method of getting a point across. Here, we simply write a memo regarding something that you want to say or do but its not expedient to do it directly through the formal system - so you ask for a second opinion. If your cards are played right, the person giving the second opinion is in a position to do something about it. Let us go back to Piles

208

Bumrubber and his little scenario. Assuming that he did not know his second line supervisor Switcho Maggotbrain well enough to belong to his SIC, but that he wanted to convey his distaste for his boss, It would be difficult to do so by sending his boss a memo - he might get fired for telling him that Clone was an incompetent asshole.

Instead, Piles could write a memo saying that his boss was incompetent because he did not understand the nature of the work station situation, that he was flirting disaster if it broke down, that given any increase in work volume, the department's credibility would be lost, and that saving a few dollars by waiting a few months was irresponsible subjective action when existing equipment was poor. That anyone jeopardizing Company ability to perform was a jerk subject to severe reprimand, and that if he had half a chance, he could develop alternatives, etc.

Now if Piles gave such a memo to Switcho, via formal channels, he would be in trouble for jumping around his immediate supervisor. If he gave it to his boss, he could be equally up Shitcreek. So he asks Switcho to read it and give him an opinion on how and where to send it, or even if he should. When Switcho reads it, he automatically is being conditioned to the situation, and Piles' position. Needless to say, he will advise : "*Holy Shit that's too strong - you can't send that out, let's tone it down a bit - here is what you should do.*" But you have already imbedded in his mind the stupidity of your superior - without doing it formally. The action has potentially resulted in modifying his behavior. He just might take action on the memo even though it was not a formal paper. In this way, even if the memo is never published, you have conveyed critical information to a key person - you have conditioned him to modify his behavior. He may even take action on your behalf to serve your cause. Thus the Phantom Memo approach serves to manipulate people indirectly without even committing yourself formally. Needless to say, the same technique can be used without writing the stuff on paper, but when people put it on paper, it usually has more impact - it is a serious situation.

WATCH THOSE PEERS - TRADE OR FADE

We have seen how to apply the ingredients of instrumental positioning to superiors. But what about your Peers ? When you are positioned in Middle Management, there is a tendency for various peer SIC's to form.

Technically, these peers are equals to you in the corporate hierarchy, each with no direct power over any other peer. As such, you have no control over them. Sometimes you could easily be in direct competition with a peer and it may therefore be difficult to be genuine friends.

Peers may even know your weaknesses more than you or your bosses do. The trauma is that you must cooperate and compete at the same time in many cases. One key is, however, that you trade cooperation and information. Effectively, peers can give the information or the critical relationships which you need to execute plans effectively. We saw this used quite effectively when Herk and Jerk, two engineers from different departments, got an impossible task done through cooperation - via the informal power system.

In that case it was clearly the favor for favor cooperation and the SIC system that allowed them to do the job in time - something that Herk could not have accomplished alone. In this case, Herk and Jerk were mere mortal Engineers - not Mid. Management types. Still the idea is the same as is the application of positioning - particularly in the cases where there is direct competition. And even if there is no direct competition, peers still belong to other SIC's where they can convey their impressions of you.

You may need a Peer's cooperation to get a job done. You may have to depend upon the Drafting Department to get your Visual Overheads ready for a critical presentation. If you, as Manager of Projects, have no control over the Manager of Drafting & Design and in addition, he thinks you are a pompous jerk, you will quickly understand what a critical peer relationship really is when he tells you he is too busy. It is the peer cooperation, therefore, and the informal power system that maintains the critical relationships that get things done. But if you and Moon Flasher, the power in Drafting have a good relationship then such a job will be done on time, regardless of how busy he is.

Your peers have the same needs as you so they are also influenced by information, trust relationships, and assistance. These are the three key trade items (and conditioning instruments) you need to activate instrumental positioning. Again, the techniques are the same once the three ingredients of positioning are defined.

One more thing should be noted about the concept of instrumental positioning. We have seen a fairly complex process as illustrated with Piles, Clone and Switcho. We then reduced this to a simpler scenario between Piles and Clone. In many, many cases, the process is even simpler, involving one step and two people. The complexity of the scenario will undoubtedly depend upon what you really want that rat in the cage to do. And if you have two rats in the cage, your task will be even more complex.

MOTIVATE THOSE SUBORDINATES

The subordinates form the third group that the Middle Management type must deal with. "Subs" are the ones that do the work so you must get them to work - effectively !

It is with subs that the whole idea of instrumental conditioning is most easily applied. Unlike dealings with superiors and peers, you are in direct control of subs. This gives you an additional instrument to work with since rewards and punishments are under your direct control. Unlike the situation where you must operate indirectly to create punishments or rewards, you can issue them directly. What you need to determine with subs, is what their needs and fears are.

If we should look at subs as a group, we can apply the following :

- Subs, particularly professional ones, are highly motivated to better themselves.
- As long as subs learn from you, they will support and even respect you.
- Subs will like to know how the system works and they will want their own roles carved into the organization.
- Subs will increase loyalty when they know that the superior is willing to assume a share of blame and also protect them.
- Subs will want more money, power, training, explanations or rewards.

- Subs do their best when you remove obstacles from their path.

When you enter a SIC, particularly after a few of the participants are half pickled by booze, you will hear the same old bullshit over and over, like a broken record:

- No one appreciates any talent or hard work.
- Nothing ever happens here.
- Management doesn't know what the hell goes on.
- Nobody gives a shit.
- They are a bunch of cheap bastards.
- How do they survive under such incompetence?
- The boss is a jerk.
- Management is chaotic.
- The current process is unproductive and inefficient.
- Did you hear what happened today?
- Nobody ever tells you how or why.
- I'll tell you what I would do.

Now bullshit or not, if you had access to these discussions, you as a supervisor or manager could be in a much better position to act and decide on many difficult matters in your department before problems occurred. The fact is, however, that you seldom hear about them until it is too late - someone got so pissed off that they boiled over and told you to stick your procrastination where your proctologist does his work.

Many ideas and thoughts are also wasted this way - never ever getting to the point of constructive use.

Once again, the SIC Network is where all this information resides. In addition, the information resides in the informal meetings and discussions with individuals. The more informal and personal, the more it flows. Actually there is nothing unique about all the gripes and bitching that goes on at any subordinate gatherings. Middle Management and Executive gatherings can easily produce the same bullshit. But this same bullshit reveals the potential ingredients of positioning. The process is the same: first, what is it that you want him to do; second, what does he want and what is he afraid of; third, what are the steps required to get him to do it. Fourth, get him in a box.

Let us illustrate instrumental positioning at work on some subordinates. Garfle Greymatter is one of those weird technical types who you would like to keep enclosed in a closet with the chains well locked. Then once in a while you would rattle them to see if he has discovered something.

Garfle's main ambition in life is to do things no one has ever done before. With a Phd. in Micro-Electronics and an Engineering Degree in Engineering Physics, (as well as a Masters on Interstellar Telecommunications) there is no question as to Garfle's credentials. Additionally, to add to his character, Garfle's appearance and weird behavior are what Personnel Department Manager's nightmares are all about.

Clepto Superbyte is Garfle's boss. Despite what Clepto's boss, and the personnel department, said about Garfle, Clepto saw potential in Garfle's abilities. So he hired him as a programmer. After spending some 12 years at numerous Universities, Garfle was happy to get any job close to a real computer. Clepto gave Garfle some behind the scenes programming tasks to check him out. Here Garfle would hang about with Quirk Multiplex and Warp Monkeynuts, both micro-computer fanatics. Between the three of them, there wasn't a computer in the world that they couldn't interconnect, especially when the beer flowed after work - the Universal Protocol they called it. Garfle even had ideas on an Intergalactic protocol.

This aspect caused a difficult problem for Clepto since it was impossible for Garfle to keep any continuity on any really useful projects. He would get side tracked very easily. Before you could blink an eye, Garfle is off connecting up various devices. Despite all this Garfle was very capable. So how must one teach Garfle the importance of projects and time commitments? Clepto decides that it is worth the effort to condition this guy.

Clepto sits down and lists out a conditioning plan. Through a few SIC gatherings, Clepto has learned a few things about Garfle. So Clepto begins to list out the scenario in terms of the Ingredients to Instrumental Positioning :

GOALS:
- needs to become more reliable and dependable
- needs to realize the importance of deadlines
- needs to be able to focus his energy on important issues
- needs to learn that he sometimes may have to rely on others

INSTRUMENTS - POSITIVE
- likes a challenge particularly with computers and telecommunications
- is a self starter and is extremely intelligent
- prefers to work alone
- technically superior and likes recognition

INSTRUMENTS - NEGATIVE
- becomes bored quickly and looses direction
- doesn't like being told what to do
- is arrogant and feels superior
- does not like to depend on others for help
- can be stubborn and uncompromising
- blames others for unrealistic deadlines and demands

Here we have a typical hot blooded PhD. type who is trying to work his way through a Corporation but finding at every nook and cranny that things are not quite the same as it was in those schools of higher learning. And if things continue, this perfectly capable fellow will become more and more of a problem to Clepto. He will become more isolated, disgruntled and embarrassing, especially since

Clepto stood up for this technical turkey in the beginning. Garfle may just get more and more pissed off, to blame others for stupid commitments and lack of precise definitions. Even worse, he may become more of a problem since he will believe that no one really appreciates him nor his abilities. We have here a delicate deadlock. What does Clepto do? He must create an Instrumental Conditioning Process from the Ingredients he has listed.

First, he must set up a harmless project to see if Garfle can do better when Garfle defines the time and project constraints. Second, he must teach him the meaning of other peoples' input. This means that Garfle needs another project which depends upon some outsider input for success. Failure would precipitate another try. Third, there must be some reward at the end if he succeeds - say a paper at the next convention. Fourth, he must set up a more serious, high profile project if it all works out.

What Clepto is setting up here is a self perpetuating process which has its rewards and punishments controlled by Garfle himself. In other words, if Garfle contemplates and sets a deadline himself, his pride in himself and his inability to blame others will serve as the punishment mechanism should he fail. Clepto does not need to reprimand him in this case. He just sets up the process, and needs to ask Garfle what happened. This is like having an electrified V-shaped maze with a reward sitting at the apex. The rat quickly learns about the shock from the wall and the goodie at the far end - after he has the hair on his ass stand straight up from a few shocks. He soon learns to stay within the bounds. So let us summarize a process. This is the same as the BOX. The box is created by properly using fears and self commitment.

PROCESS - 4 ITERATIONS:

STEP 1: **The Harmless Project**. This is a short duration project which involves objectives, plans, time schedules, reports, and so on - at a simple level. This is all done by Garfle. This creates commitment, allows independence, creates challenge and shows trust in abilities. Success generates confidence, arrogance, independence, aggression. Failure generates a knock down in arrogance but done by himself since he set the terms. He will quite likely admit where he miscalculated. Either way he is ready for the next step.

STEP 2: **The Real Project**. In this case the project is a bit more extensive, requiring some planning up front. As with Project 1, Garfle must define objectives, schedules, plans, costs, etc., but this is done formally - and circulated for wider recognition. This is a bigger "BOX". This time other people are involved and the plan must involve other's input as well as other's cooperation. A failure in this case will undoubtedly highlight the independence problem. This time he will look stupid to others. This will serve as negative reinforcement. If he succeeds then he will be even more arrogant but less independent since he succeeded only by involving others and getting their cooperation (positive reinforcement). This would be further reinforced if Clepto had a "project recap" with Garfle getting him to admit the success factors. But in reality, Garfle, being the stubborn asshole who could only do things his way, would fail. The injury in pride would be harsh. A project recap would identify the failings. Here a new project of similar structure would be launched or else a second attempt at the same project made. This time Garfle would be much more cooperative and likely to listen and learn.

STEP 3: The Reward. At the end of the first two steps sits some reward to turn Garfle's hot button on. The condition is, however, that the Project must firstly be finished on time and be successful. Obviously, for Garfle, this could be working on a technical paper for publication or some pet telecommunications project for a few weeks. Needless to say, he cannot do it if he fails - but, again, the failure must be of his own doing.

STEP 4: The Serious Project. This point is reached only upon successful learning (behavior modification) through the previous steps. At this point Garfle should have been humbled and rewarded sufficiently to make him realize what he can and can't do. He would be ready for the next level of Project more involved and more dependant upon others ideas.

It should be noticed how Clepto modified Garfle's behavior to become a good project coordinator - more dependable and more useful. He could have either waited for Garfle to learn or he could have told him what to correct. Both methods probably would have not worked within a time period that Clepto had available since other eyes were upon him. Through positioning, he needs less supervision and has less conflicts. But he needed to set up the three Ingredients of Instrumental Positioning. It should also be noted that Garfle could have bitched because the project was unfair or he was not given sufficient education. Technically this could be true - there could indeed be certain obstacles. But if Garfle required a project management course then he could have been given one - then tested to see what was learned.

Quite typically, the Mid Management Group uses these methods all the time. Human Resources Courses in "Employee Motivation" or "Making Subordinates Productive" is typically a disguised Instrumental Conditioning course. And the bullshit that surrounds these courses is staggering - just to talk about the three Ingredients to Instrumental Positioning. Although all cases are not like Garfle's, and some are much more complex than others, most cases can still be reduced down to these three ingredients. The key, of course, lies in defining the positive and negative instruments which need to be balanced in some step by step process. Here lies one of the keys to tactical manipulation that the Executive group uses.

It goes without saying that the SIC Network is the decisive means of defining the ingredients. If you have ever gone to have a few beers with your subordinates - and really tossed a few back - you would know how revealing the process can be. The fears and needs can come frothing forth in a deluge of drunken words quite easily. But everyone's fears and needs are different and some are harder to use (or get at) than others. More over, your style may be different as may the subordinate type of problem. Let us now look at some of those problems. :

DISPENSE WITH PEOPLE PROBLEMS FAST

When you move into the Middle Management category, you come to realize that you no longer control the actual process that accomplishes the work. Rather, you control the people that are responsible for the actual process. As such, you cannot govern directly the speed or efficiency of the work because you do not do it. As we have seen, moving up the ladder gets you further and further away from the real process of doing the work. So you must depend on making sure that people work effectively through other means. In the previous section we saw how to apply Instrumental Positioning to correct (or change) peoples' behavior so as to make them more productive, efficient, and in line with what you and your superiors expect.

The whole idea of management, however, is conducive to the AQ process and potential conflicts. Subordinates will place Superiors on their AQ lists because they do not agree with or do not like them. Superiors will always try to make subordinates do better and change things to suit them and the Company. It goes without saying that it is inevitable that the people involved in this process realize this and eventually get pissed off.

This always leads to some sort of people problem. Garfle Greymatter was such a problem.

One thing that becomes fairly clear is that many of these problems are destructive to efficiency. It is this that Middle Management must learn to cope with. Your Management style will undoubtedly set the scene for how you will cope. The Commando would simply tell a slackass *"It's my way or the highway you lazy bastard!"* The SYMPATHIZER on the other hand would say *"Lets have lunch and talk about your attitude".* Whatever the style is, however, the need is for correction and it involves the use of reward or punishment. And this process, as we have seen, involves the detection of individual subordinate needs and fears. But one thing is a sure bet, people problems effect productivity, poor productivity affects your position and your superiors will measure you by your production and your ability to resolve people problems. So let us look at some of these people problems.

SOME PROBLEM TYPES – GETTING ON TOP

People will always exhibit various symptoms that will manifest themselves in some corporate problem. They will show stress, burnout, exhaustion or depression. They will have poor concentration or not listen well. They may be tired all the time, forget appointments, or require extra attention. They may never finish something or they may complain constantly. Some may forget orders while others have no sense of responsibility. Others may think everything is just too much while others have nothing to look forward to. A few could be lazy and stupid while others seem to never learn.

Whatever the problem is, however, the superior's method of finding out and dealing with the problem will clearly dictate the success of both sides. The majority of people in corporations are there to improve themselves and their lives. So many are greedy and self centered egoists like anyone else. People do not usually deliberately set out to cause problems - they just precipitate problems, or they encounter obstacles which cause problems. Your task as a mid-management type is to therefore remove those problems or obstacles so they can work effectively - but at a price to them. But first, some problem people :

WALLOWERS   These types seem to enjoy their condition of perpetual complaining. They are always victimized by others and the system. Wallowers will, of course, never want to do anything. They just seem to like the feeling of telling everyone what rotten bastards the rest of the world is.

DEPRESSERS This type, unlike the mouthy wallower, withdraws, feeling sad and hopeless. They blame themselves saying it is all their fault but feel helpless and guilty, regardless of who did them in.

HIGH TECHIES   The high techies have a tendency to make technical mountains out of simple molehills. They complicate things to the point of absurdity. There is never a simple solution.

COMPLAINERS   This type is like a seagull. All he does is eat, squawk and shit. There is never anything that is right. Everything is wrong and if he had the chance he would fix it.

PISS TANKS These are the guys that come in pissed after lunch. They love to think that no one can see they are pissed and they like to slob around dribbling on everyone, giving advice.

DENYERS   Denyers pretend that all is well and that nothing is wrong. They feel that by not admitting it they are real tough.

WHIZ KIDS   These types have huge egos and always like to shatter world records. They have little respect for rank except to aspire to it.

UNREACHABLES   These types don't communicate. They avoid eye contact and show vacant stares. They are unsociable and live entirely in their own vacant space.

LIARS .Liars will tell you that you gave them instructions which you did not. They will lie to your face to protect themselves.

BLAMERS The blamer will never ever take responsibility for anything, particularly if something went wrong. He is always quick to identify someone or something to blame.

DREAMERS These types are always dreaming up solutions which are not practical. They would work forever on hypothesis and theoretical solutions to make things better.

PUSHERS These types like to tell others what to do and when to do it. They are ambitious and abrasive egotistical types.

GOOFERS Goofers are lazy always looking for a way to get out of work by doing something the easy way. They can be quite clever at being lazy.

DIMWIT Dimwits need 300 explanations before they can execute a task. They just never seem to learn anything and also appear to forget quickly.

APATHETIC. This guy just doesn't give a shit. He just does his work and never seems to care about anything. He is like a robot.

PROCRASTINATOR This type never seems to understand what time deadlines are, except to start the job close to it. He just loves to leave things to the last minute - then panic.

DROP-IN The dropin is always seen carrying his coffee cup into someone else's office to waste time. DropIns like to solve corporate problems in your office.

SCABS Scabs are always looking for ideas to steal from others. They are plagiarizers, seeking recognition by using other's work.

CRITICIZER These people spend most of their time criticizing others and others work. They don't complain, they just tell others that what they are doing is wrong.

BLOWHARD He is the one who likes to pretend he is tough. He curses before women and always has alternative jobs to go to (if he wants to).

TARDYS Tardys are always late. They are late for work, late for meetings, late for anything. It is never a lot, but just enough to irritate you because they won't improve.

WHINERS These types are prone to whine about anything they are asked to do. How can they do it or will they get help seems to be their biggest concerns.

SNOT The snot is the guy who figures he is above everyone else. He thinks his shit doesn't stink and that it never ever did. Moreover, he never minds telling anybody how great he is.

SUCKHOLE The suckhole can be extremely painful as he slurps around trying to get away with doing as little as possible. He gets the boss coffee, asks if he needs anything, etc. - trying to attain favoritism.

TWO-FACER This type is the untrustworthy creep who likes to tell on everybody. He sneaks around creating trouble for others by telling secrets, even lies.

BRICK WALL This type never does what he is told to do. He appears to listen but never seems to absorb anything. He typically just goes away and does whatever he thinks he should do.

PESSIMIST The pessimist never sees anything any other way but dismal. He has no confidence and he always thinks that failure is inevitable.

BULLSHITTER These types tell you what you want to hear but what is untrue. They try to cover up failings with bullshit and smoke screens.

Here we have but a few problem people. There are many, many others. Some have combined problems and others are just more severe cases. All of these types can in some way disrupt productivity, undermine authority or cause trouble. Basically they all represent two simple types of problems, either productivity or personality related.

- They are not or can not do something as expected.
- Their personalities do not fit with what is expected.

If you look closely at all the types listed, they are problems because they do not fit a corporate personality mold or they do not perform according to a productivity mold. In most cases, these moulds are created by a Middle Manager as an interpretation of what the Corporation wants and what he wants. And what he wants to see is quite likely a reflection of his own personality and management style. These are what we call the DUAL OBSTACLES.

The moral of the story is that these Dual Problem Obstacles are usually quite easy to identify - just as we have done so above. Quite obviously, one can then identify the INSTRUMENTS and the GOALS. The positive and negative INSTRUMENTS are just a list of fears and needs for each particular problem type. So no matter what the problem or the problem type, the process is the same. The next trick is to get the PROCESS.

PERSONALITY OR PRODUCTIVITY OBSTACLES – "PPO'S"

Let us labor on this aspect a little longer. Most problem people are a problem because one of two main obstacle types is causing the problem. Type one, mainly personality, is potentially an obstacle because you may not have certain habits or traits that your supervisor appreciates.

This could be as simple as talking loud to being a recluse. It could involve being radical or not conforming to policy (ie. dress code). Type two, mainly productivity, involves obstacles which limit productivity. Clearly, this can involve vast problems ranging from lack of experience to an inability to learn or cooperate. Most Management problems (as related to subordinate problems) will involve some combination of Personality or Productivity Obstacles. Thus the identification of PPO's is a key ability that needs to be included in a Middle Manager's Arsenal. Productivity and harmony can then be accomplished by removing these obstacles - usually through Instrumental Positioning.

If we look at any problem type such as a "snot", it is easy to understand that the problem is that this person assumes that he is better. To get rid of the problem is the "goal". If we look at why, mainly that he is overqualified, under challenged or is of shitty personality, then these are his PPO's.

These PPO's, like most problems, stem from a combination of personality and productivity. It is difficult to identify, however, which one has caused the other. So as soon as you can identify the problem, you have a GOAL - mainly get rid of the problem. And when you can list the why's of the problem, you have identified the PPO's. These PPO's will usually include the fears and needs required for the Instrumental Process.

Another clue to creating a process resides in the idea of the "BOX". The box in the rat scenario, was a physical box within which the victim could not escape his "training". In our human case, the box usually takes the form of rules, power and commitment. If you can get a commitment, which if violated, creates humility, embarrassment, loss of pride, etc., before those that a commitment has been made in front of, then you have a box! Clearly, if someone has been boasting that he can do better - at coffee break - and you "call his bluff" (at coffee break) by giving him the opportunity, then his peers and his commitment to accept will automatically create the BOX.

The PROCESS, as we have seen, is a step by step iteration process which narrows in on the desired GOAL. In forming a process, one must keep in mind that the main reason that a subordinate is having trouble doing his job is because of some obstacles in his way. As part of the process you must remove these obstacles - but at a price to him, just as we saw with Garfle Greymatter. Consider an example.

Harvey Hotshit is a problem. He works for Bill Blastoff as a planner. Harvey is a fairly dependable worker. He always gets the job done but he alternates between a HIGH TECHIE, SNOT, CRITICIZER and DREAMER quite a combination of problems for his boss. Harvey, it seems, always has a better way of doing things but he never gets a chance - so he says : *"These two nerd turds above me don't know shit about planning. I could have done a superior job if the dinks let me. Christ, we could have used linear programming to optimize the critical path."*

Typically, Harvey vents his emotion after the fact, at his SIC. Sometimes he does it at coffee - in front of Bill Blastoff. Needless to say, Harvey has a tendency to undermine authority and make Bill seem quite stupid. But because Harvey does his job, Bill finds it hard to reprimand him for his smartass lip. Harvey, because he is getting away with it, is becoming more obvious about it. So what does Bill do about this lippy bastard? He activates some INSTRUMENTAL POSITIONING strategy. First, we identify the PROBLEM: Harvey is a smart ass lip who undermines authority by insisting, afterwards, that he could do a better job. So we have a goal.

GOAL: Teach the lippy creep a lesson in humility so he does not undermine authority.

Obviously, the Goal is to solve the problem, right? Next, let us try to identify the PPO's :

PPO's Needs a challenge to see if he is indeed capable. Does not understand the problems properly. Thinks he is smarter than everyone else. Doesn't like the boss or authority. Is out of control. Needs to grow up and become more practical.

It doesn't take a genius to deduct from this list that Harvey Hotshit needs to be served a challenge in such a way as to commit him in front of his peers. By doing this you put him in the BOX where escape means a failure - and a justifiable reprimand from the boss. Best is a failure in front of his buddies.

Actually there is little difference here than what had to be done in the case of Garfle Greymatter, where Clepto Superbyte had to do a bit of "training". So we need a training process.

PROCESS Commit him to his loudmouth ideas in front of his peers the next time he mouths off.

    STEP 1 Catch him at the next coffee break and tell him that it was a good suggestion. He will be given authority to use it next time.
    STEP 2 Set up a meeting where all involved will be informed of the new strategy - as presented by Harvey Hotshit.
    STEP 3 Let Harvey and everyone know what is going to happen, then activate the project.

Note that the process involves combining the needs and fears from PPO's in such a way as to have them work against each other. Commit the big mouthpiece to real life instead of theory in front of peers where he could fail and show incompetence - that which he detests. If Harvey fails, it is not likely that he will be so lippy for quite a while.

If he succeeds, then he may be even more lippy, but Bill Blastoff can't be criticized for being unprogressive, and his production has been improved - nothing wrong with that ! Anyway, if Harvey gets too lippy again, a new strategy, more complex and demanding could be applied to him.

There is nothing difficult about the idea of Instrumental Positioning once you have identified some key ingredients. The idea can be summarized in the Strategic Positioning Profile (SPP). Again, some of the "most successful" managers and executives are so good at this, one does not even know they have been "conditioned" like the rat in the cage.

STRATEGIC POSITIONING PROFILES (SPP's)

By now you may have realized that there is really nothing complex about Instrumental Positioning or People Conditioning. In reality we involve ourselves in determining peoples PPO's every day, regardless of whether the person is a superior, peer or subordinate. Usually PPO's are why the others get on our AQ lists - right? So it should be easy to identify someone's PPO's.

Some attain a position on your AQ list because they have a problem that affects you in some way. But that problem may also be the potential goal which needs to be corrected. In looking at the PPO table which listed some problem types, we see that the problems are not really, hard to identify. A LIAR lies and a SCAB steals others work. A DREAMER is impractical while a WALLOWER complains. But the other question one must answer is why - why is this person a problem and what is his problem. A SCAB steals others work because he is lazy, he is not creative or he just likes to steal - in either case the result is aversive and it must be corrected. So the next time he steals he must receive an "electric shock" to punish the action.

So you create a little Strategic Positioning Profile of your potential victim:

Why is this person such an Asshole?
GOALS: What is his problem & what does he want?
TOOLS: What would you like to do to him? What have I got that he wants or is afraid of? How can I get a commitment from him?
BOX: Can I do it in such a way as to benefit me and him?

Corrective action to the problems become GOALS. NEEDS and FEARS are the instruments of correction. How and where you put the GOALS and TOOLS together becomes the BOX.

THE BRAWLERS' HANDBOOK

If you remember the Chapter on the Executive Arsenal, you will recall the various methods used at meetings. Most were not nice. It does not have to be that way. The techniques of boardroom brawling were highly developed and refined. It turns out that the "undergraduate course" in boardroom brawling is effectively taken in Middle Management - in dealing with people problems. Remember that building a good solid AQ in equilibrium with your position is essential. When you move into Middle Management you must learn to Call and Tell people that they are assholes - and get away with it (under the AQ virus spell). If not, you will not handle people and problems properly. You will eventually be judged as non-management material.

In identifying those PPO's (Personality or Productivity Obstacles) we developed a manipulative means of instrumental positioning. This is used to position those who are worth positioning. If a guy is just an unchangeable smartass and won't really produce, then he is hardly worth the effort of developing a process. It is much easier to tell the dork to his face or embarrass him so as to keep your AQ growing fruitfully thus solving the problem directly. Moreover, you need to practice developing direct Brawling Methods for the next level of your career. That is what happens mot of the time when you have the AQ Virus.

THERE IS ALWAYS THE TRAP

Subordinates are essential to progress. They can make or break a middle manager. If they don't produce and they cause problems then you will be on the carpet. So most of the time you are trying to make people productive. But what happens if you can't make someone productive? Or what if this person is a real trouble maker. Or what if he is not worth the effort. Well, clearly you must fall back on your authority and get rid of the asshole so you resort to not nice tools.

This is not always as easy as it may appear. In many cases setting up a box may be difficult and it may not be easy to trap an asshole let alone fire him. A premeditated set of traps where you know failure will be the result is then the best alternative. But note that the Positioning Process is still the same, only the Goal has changed mainly get the asshole out but it can be done constructively in most cases.

PROCESSES - PRODUCE OR PERISH

When we talk about processes, we include all those procedures, methods and functions that companies develop, use or follow. Typically these processes are followed by people (workers) to produce whatever services or products that the company makes its living from. A process not only involves people, it involves equipment and goods. Capital and materials are put together in such a way as to produce for the company. Ensuring that these processes are run efficiently is one of the prime functions of a Middle Manager. To fail in this function is to surely flaunt disaster.

In learning to run processes efficiently, we find that buzz words surround the functions. Organizing, planning, evaluation, monitoring, improvement, teamwork, projects, etc., etc. There is no denying that much of the process of efficiency depends upon technical capabilities and knowledge of a middle manager. This book, however, is not about technical matters. Nor is it about the skills of project management or organizational planning. These are taught in schools. It is more interested in those untaught processes by which technologists are controlled.

Several previous chapters were dedicated to the Executive. There we saw the tools he used to maintain order and control - in a corporate motive of profit and efficiency. The Middle Manager, needless to say, must also learn these tools. This is part of the "Big Transition". The Manager is usually less advanced than the Executive is in the use of the Arsenals. Middle Managers, less refined in their tactics, get their experience in Backroom Brawling. This experience is used to gain entry into the next level.

But together with all the buzzwords of Project Management, Organization and so on, comes a need to still deal with people and processes no different than that used by the Executive.

THE PROFIT PICTURE - BEAN COUNTERS INC.
There is yet another aspect of the growth process that has its important beginnings in Middle Management. Commonly referred to as "bean counting". Managers find that its importance becomes increasingly more vital to successful climbing up AQ mountain. Accounting, Budgeting, Cash Management, Forecasting, Cash Flow and Financial Reporting all become increasingly important concepts upon which decisions are made. It is not a surprise, therefore, that those most comfortable in this terminology and its use will also be the ones most likely to move upwards. Again, this is not the place to discuss bean counting - there are many courses available. The topic has already been discussed as part of Executive and Managers arsenals. Let us move on.

II
MIDDLE MANAGEMENT MEETINGS

THE IMPORTANCE OF MEETINGS

The main difference between Executive and Middle Management meetings is that the Executives are usually more skilled at Focus, Control and other Arsenal skills. So keep this in mind in your upward climb. The sooner you learn the skills, the sooner you will be able to climb upwards over the people you have in your meetings. Sooner or later you will take charge of meetings. Have you ever sat in a meeting and wondered one of the following :

- Who the hell is in charge of this meeting ?
- What is the purpose of this gathering ?
- How long will it take to reach a conclusion ?
- Why don't they focus on the real issues ?
- Why are we wasting all this time ?
- What a bunch of emotional jerks wasting time.
- Why wasn't anyone prepared for this stuff ?

Regardless of topic, these aimless, wandering, boring meetings prevail in the rooms of Middle Management. As silly as the example

Executive meeting seemed, the focus and control was always there. This is not quite the case in lower levels since the experience is usually less developed. To illustrate this, let us first get to know some new people lower down the ladder at Steadfast Meats. Let us then see how they carry on at a meeting and learn from their tactics (and folly).

THE BIG TOILET PAPER MEETING

If we can recall the Executive Meeting on the issue of Bathroom tissue (Book 1) we will note that Randolf Snooper was made a fool of because he couldn't explain certain numbers. Actually, it served him right for plagiarizing on his staff, despite the fact that the report originated from misguided ideas. Remember that this whole thing started as a result of Pomp Crotchley and Brenda Breeder attempting to hide the fact that they had leaked information. We also recall that although the magnitude of the decision and the financial impact was trivial, certain things had been brought out which needed immediate attention:

- Scab Dancer was "not pleased" with Mr. Snooper's poor presentation.
- Policy of other divisions needed clarification.
- Randolf could not explain the cost justification segment.
- New quotations on toilet tissue were required.
- Security leaking needed to be addressed.
- Efficiency surveys or wiping habits needed attention.
- Use tests needed to be set up and analyzed.
- Payout analysis would have to be redone and presented.

All this was required for the next meeting in formal report form. So Randolf has to mobilize his department swiftly. His department is made up of six staff members :

POMP CROTCHLEY: **Supervisor of Personnel**
BRENDA BREEDER   **Personnel Clerk**

233

SAC MEDDLER.   Personnel Clerk
KEVIN BALONEY: Supervisor Industrial Relations
TINA TINKLE: W/P Operator
ERIC VON SHITHEAD   Industrial Relations Clerk

FIRST THE MEETING PLAYERS

RANDOLF SNOOPER is the Director of Personnel. He is, in terms of our AQ birdies, a Kite. These birds are noted for being very swift at stealing from others. They also have a slick appearance. Randolf is one of the slickest, cunning backbiters around. He is concerned with one and only one thing - himself. Randolf got to be the Director because he was the owner Boomer Steadfast's personnel clerk from twenty-five years ago. He has simply outlived everyone in personnel and he has indirectly black-balled any others that appeared to be a threat.

Randolf likes to take credit for other's work and he likes to sneak around spying on others so he can tattle. Randolf, being uneducated, never had great expectations as a professional. When he achieved the height of Director, without the fancy credentials held by others, he became an unbearable creep to listen to. As he became more and more protective of his position, he just became an obnoxious and despicable asshole. In fact, he is an evil corporate Slink, of Pecker species, looking for any opportunity to peck someone if it means an opportunity for him.

Randolf's background is all relatively insignificant since he has really accomplished nothing except to be able to steal, cheat and lie well. Even as a kid he would always try to cheat someone - he was just a bad case right from the start. It was not surprising to see him recognize the power behind Scab Dancer, his boss. He was fast to "attach" himself to Scab, picking up scraps whenever Scab would leave some. His AQ is well beyond his position because he just thinks that everyone is either out to get his job or everyone is just an asshole. His position, therefore, could easily be in jeopardy -

a fact that even Randolf recognizes - so he steals and tattles even more to keep his position.

POMPY CROTCHLEY is the Supervisor of Personnel. As supervisor he has two clerks working for him. The prime responsibility is to keep track of personnel files and personnel matters. So Pomp's major responsibility is to supervise records and filing. Pomp is like a fat seagull who has just learned to fly. He has also learned that in flight he is able to shit upon people. Pomp thinks that he is super great.

Pomp's main concerns in life are like a seagulls in that he must eat, shit and squawk. He also thinks that Randolf, his boss, is the most dynamic leader in the organization - this is why Pomp, after five years of filing personnel folders, was promoted to supervisor. *"I really have a feeling of accomplishment and purpose when we have a meeting with Mr. Snooper"* he squawks, *"he really activates constructive discussions and solves problems"*. Pomp is a fairly stupid individual. He is fairly overweight and quite sloppy in appearance. He has recently taken to one of his clerks, Brenda Breeder. If you remember correctly, he was having sex on the side whenever possible. In this regard, too few of Pomp's brains seem to have been dislocated in the head of his crotch member. It was, in fact, such activities that precipitated the "toilet paper leak".

BRENDA BREEDER is a Personnel Clerk, with few ambitions in life but to get laid. Being a pudgy little thing, she has been endowed with fairly large breasts and constantly seeks opportunities to display them. Brenda simply does her job as she is told, never any more, with a constant lookout to satisfy her "crotch fever". It was not surprising that Brenda and Pomp would hit it off. Whenever possible she will wear deep 'V' tops and bend over in countless ways to expose her prized possessions. At coffee breaks, at lunch, while typing, filing or whenever possible, Brenda can be seen trying out another pose. Brenda is clearly a penguin, with a rather prolific desire to breed - and everybody knows it. It turns out that she had to be transferred out of Office Services. It seems that Flirt

Shameless and Jock Flasher, according to Bertha Bitchalot, were constantly performing some fairly lewd acts with Brenda in the central file area. There was a time when vast numbers of employees would sneak up to hunt for files, hoping to get a look at the bizarre acts. Since no one could really prove anything, it was suggested that Brenda get a 'promotion' to personnel, where Pomp had already taken an interest in her. Needless to say, Pomp spends a lot of time hanging over Brenda's desk.

SAC MEDDLER is also a Personnel Clerk, reporting to Pomp. Sac is a skinny fellow who is always looking to be helpful. The problem is that he is, more often than not, over helpful to the point of being a pain in the ass. Sac doesn't have great expectations in life - he just wants to do a good job. If it wasn't for Sac, many of the functions just wouldn't be done - something that others in the department do not appreciate and constantly take advantage of. Sac doesn't complain, he just tries to do more. Sometimes people become worried that he will take away all their work. Sac even tries to show the word processing operator how to run the machine. He tells people how to file things when all they want is a file. If you ask him about a policy or a plan, he will give you a rambling speech lasting an hour - he will even follow you into your office or the bathroom to continue the answer. If he walks by your office and sees you with anything to do with personnel matters, he will pop in to give an explanation. Needless to say, Sac is a walking storehouse of information, just waiting for someone to knock on his door. So in terms of our AQ Birdies, Sac is a Chicken with a certain amount of economic significance to the Company.

KEVIN BALONEY is the Supervisor of Industrial Relations - the other part of the Personnel Department. Kevin is a Parrot, with several years of experience in matters of Industrial Relations. He has had the same position for six years and is the only one in the group who has an ounce of brains. Furthermore, Kevin has had a formal education in College (Business) and has taken various courses in Negotiating and Bullshitting. Kevin has found these courses quite useful in his work but they have gone to his head. He has a tendency to bullshit the importance of his work. His one staff employee, Eric von Shithead, has picked up the same idea quite obnoxiously. Together they make quite a pain, each working the other up more and more on matters of the importance of Industrial Relations. So Kevin has learned to bluff and bullshit quite successfully to get his way. He doesn't see eye to eye with his boss, Randolf Snooper. "*Just a useless turd stuck in the corporate asshole*"- he says. Kevin seeks any opportunity to display superior qualities and make Snooper look stupid. Randolf, of course knows this and acknowledges Kevin as a serious threat. So Eric and Kevin take responsibility for industrial relations, labor contracts and all matters pertaining to staff benefits, pensions and so on.

TINA TINKLE is a Word Processing Operator, who happens to be a leftover from the old secretarial pool. Tina was such a precious, cute little worker that no one could let her go. In addition, she was so good on one of the old word processor systems that it was a shame to take it away. She was therefore moved into the Industrial Relations area. They needed considerable help in typing labor agreements at the time. She was later moved up as Randolf's secretary and general typist for the group.

Tina almost seems fragile - radiating purity and uncompromising politeness. She always smiles and has a little twinkle in her eye - eager to work. She is efficient and tidy - it is indeed difficult to find fault with her. Although she would never admit it, she shivers when Pomp Crotchley comes near. And Brenda Breeder, she thinks, is a despicable creature who makes a mockery of true womanhood. But she bites her tongue and smiles, just quietly adding to her AQ list.

ERIC VON SHITHEAD is an Industrial Relations Clerk. Eric is down to the very core, a loud mouthed, smart assed shithead. He is an obvious suckhole and has a terribly gritty personality. His main objective in life is to tell everyone how important Industrial Relations is and how important he and Kevin are to the company. Eric is protected by Kevin who insists that Eric is unusually conscientious and a most dedicated employee. Because of Eric's personality and attitude, he has achieved a fairly high AQ and is clearly in precarious disequilibrium. Eric has been working in the area of Industrial Relations for the last ten years, moving through four positions as a Clerk. It is easy to understand why his previous positions have lasted about two to three years. Eric is now at the three year mark at Steadfast Meats - his main salvation is that Kevin Baloney protects him. Eric is an ostrich - too big for his boots, with his head in the sand most of the time. He has little significance economically to the Company and is probably more of a nuisance than should be allowed.

NOW THE MEETING

Here we have the Personnel Department, headed by Randolf Snooper who has called a meeting in order to do several things. Firstly he needs to inform his staff of the status of the proposal. Secondly, he needs to get ideas on how to accomplish the tasks as set out by the Executive Committee. Thirdly, he must activate a plan of action - and rather quickly - to get a final report. Fourth, he needs to give a few people shit for putting him in a bad situation in front of the Executive Group.

Needless to say, he is still steaming from the meeting where he was 'caught' on the numbers. But Randolf is smart enough to try to keep cool and seek out carefully the reason for the non-accountable figures as done by Pomp Crotchley. The meeting takes place in the Personnel meeting room early the day after the Executive meeting. This way Randolf is able to play king without any superiors to observe his habits.

SNOOPER *"I have called this meeting because we have been asked to follow up on the important report that we have submitted to the Executive committee. It is so important that the President has insisted that it be ready for the next meeting. I have also noticed that some of the monthly costs do not balance and I have pointed this out at the meeting to avoid any embarrassment. Pomp, you* *assured me that these numbers were correct. I came up with $200.00 per month as the net increase of moving to the Executive paper, not $40.00 per month."*

Notice how quickly Snooper gets off the real focus and heads after the area where he suffered the big embarrassment. He even lies about the meeting.

CROTCHLEY *"Let me check the figures in the report.* "

SNOOPER *"Kevin, we need to know what the policy is at our plants and the walkout ramifications of ignoring employee grievances. Pomp, we need to know that our prices are the best prices. And Kevin, how did the staff get access to executive washrooms anyway ?"*

BALONEY *"We have no policy on toilet paper. I have no idea what they use at the Plants - why is it even a concern ?"*

SNOOPER *"It is of concern because I said so, I want a complete report on my desk tomorrow on what they use and how much it cost them !"*

Notice the little jockey for position and the use of power.

CROTCHLEY *"Randolf I have checked the numbers in your report. They are not the same as all my notes given to Tina for typing. The numbers should be a net increase of $66.00 per month, not $40.00 per month like the report says."*

MEDDLER *"That's right. You probably got $200.00 before you applied the 3 to 1 efficiency factor. Do you want me to work it out on the board ?"*

TINKLE *"But Mr. Snooper, I typed what Mr. Crotchley gave me - honest."*

CROTCHLEY *"Sac, how did you work yours out ? Did you divide the number of rolls by 3 or 4 ?"*

BALONEY *"I think that security is not our business. If you have concerns then we should send a memo to the security department about tightening up."*

SHITHEAD *"It is our duty in Personnel to get these things sorted out for the Company."*

BREEDER *"I think we should get a memo sent off right away."*

TINKLE Sobbing, *"I really didn't type in the wrong numbers Mr. Snooper."*

SNOOPER *"Where are the original notes - do you still have them?"*

Notice how focus and control have been diluted. People are starting to wander off in tangents.

TINKLE *"Mr. Crotchley took them back."*

BALONEY *"I think that the legal department should address the issue of walkouts and whether they are legal or not. We have no records of these types of grievances.*

Now by this time it has become quite evident that the meeting is out of control, with no focus or direction. Snooper tries to regain some order.

SNOOPER *Loudly "Quiet, all of you, we are here to get things done not hold a social event. Before we go any further, I think that we better make sure that the results are all accurate. We will need to survey the habits of the employees to see that the efficiency factors are correct. In addition how do we know that $2.00/roll is the best price? Pomp, you must set up an efficiency survey."*

CROTCHLEY   *"What do you suggest ? Do we stand in the washrooms and count wipes?"*

BREEDER   *"Why don't we set up video cameras to watch and count."*

SNOOPER *"I will authorize the purchase of the Executive paper. You must place it in the staff washrooms to see if the number of rolls used decreases by 3 to 2."*

BREEDER *"Then we can put in cameras, right?"*

SHITHEAD *"Brenda don't be so stupid. You could cause law suits if anybody finds out, even though you'd like to watch."*

BREEDER "You should talk you big creep - how come you wanted to sneak in to washrooms with me the other day, hey - didn't you want to watch ?"

SNOOPER Loudly *"Hold it, lets not get involved in private problems."*

TINKLE *"Mr. Snooper, would you like me to go down to the Safeway and get a list of prices ?"*

SNOOPER *"That's a good idea Tina but we don't know how much any one would use."*

BALONEY *"So what do you suggest ? Are you really serious about this?"*

MEDDLER *Why don't we check with Systems - Garfle Greymatter knows all about setting a sampling procedures."*

SNOOPER "Ok, Sac go ahead on that immediately. Tina you can do that survey too."

By this time it is clear that this meeting is not going very far. It is disjointed and going in various directions all at one time. The focus points change and after two hours of back and forth bickering, all that has been accomplished is to raise AQ's. Randolf finally breaks up the meeting by concluding that they will hold another meeting in two days. He will call each in to his office one by one, giving specific tasks this way each situation is under his control. Within two days he will be able to assess what needs to be done.

It should be clear that, if any meeting like this was held at the Executive level, it would not last too long without some reprimands and embarrassments. Why? Because they are usually capable of using Arsenals - that's why. Randolf just didn't know how to get order back into the meeting so he could only rely on his seniority to stop the nonsense. Putting people in their place not only raises AQ's properly, but it gives you a place (in the Company).

So we have seen that the BIG TRANSITION is only a prerequisite course to the GREAT TRANSITION. And how well one learns the course material impacts directly upon how well one climbs up AQ mountain. But what about those poor souls who fail the course to fall down those productivity slides. What about the vast majority of people who live in AQ-Disequilibrium? Let us examine these people and their options more closely in the next chapter. Let us drop to the lower reaches - into the working class.

12
AQ TOOLS??
FOR THE REST

WHAT DO YOU DO ABOUT A HIGH AQ

BEFORE WE GET TO THE NITTY GRITTIES

This chapter is devoted to the millions of professional workers, middle managers and executives who have not achieved the status that their AQ's demand. These are the people in AQ Disequilibrium. It is not easy fall prey to AQ'ISM when there are so many assholes around you that have the power or the stupidity to affect your life. How can you avoid it? And for those who are not in AQ Disequilibrium, consider the possibility of being in such a state sooner or later. Clearly, not everyone who works in a corporation can be an Executive or a Manager.

Moreover, not everyone even wants to be in such positions but most want to just do a good job, get paid and be passionate about what they are doing. AQ'ISM does not allow this. And furthermore, there are many who are in power positions and shouldn't be. We have seen people in lofty positions with AQ's higher than their positions allow. We have seen lowly people with lofty AQ's. We have also seen how through any normal working environment, the

Laws of AQ'ISM are working against you to damage productivity. We have even suggested that the vast majority are in a state of AQ-Disequilibrium within three years of any particular employment. So what does one do about all this high AQ stuff. How does one keep any sense of pride in his work and how does one progress sensibly in any Company?

How do you avoid the AQ productivity dilution? Remember the AQ saturation issue?

At one extreme end of the spectrum one can quit his job and get out. This would surely bring the AQ down and job enthusiasm up. At the other end of the spectrum, one can accept his fate as an asshole and take advantage of it. Not everybody wants to quit, however, nor does everybody want to behave like an asshole. Moreover, if you don't watch how you progress in being an asshole then you could create too many assholes too quickly, jeopardizing your position. Most people - probably the vast majority - try to stay within a company in spite of their Disequilibrium. It is this assumption that we must address in this chapter - what do we do about a high AQ ?

FIRST TO REALIZE THE REALITY

It is not always obvious that you are a victim of AQ Disequilibrium. If you were a Vice President one day and were told to take a job as bathroom attendant the next day then a potential problem would be obvious. Similarly, if you had been a Payroll Clerk for the last 30 years, then you would also acknowledge a message. If you just missed a promotion, however, the message may not be so apparent. And if you didn't know that you were a candidate for a promotion, then Disequilibrium would be well hidden. Well, we all sit in various stages of this type of reality, so the first step is to attempt a quantification of how bad things really are. In the previous book we dedicated a chapter to this quantification through the AQ-Meter. This is the first step. The second step is to decide what to do about Disequilibrium or whether you should even bother at all.

Remember that the higher your AQ is from your actual position, the more likely you are to go down one of those productivity slides. And if your position has gained any height, you could easily suffer a demotion. You must either protect yourself or get out. And depending upon the size of the disequilibrium, you may be fighting some very adverse conditions. As such, the manner by which you protect yourself may also seem adverse and even hard to digest, but nevertheless, harsh action may be essential to survival. In looking at the various alternative strategies available for protection, we must assume that somewhere you have failed in the corporate climb - failed to use effectively the arsenals outlined in the previous chapters. But yet there are still other strategies that some "successful" climbers have used. These can be of great benefit through the adverse disequilibrium. It is these strategies that we need to look at next.

A CAVEAT

I want to point out an important aspect of this next section. That is, these are examples of the ways that these issues of AQ'ISM are handled in the lower reaches of corporate life, albeit unknowingly. These are tactics and tools that seem to prevail are anything but desirable strategies.

But, they serve to show an example of what you may <u>not</u> want to do. Of course you cannot determine what you <u>want</u> to do until you know what you do <u>not want</u> to do, can you. Or perhaps to avoid infection, you may <u>want</u> to do so of these things?

Remember, we said you had four choices once you know you are infected:

1. **Raise your AQ to be in line with your position.**
2. **Raise your position to be in line with your AQ.**
3. **Leave and zero out your AQ.**
4. **Don't engage in the AQ'ISM addiction**

In reading the following example see if you can learn from them and laugh about it once you see this AQ process clearly. This is your 4th choice. It is however, the most difficult. Many of these are not strategies as much as habits. The point is, however, once you see how you have been infected by the AQ Virus, what do you do about it? Well, there are many example of people that are quite immune to the dark side of attaining posh and power!

THE AQ DISEQUILIBRIUM STRATEGIES

Disequilibrium strategies involves those tactics which prevent the Corporation from further injuring you, getting rid of you easily, and which may even help you to repair yourself. They can vary from subtle to extreme and can be used to prevent progress as much as they can be used to protect progress. They can be devious and crass and they can be useful and enterprising, but essentially they fall into two groups.

The first group is the PERVASIVE STRATEGY. These are the more aggressive ones designed more for some form of repair on, or protection to, progress. The EVASIVE STRATEGY group is more in tune with prevention of progress or avoiding reality completely.

The best way to examine these strategies is to take examples from some of the more skillful users of the Arsenals at Steadfast Meats. It is also useful to look at some of the employees who are not so skilled at using the Arsenals, but nevertheless are accomplishing certain strategic actions - whether they know it or not!

PERVASIVE STRATEGIES and LAWS OF PROGRESSIVE CONTRADICTION

Pervasive strategies involve aggressive tactics applied to repair or protect progress. The key here is that some form of progress is wanted (as opposed to standing still). Each strategy is based upon some fundamental Corporate Law of Contradiction. Although there are many strategies, here are the main types, as exemplified by some of our favorite Corporate citizens at Steadfast.

DECEPTION BY DELEGATION like SWITCHO MAGGOTBRAIN

The basis to this strategy is to abide by the Law *"Never make a decision that you can get someone else to make"* or "*Never do any work you can get someone else to do*". People who learn to do this well can get away with the grossest of injustices. Just consider Switcho Maggotbrain of Steadfast Meats.

Switcho is the Manager of Engineering where he is responsible for the engineering segments of Plant Operation and Design. His unique trait is rooted in the firm belief that all successful people attained their positions through delegation. This means that he not only delegates work, he even delegates decisions. Switcho also believes that you don't need to be a gifted person to do this (and he most certainly isn't) - you just need to show the subordinate serfs that you are aware of the details but you are really too busy with more important work. No one really understands whether Switcho does this through design or whether he was just born an incompetent A, but nevertheless, with a head filled with the most stupid, trivial and irrelevant details, he delegates work in great profusion.

Once a day Switcho makes his rounds from office to office making up stupid projects to give people - sometimes even delegating the same project twice, or to more than one person. He even tries to do this trick on people who are not in his Department. His primary statement is "*This is really important so we will rely on you to take responsibility*". Occasionally, he attempts to "get to the bottom" of things by immersing himself in some useless details which he really never understands - bothering people to unbearable extents. Because he works in a maze of disjointed ideas, he constantly forgets what he has delegated, and switches directives - causing frustration and confusion in the ranks.

Switcho's second most important statement, particularly when asked a question, is *"What do you think? I am willing to listen ...."*. Needless to say, this statement hides his ignorance and inability to make a decision. Switcho's next important statement is *"You should submit your recommendation on that matter ...."*

So Switcho, despite his ability for unparalleled ignorance, has managed to keep his position. To his Management, he is constantly busy and "*on top of his people*". And if any thing goes wrong, he issues his fourth statement of *"I had a feeling that I should have done it myself - he had full responsibility for that ...."*

SOCIALIZING FOR PROTECTION like WILLY LIPLOCK

This little law of progressive contradiction states that *"It is difficult to soar with eagles when you hang around with turkeys"* and *"bullshit goes a long way if spread on the right place"*. Willy Liplock is a good example of this law.

Willy is the Assistant Manager of Operations. Basically, Willy is the errand boy for the boss but he has a handsome salary, excellent fringe benefits and he is the "up and coming star". Considering his age, Willy has moved very rapidly into a Senior position. Now this guy has a very interesting tactic - he always tries to fly with eagles.

Willy naturally gravitates to company functions, socials and clubs where senior executives can be seen. If Willy knows that a Vice President goes to a particular club, then he will join that club. Willy is almost prepared to hire private detectives to know the nocturnal habits of others. And he is merciless in his capacity towards flexibility. He will join a religious club, or even go to a brothel - if he figures it will yield him some protection and progression.

In this way, Willy is always in the personal category of the minds of people in power. And what does Willy talk about at these social meetings ? He talks about doing good for the Company and he gets to know where the power is. So when new positions come up for discussion guess who's name comes up first?

And on the other hand, what if Willy gets in trouble, or is accused of being incompetent? Guess who stands up for Willy? So Willy operates on the basis that no matter how much of a hardass someone is, he is more likely to attack someone who he does not know personally - just as he is more likely to choose someone he knows first.

RIDING THE POWER TRAIN like BARF CHAPSTICK

This Law is summed up in *"the higher the level of power behind the idea, the lesser the chance of abandoning it"*. Expert users of this law are as obnoxious as they are effective. Lets look at Barf Chapstick.

Barf is now the Manager of Legal. This position he got because he was previously a legal advisor and when his boss retired, he got the job. Before that, Barf was a Support Administrator and before that he had the title of Project Assistant. Typically, Barf strives to be close to a source of power. In this way he can use someone else's influence to get something done. Better still, he is able to get other people to do things indirectly. So Barf typically writes a general horseshit report to his boss, preferably on an idea that he has heard the boss mumble about. He suggests that certain people take various responsibilities and execute the details. By therefore building on the boss's idea, he gets strong support and is able to effectively manipulate him into telling others to do a job. The beauty of this procedure is that Barf not only has the prestige of higher status but he never has to take final responsibility. And in addition, he doesn't even know anything about the details.

In reality, Barf is just an obnoxious, presumptuous, educated jerk. He has a personality like a torn boot and he thinks that he is hot shit. Nevertheless, it is hard to knock him off a good seat on the power train.

PLAGIARIZE AND HYPOTHESIZE like HORACE LaPRICK

Have you ever heard the adage *"to steal ideas from one person is called plagiarism, but to steal ideas from many is called research"?* Let's meet Horace LaPrick.

Horace is the Supervisor of Ranching Operations. Without a shadow of doubt, this fellow knows everything in the book about plagiarism. Horace actually makes a point of going out purposely to suck out other people's ideas. Because several people know about this tendency, they avoid Horace like the plague. So old Horace has learned to draw people out by throwing out somebody else's suggestions to generate new ones.

At coffee breaks, meetings, and after work piss-ups, Horace can be seen scavenging information from other people. Once he has gathered ideas from others, he immediately goes to his boss and says, *"say Mr. Muddler, got a few minutes to discuss some new ideas?"* On occasion, Horace even goes so far as to publish material that he has taken from others, or he even brings out other people's suggestions at meetings - right in front of the person who made the suggestion !

In reality, Horace is fairly clever and has become a Supervisor because his superiors have viewed him as a "great idea man" and an "asset to the Company". Horace tires hard not to scab from anyone above him since he feels this would be fairly dangerous - instead he gets ideas from peers and subordinates. It is not surprising that he is not well liked - being a fat beady eyed and hairless crass individual doesn't help. Dork McPork, his sole subordinate and he get on well because Dork himself has picked up some tricks from Horace. In addition, Dork even looks like Horace just a more hairy version. The talk of the company is to see Murk Muddler, Horace and Dork waddling down the hallway - the "Three Thick Trolls" they are called. But nevertheless, Horace and Dork constantly put others' ideas together to get recognition from the right places.

PLEASANTRY FOR PROTECTION like VERA SPARKLE

Ever heard people say *"she sure is pleasant to have around"* or *"he wouldn't say shit even if his mouth was full of it"*. Well if you think about the Law "friends come and go but enemies accumulate" you can understand how little Vera has moved up in the Company.

Vera is the Receptionist, a bubbly little thing with an everlasting smile, a sparkle in her eye and an unusual warm glow that consumes anyone that comes close to her. She is a pretty little thing, always well dressed and immaculate. Vera, however, is a complete klutz, with a memory like a sieve and a flippant brain. On top of this Vera is a physical nightmare when it comes to any effort which requires any physical coordination. Although it may not seem that being a receptionist is much of a significant position, it must be noted that Vera has been promoted through three positions - within a year !

Vera's first position was as a washroom attendant - cleaning the ladies washrooms and ensuring that supplies were always in place. The problem was that Vera always forgot which washroom was the ladies - coming into the men's washroom at the most embarrassing of times. This didn't matter to Vera - it was all part of the job. She would just walk over to the urinals, with a big cheery smile on her face and reach down to put in a new deodorizer disc.

The highlight came one day when old Angus Steadfast was having a leak. Vera just said "*Oh, excuse me Mr. Steadfast, my goodness, your thing is so big I won't be able to reach in to change the disc..."*. Angus got an immediate erection which only made matters worse. But the next day Vera was promoted to Xerox Attendant. Here she did nothing but mix the wrong solutions together and order wrong supplies but she just couldn't be more pleasant and helpful to anyone who had some copying to do. This job lasted three months, until the maintenance costs on the Xerox skyrocketed. *"But Vera is just so bloody pleasant to have around"* said Prim Strutland, *"we just can't get rid of her".*

So she was promoted to Filing Clerk. Here Vera would screw up the files to the point of total chaos but because Vera was so helpful and pleasant - everyone started to use central files. Of course she could never find anything especially if she filed it, but is was fun looking. When Vera started wearing sexy little dresses to work, things got a bit out of hand, as guys like Feelo Ballsack, Moon Flasher and Hump Pussywhip would spend hours a day looking for files.

So Vera's smile and her pleasant grace protected her and even promoted her because nobody could be mean enough to fire or demote her - despite her job failings.

FOOL THE REVIEW SYSTEM like BULA BUGLE

This strategy is based on the Law that *"Corporate Memory is a fickle matter"* or *"the further away you are from the past the more you believe the present".* Let us look at one of Steadfast Meat's employees.

Bula Bugle is a Business Analyst. She has learned from experience that any good performance if made too far back, is not remembered. In fact, she has learned that only the most recent months are really important those recent months prior to a performance review. Bula is a fairly outgoing business lady, is very money conscious, as she is work conscious. *"But",* she says, "why should I bust my ass for nine months of the year when all *they give a damn about is the last few months before the review?"* Now although Bula's boss, Dona Dingdong is considered to be somewhat of a fuzzbrain, she does reflect a common review phenomenon. When review time comes along, she attempts to recall the most significant positive or negative things her subordinates have done - in reverse chronological order. It is not surprising that the most recent events have the greatest importance, particularly if the review period is a whole year. So Bula just quietly does minimal work for most of the year, saving up her energies and ideas for the last three months just before her review - and before the raises come out. At the critical times, Bula then goes to her supervisor with new ideas - all which require extra effort and overtime of course.

"Dona," she would say upon rushing excitedly into the office, *"we should be able to get a better handle on our cattle price data base. If I go down to the library in the evenings, I can get historical prices on various grades of cattle. Maybe we could get Wino Dingbat to do some regression analysis to give us some future trends ...?"* "*That's an excellent idea* " says Dona, and guess what appears on Bula's review a month later? In fact, because Bula had suddenly started performing, she looks better than if she had excellent performance at the same pace all year. In that cases it would have been expected, but in the earlier case, she improved! But what if she had just done average work all year? Then there would be no reason to show any significant performance on her review - except average. Anyway, it is usually much easier for a supervisor to give a nice review.

Well, Bula is like a clock, coming to life with the greatest of zeal and vitality starting in October of each year, just before review time, Christmas bonuses. And it isn't that Bula is a suckhole or a plagiarizer - she just has learned how the system works - for her.

REPLACE THYSELF like BUFF WINDBAG

This relies on the principles of *"the one who does the least work gets the most credit"* and *"no one really cares or understands what anyone else is doing".* Buff Windbag is a good example.

Buff is a Senior Financial Analyst, having evolved to a senior position in the Marketing Department. Buff is basically a lazy creep but with a hidden talent. Buff likes to train subordinates to do his jobs, particularly useless jobs. He would go to his supervisor and say *"you know that new junior guy we hired - he really seems quick. I think he can really do a great job on this project of mine if I train him"*. Before you know it, the kid is doing Buff's work, even though it is useless work. Then Buff goes in to the Boss and says *"Goddam, is that guy ever doing a great job. He is really an asset to this Company! You know, that's a really important segment of my job"*. And before you know it, the Junior works for Buff. And shortly thereafter, Buff is promoting the junior so he can move upwards in seniority. He can even suggest that this "highly capable" individual take over his job - so that he can move up in position.

Buff always creates extra jobs for poor unsuspecting juniors to do. And actually many of the people like Buff because he appears to be constantly trying to help them. Yet to his superiors it is hard to fault him because he is "keen on developing people and responsibilities".

SEX FOR POWER like MILA MEATSEAKER

Whether anyone likes to admit it or not, sex plays a role in a Company. If you can believe that the way to a mans heart is through his stomach, then you can believe that the way to a man's brain is through his hormones.

Mila Meatseaker is an Executive Secretary. Now she is not just any

executive secretary, she is the secretary on the move, with the presidential spot in her view port - Moira Mouth's job. Five years ago, Mila was a mere typist down in some insignificant corner of the Accounting Department. There is no doubt that Mila is a looker, aged in the mid twenties, she is both physically and mentally active with a body and face that would force even a Preacher to take a second glance and suck wind. Mila knows the power of sex - if used effectively. And the fact that she is well endowed even makes her more effective.

Mila has learned that men run most companies and men are in most power positions. Mila knows that most men have some secret little sexual fantasies - which if given the chance - will come out. Just a sequence of seductive encounters, follow-up and eventual after work sessions, she has realized, is usually all it takes to produce the seduction process to activate what she wants. Mila is never direct - she is always indirect.

Mila used to work in accounting as a junior typist. Here she sat close to the Administrative area of Prim Strutland, the local Supervisor. Prim, a self centered snob, semi religious in fact, would seem the least likely victim for Mila. Mila noticed Prim notice her a few times so Mila just made her body a little bit more available for Prim to view. One day, all dolled up, Mila came in to Prim's office and asked if she could have a few words. Quite shocked, Prim said yes and watched as she seductively placed herself in a chair so as to display as much skin as possible. *"Mr. Strutland"*, she bubbled, *"I would be very happy to help your secretary with any overload typing - or any other job you may have".*

As she strategically flashed her crotch, Prim took the bait and with eyes-a-wandering he said *"Why thank you Mila, that would be very nice".* After that Mila got a lot of work from Prim. She knew how to lean over his desk with a boob exposed enough to get Prim's interest so as to immobilize his brain. It wasn't long before Mila was accidently rubbing or bumping Prim. And before you knew it, she was having the odd discussion of Prim's interests and even desires. *"Gosh,"* Mr. Strutland she would say *"isn't that a coincidence ...."*.

So Mila would seduce personal information by merging her ideas - then desires - with his. It wasn't long before Prim took quite an interest in Mila, and it wasn't hard for him to get her a job as his secretary, particularly when Mila kept suggesting that she would be much more interested in the job than his current secretary. Now Mila knew exactly how far to carry this one before it got serious or conflictive. And Prim - this "happily married man" had no problem with having this sexual goddess in constant view.

Well it wasn't long before Mila picked out her next target - old Angus Steadfast - an absolute natural. This time Mila carried it to the after hours work stage before she got the job.

WATCHING THE PREVAILING WIND like CLONE MIMICKER

This system is based on the idea that *"your sailing speed is determined by the angle you move with or against the prevailing wind"*. If you want to get somewhere fast choose the wind and the angle but the least effort is required by simply moving in the same direction. Quite often, however, the wind doesn't blow in your direction.

Clone Mimicker is the Supervisor of Industrial Engineering. Clone did not get here because he was always fighting his bosses. Nor did he get here because he disagrees with people in influential positions. He has learned that no matter how big an asshole his boss is, he is still the one who controls his promotions and his salary. And even if the asshole's ideas are total dribble, it is best to bite your tongue, swallow your pride and work in agreement rather than in frustrated opposition. If Clone finds out indirectly what the boss's ideas are, he will come into his boss's office and say *"I got this idea the other day. Got a minute?"* If Clone hears his boss come out with an idea he says *"You know I never thought about that, that's a hell of a good idea"*.

Clone will therefore reinforce, or reiterate superior's ideas or suggestions. If he receives a directive he says *"Okay I'll get right on it"*. So Clone always is the one who gives the boss the least trouble and produces the best work - the one who the boss will recommend. This is not hard to understand since Clone becomes a mirror image of his boss.

It should be noted that Clone is not a particularly bright person, he just works with prevailing forces for a free ride. A more intelligent use of this principle was show by our Vice President, Scab Dancer - whom we got to know earlier.

CORPORATE CHARACATURES like OINK FREAKER

This strategy simply involves being tuned in to the various department characteristics. Learning how various departments think allows one to focus dealings on that group. Oink Freaker has learned how to get his way and also minimize frustration when dealing with the Corporate Players.

Oink is an Administrative Assistant - not the greatest of positions, but nevertheless important to Oink. A funny looking character, Oink is so funny that it is difficult to be angry with him. But people very rarely get angry with Oink even though he is constantly costing everybody money. His efforts to get new furniture, pictures, copiers, services, typewriters, office equipment and you name it, is endless - even though each Department must foot the bill. You can always hear "*Oh, christ, here comes Oink again. I wonder what the hell he wants from us now*". It just freaks everyone out to think that Oink can get money so easily.

Oink has learned a few simple things about department personalities and he tunes his strategy towards those personality traits. Here are some examples :

Finance Dept. They only know one word 'NO'. It is best to keep away from them unless one has a financial justification.

Personnel Dept. They are always concerned and must check the policy manual. One must therefore always be concerned.

Legal Dept. These people review things forever. Oink always gives them something to review.

Operations These people always want action and decisions. Oink just says "*you are action people, here is some action for you*".

Engineering Dept. Will always want to solve it logically. So Oink comes to them with a problem to solve.

Marketing Dept. Will always say yes so there is no problem.

Accounting Dept. Will want everything justified according to budget.

Whether one needs to get something done or whether one needs to do things in such a way as to minimize wasted time, paying attention to corporate caricatures is important.

SLURP YOUR WAY AROUND like SLIME MEALYMOUTH

Although a repulsive tactic to those who observe it, slurping has, on many occasion, proven itself to be effective. Let us look at an expert in his class.

Slime Mealymouth is the Supervisor of Engineering - Mechanical Division. He looks like his name infers. Slime has beady eyes and lips like a catfish. He has a bald head, so he has grown a huge moustache over his lip. Slime is always in first before the boss, with his desk looking "busy". *"Say Switcho*", he says, "*I'm just going to get a coffee, do you want one? I'll get it for you*". Slime would wipe his boss's ass if given the opportunity. He runs errands, he reminds his boss of appointments, he phones for him, he even offers to do the boss's work for him. At 11:45 Slime walks past the boss's office and says *"Can I buy you lunch Switcho?"* or *"Mind if I join you today?"*

An obvious suckhole, Slime does his best to pamper superiors without being a pain to them. It is through this method that he got his promotion to Supervisor. "*Boy, did you ever do a good job on that last project*" or "You sure know how to put those people in their places" or "*They just don't appreciate your talents*" are all common

259

statements which help to keep supervisor's wrath off his back - and to keep his position. Such procedures have worked well on his boss Switcho, who just loves being catered to. In fact, Switcho manages by confusion so that many subordinates are not always as agreeable as Slime. The grumbling and bitching only amplifies Clones superb behavior.

So Switcho takes care of his "bum brother" as Slime is referred to by the others in the department. In addition, Slime "tattles" on others constantly - this being a useful characteristic to his boss.

SAFETY IN NUMBERS like WIMP WISHWASH

The strategy here is based on the idea that "Teamwork is the essential means of blaming others" and "*If more than one person is responsible for a screw-up then no one is at fault*". Wimp Wishwash is a good example of this tactic.

Wimp, the Supervisor of Support Services works in the Information Systems department. It is impossible to get a decision out of Wimp - no matter how you press her. "*Well, what do you think?*" or "*I will have to check with my boss first*" are standard answers to one on one confrontations. "*We will have to put a task force together first*" or "*Let's have a vote*" or "*What do the others say about this?*" are all typical answers to group confrontations. And if something goes wrong, the answer is "*We all agreed to this before we began*" or "That was not part of my job" or "*Talk to Blam about it, he was the one who supported the idea*".

All in all, Wimp is most frustrating to others who want decisions or action. Her procrastination is especially irritating. But she knows that the more proficient you are at procrastination, the less proficient you need to be. It is procrastination that allows her a means of setting up the pawns so she never gets the blame. Wimp is even smart enough to get others to write their convictions on memos and have others agree first. This way if anything should go wrong, Wimp can say that she never did agree with the concept.

On the other hand, if it worked out, Wimp can also slop up the credit.

Needless to say, it is difficult to trap Wimp even if you know what she is up to. One would have to purposely set her up to trap her, since she is always "looking good" to her superiors. The fact that she is a complete indecisive manipulative, spineless asshole to her peers and subordinates is of no consequence.

JUST KEEP TRUCK'N like NOSE GRINDSTONE

This strategy, one would think, is the only one that anyone should use in a company - if they are to get ahead. Your mother always told you to work hard to get ahead. Well, as we have seen, this is not always so. Nevertheless it sometimes does work, with a few added ingredients.

Nose Grindstone is a Design Engineer, even though he was not formally educated as an engineer. Nose has an uncanny ability to ignore surrounding confusion or distractions. His tenacity towards work is only likened to a bull dog with new teeth - once he bites he never lets go. You can beat on him, scream at him, but there is no way to dislodge him. Nose listens well, talks well and analyses well - all those great qualities of hard work. Nose also lies to difficult questions and stays cool when things get hot. To illustrate his method, consider and example.

One day Nose was working diligently through coffee break, head down, drawing without distraction on his table. His boss was furious because he had just had his rectum chewed to bits by a Vice President for sending a drawing up with a Divisional Logo drawn on the design document instead of the Corporate Logo.

He walked over to Nose and said *"Grindstone, you have fucked up the reputation of this group with this inexcusable blunder. You, my fine friend are in deep shit"*. As everyone stopped their conversation, bewildered at the rage and language of the boss,

Nose looked at his boss and said *"What's wrong with it Mr. Flasher?"* *"Why goddamit can't you see the Logo, you jerk?"* screamed Moon Flasher. *"Mr. Flasher, the Vice President told you specifically to put this logo on, three weeks ago in your office".* Nose said this as he realized the mistake. You could hear a pin drop as Moon tried to recover his superiority. What does Moon do in such a case? Go tell the VP he is a liar? Stand and say Nose is a liar? Call the pissed off VP and Nose into his office? Back off? How? Clearly Moon is in a dilemma because it is difficult to counter a lie - if it is a lie. He can't even say *"you better be right"* because he just got shit for the wrong logo. All he can do is pull a typical supervisor statement : *"Well he wants the company logo so fix it by 2:00 pm."*

So Nose just works away without complaining, doing the best he can but always prepared for a direct lie to protect his domain.

CONFUSION IN THE RANKS like FRED FANTASY

Have you ever heard the saying *"If you keep the troops confused enough they will not see that they are being led to slaughter"*? This Law of progressive contradiction is best illustrated as Management by Confusion a means that Fred Fantasy is skilled at.

Fred is the Manager of Planning, and basically a hair-brained dreamer. This doesn't much matter since the Planning Department is made up of a group of has-beens, sots and goof-balls. Nevertheless, Fred is the Manager and the group is the busiest group in the company. Now because Fred is a complete twit when it comes to organization and coordination. So he manages by confusion without even knowing it.

Fred likes everyone to report to him, he makes everyone equal and he mangles any existing communication channels. He never defines anything, and he never lets anyone know what the others are doing. He changes responsibilities constantly and he assigns the same projects to several people. He relays ambiguous information and creates chaos. If any one gets pissed off at Fred he says: "*I know exactly what is going on. You just worry about your part!*"

So Fred has a group that looks frantic and busy. If they are not busy, he just assigns some hair-brained ideas that he has dreamed up. Thus, it looks like everyone is working at 150%. Now the interesting thing about this process is that sooner or later one of three things takes place. First, eventually a strong personality will evolve to lead the chaos; secondly, the responsibility will fall to those willing to accept; third, someone devises a system that allows the work to be done. But Fred, in his confused brain, doesn't realize the method behind his madness.

Nevertheless, he looks busy, is busy and appears to be doing great things.

EVASIVE STRATEGIES AND LAWS OF REGRESSIVE COUNTERACTION

You will note that the Persuasive Strategies have been exemplified as methods of maintaining or even attaining positions - despite AQ-Disequilibrium. They are both bad and good examples. We have seen in earlier chapters, the use of some of these strategies in a more planned "professional" manner. Most of the Vice Presidents and Managers used some forms of these in their Arsenals. But here we have seen some use of similar strategies by people less senior and perhaps even less skilled in any planned execution. In fact, most of the players that we have just studied just seemed to have a peculiar trait that turned out to be an asset rather than a handicap. Actually, as we proceed lower and lower down the Corporate Pyramid, we just simply encounter more and more people who are less skilled in the application of the Laws of Progressive Contradiction. When people learn how any of these rules work to their advantage, they then become candidates for learning the Executive Arsenals, thereby proceeding through the Great Transition.

But what of the people who are in AQ-Disequilibrium and have not developed weird traits for protection? What about those who have no interest in climbing any higher? And what about those who just want to be left alone? For these people we come to Evasive Strategies. They are evasive because they are used to evade the issue of promotion and of AQ-Disequilibrium. There are many people who just like working at something they know best. Some people don't want more responsibility. Others can't deal with a widening AQ-Disequilibrium gap. Lets look at some of the evasive strategies. They are usually designed around the LAWS OF REGRESSIVE COUNTERACTION because they counteract progression in a Company and are therefore considered regressive. Here are some examples:

JUST A BIT OFF CENTRE like CALC THEOREM

This strategy relies on the fact that there are little unwritten codes within Corporations which define "Corporate Normality". If you have ever heard (or even said) the expression *"He is an extremely capable person, but he is just a bit off centre"*, you will clearly understand.

Calc Theorem, is a Marketing Engineer, a rare breed. He is involved in the development of marketing analysis strategies and developing forecast models. Calc likes his job and he does his job well. He has done the job for some 10 years and it is not surprising that he can do it well. On several occasions, Calc has been considered for promotion to a managerial position but he has never yet gone past the consideration phase. This makes Calc quite happy since he admits that he doesn't like to work with people - he prefers formulas to work with. Over the years, Calc has realized that he does good work and he takes pride in his results - as he should. But he also knows that good work makes him a candidate for promotion so he has developed a little counteractive ploy.

For years Calc has made some fairly good predictions on cattle prices and various supply and demand figures. As such, he has gained a reputation for being a good source of economic forecasts. So on many occasions, senior Executives have "popped in" to chat with Calc about the future particularly to get some clues on the Commodities or Stock Markets. When someone asks Calc a question, he typically already knows the answer and he is prepared to substantiate it. But before he does, he pulls out a dart and flings it across his room at a big "Marketscope Trendagram" with a bunch of coloured circles on it to get a "Random Unbiased Coefficient of Stocastic Trending" as he calls it.

He then writes a few numbers on a sheet, pulls out his abacus, flips the beads around and writes some more numbers down. He then turns on his computer and keys in some numbers, writes a sentence down and gives an answer with some word clouds. This little ritual of Calc's, as predictable as it is, seldom forces the question of "*what are you doing?*" any more - because the answer would eat up an hour.

So Calc, to the Executives, is just a bit off centre - "*not really management material*" they say. The truth is they would never be able to explain his procedures and his accuracy - could be a bit embarrassing ! He's doing a fine job - lets leave him where he is. This is just fine with Calc.

IMMERSE THE GREYMATTER like QUIRK MULTIPLEX

Remember Herb Hoyle? He was the VP of Engineering - the one who had an insatiable need to solve problems. Herb was lucky enough to get a lofty position in the company because someone higher up liked that trait. In other cases, the results may not be the same. Let's look at someone who uses the same tactic - Quirk Multiplex.

Quirk, is a Systems Analyst. He has been a system analyst for some time now, having been demoted from a supervisory position. It is not that Quirk is incompetent - he just rubbed too many people the wrong way, getting his AQ much too high for his position. Once too many times, Quirk called a spade a spade, his final "waterloo" being when he told his boss that he was wasting his time trying to convince an incompetent dip stick, as he put it, of anything technologically progressive.

From then on, Quirk's boss did his best to slowly move Quirk's people into new areas - away from Quirk's grasp. It wasn't long before he just did all the work himself. Oddly enough, Quirk did not get fired at the time he mouthed off - simply because others knew that he usually did his work well.

Well Quirk just withdrew further and further away from the Corporate Scene, becoming more involved in whatever task he was assigned, but to depths no one else would attempt. If Quirk was asked to write a program to sort and report some statistics, he would include a data base management utility which would exceed the users' expectations. In this way, Quirk focused on the extra quality and challenge which he himself would add. His immersion in this manner made him oblivious to the jerks which surrounded him and impervious to criticism.

EXTRA CURRICULAR VARIETY like PERKY SHORTWIP

Sometimes when things go wrong with AQ's, one may not be as keen as Quirk Multiplex was. The 'Nine to Fiver' does things a bit different for example. Lets look at Perky Shortwhip.

Perky is an Advisor in the Corporate Affairs Section. How he got the job, no one knows or cares to explain, but he has been there quite a while. Perky comes to life with a dashing fury at exactly one minute prior to coffee breaks, lunch and especially quitting time. In fact the occasion itself is predictable from Perky's behavior. *"Christ it must be lunch time, Perky's setting his desk with his utensils"* people would say at 11:59 am. Perky abides by the work ethic: *"Don't be last and don't be first and never, never volunteer".* He works for a paycheck and he gives not a second of his time beyond what he is obligated to give as an employee. He does what he is told and no more. Should anyone suggest some overtime Perky always has an immediate excuse like: *"Golly, I wish I could but I have made other commitments"* or *"If I had known sooner I could have planned for it".*

And in fact, Perky is a ball of fire outside the office. He is involved in a vast variety of activities, living only for the time to indulge himself - away from the office. So Perky is completely immersed in non-corporate matters and interests. He just doesn't care about more money and higher positions, ever since he got reprimanded for giving free legal advice to some of the employees. Now Perky puts out only what he has to - and no more. *"Screw them,"* he mutters, *"why should I bust my ass for the extra effort? They get what they pay me for and no more".*

JUST A BIT OF GROSSNESS like GROSS FARTLY

For some people being repulsive is quite a natural function. We saw earlier how Murk Muddler seemed to succeed despite his gross tendencies. In fact one of Murk's subordinate managers,

Gross Fartly got his job because *"birds of a feather flock together"*. In many cases, however, it does not work the same way.

Gross, the Manager of Corporate Affairs, got his job because of the repore' he developed with the Vice President Murk Muddler. They got great pleasure in discussing how they could scare or affect peoples behavior depending upon the frequency vibrations of farts, as emitted after certain types of food were ingested. In reality, Gross would not be in this position if it was deemed important, nor would he be there if his boss was not there to protect him. Gross, however, is a case in point simply because people keep away from him - they just don't care to associate themselves with him so they leave him alone. Gross dresses like a slob and he looks like a piglet in pants. There is very little that one could note as an interesting or appealing quality of this man. He swears continuously and undresses women (and some men) with his eyes, even slobbering with the wicked little thoughts that invade his brain.

So Gross is tolerated as most just keep their distance from him. Even some of his staff try to keep away from him - avoiding him like the plague. Needless to say, this suits Gross quite well since his supervisory tasks are minimal and his work load is almost negligible. And interestingly enough, Gross knows this to be the case. So he sometimes puts on little "gross shows" for people or he doesn't change his shorts and socks for weeks at a time. But regardless of his tactics, the results are the same - to minimize his exposure and work load.

TRY THE RECLUSE METHOD like WARP MONKEYNUTS

Sometimes you meet people in a company that are really odd - I mean really odd. If you look at these odd people closely, upon a Corporate acceptance of their presence, they can become known as a strange, tolerable - almost a mascot type novelty within the Company. Warp Monkeynuts is perhaps a good example.

Warp Monkeynuts is a Programmer. He makes his own programs, and his own clothes - even his shoes. Warp is married to a Botanist who studies moss and lichens. They live on the outskirts of town in a very rural accommodation. Warp studies mushrooms - to the nth degree. He eats them, dries them, he draws them and he makes dried lacquered mushroom necklaces. Warp's philosophy on life is just a bit eccentric - to say the least. He believes that all life originated from mushrooms and that Darwin was a jerk. "*The mushroom is the sole derivative of humanity - it is clearly the only real evidence of man's evolution",* he would say, "*It's varying hybrid chemistry can be used to enlighten the mind and to protect one against evil forces".* It is difficult to really argue with Warp because his propositions are so offbeat that they can create a mental block in even the quickest logician, especially when Warp states his principles with such sincerity.

To see him extract tobacco from the little rattlesnake skin pouch on his belt, then to casually roll a smoke is enough to perplex anyone even before his beliefs begin to froth from his lips. And his wife is even weirder. But Warp works quietly and diligently at programming - and he is left alone. People don't invite him to socials and they don't bother him for lunch - heaven forbid that he should open his Darth Vader lunch bucket in front of friends. They certainly don't want him in meetings and they don't want him to supervise. So Warp just works away in the corporate jungle, quite immune to politics and with an independence equaled by very few corporate employees - just the way Warp likes it to be.

HIDE IN A BOTTLE like BUZZ BOTTLE

Although this tactic is not one that comes highly recommended, there are those individuals who can use it carefully - to their advantage. The obvious danger is that one becomes a "Corporate Piss Tank", either in reality or in reputation, or even both. Buzz Botttle is a case in point.

Buzz, an Intermediate Planner, began his professional career as a Civil Engineer. Buzz, working hard, like a hive of bees, worked his way up to a senior position. Somewhere along the line Buzz got his AQ out of line and bumped into the Peter Principle at the same time. He ended up screwing up a fairly critical project through an error in judgment after telling a lot of people that he was the expert - not them. So Buzz became an immediate candidate for lateral to downward "repositioning". After hiding his woes in miserable agony for a while Buzz took up luncheon martinis to "lube his brain up" as he put it. Now because Buzz had worked for some five years at a fairly diligent pace, his expense account for luncheons was tolerated.

Buzz would, at about 11:30 at least once a week, look for some poor victims to take out to lunch. Here Buzz could use the "business lunch" excuse and use the purpose as a corporate head session. This would allow the bullshit to flow profusely, with even some new ideas coming forward once in a while. Best of all, Buzz could vent his frustrations and even get others to agree to do things for him. All he had to do was write up some of the other guy's ideas once in a while to show the fruits of his dedicated work - through his lunch hour. Buzz would even carry on these antics after work if given the opportunity, always trying to pick on some "rising corporate stars" he called them. So Buzz could bitch away his troubles and temporarily float his brain into that immune oblivion until it got to be a bad habit where he could hide his intoxicated state during working hours. But regardless of this, Buzz was able to deceive the system for years.

JUST RISE ABOVE IT ALL like MOOSE BAXTER

Some people are just totally immune to corporate systems and are unaffected by their shenanigans. Some people just live on some upper plateau beyond all the squabbles and positions - above it all. Moose Baxter is a case in point.

Moose is the Special Services Coordinator. In this capacity he is free to move about looking at special problems which may occur at any of the operations. If someone is rustling cattle or some obscure land conflict has occurred for example, in comes Moose. Here he is free to move around freely without anybody really able to bug Moose about the usual Corporate policies, protocol and so on. So Moose never has to wear a tie or a suit, nor does he want to. This man truly lives in a different world, giving the Company the privilege of his time when he sees fit to do so. Moose likes his job and he doesn't care to have any other job - particularly one higher up. He doesn't even care to make more money since he tells himself that he is paid sufficiently for what he does.

A backwoods hillbilly at heart, Moose is hardly extravagant so he only needs a small portion of his income to live. In fact his dress reflects his rural attitude. But for the last 15 years Moose socked 70% of his net income into imported wines, stocks, bonds, stamps, oil paintings, undeveloped real estate, investment certificates, odd curios and so on. He hunts wild game for his meat and he grows his own vegetables. Yet he never says anything about his dealings, he just doesn't think that it should be anyone's business but his own. He just doesn't care since he is above it.

And if his boss dared to fire him because his gumboots were smelly, Moose would just casually give him the finger, ask him what he planned to do about it and tell him that his lawyer would be in touch. Moose doesn't care about gossip and truly doesn't think much of the corporate games. He is an unassuming, untouchable oddity in an alien sea of corporate policy and protocol.

IGNORANCE IS BLISS like GRUNT HOLLOWHEAD

If you are a student of logic, you may believe that anyone can make a decision if he is given enough facts. It may follow that a good manager can make a decision without enough facts. Well, then, a perfect manager should therefore be able to operate in perfect ignorance. Lets look at Grunt Hollowhead.

Grunt is the Supervisor of Projects - not a hard job since the Company hasn't had a project for years. Nevertheless, Grunt never, never knows the answers. He uses the referral system. By referring it to someone else, he absolves himself of any responsibility and covers up his ignorance. "*That's not really my specialty*" counters Grunt. "*I think Jack is into that area*", "*I'm not sure, I wouldn't want to do a bad job. You should get Charlie in on that*", "*I don't think we can handle that and I wouldn't want to steer you astray. Ask Frank*". After years of this, everyone really wonders what the hell Grunt really does know. And it isn't that Grunt is really such a dummy - he just doesn't like to be committed. So he avoids many situations, and even many responsibilities, that would possibly cause problems to himself or his subordinates.

But Grunt does have one philosophy which he expounds upon like a broken record :"*Ya never know the proper course of action until the subsequent events have occurred. So what's the big deal about planning? Good Management means ya got to have fast feet! What the hell do I need details for when we got techies to do the gritties? Hey ?*" Thus Grunt is able to operate in a vacuous oblivion - perfect ignorance, so to speak, and perfect bliss! And even when, on a rare occasion, Grunt is stuck with making a direct answer to a subordinate, what does he have as a pat answer? "*Shit man, you can handle that can't you .....?*"

PATHETIC PROBLEMS like FEELO BALLSACK

Have you ever felt so sorry for someone that you would truly have difficulty getting rid of him? Even the most ruthless manager might be hindered temporarily when the target of potential wrath has just limped into the office after breaking his arm and leg. Feelo Ballsack uses this tactic very well.

Feelo is a Draftsman. He is essentially quite thick. Somewhere along the line he lost several screws in his head and the other parts don't seem to work. Drawings are screwed up, equipment gets

272

broken, work is forgotten. The list goes on and on. And yet Feelo still works there. His boss, Moon Flasher just moves Feelo into some other task. *"I just can't bring myself to fire this guy - I can't believe the bad luck he has. It is just one misfortune after another"* says Moon to his boss.

Feelo has learned to put on a good act with the utmost of credibility. Although he appears quite stupid in one respect, he is brilliant in other respects - particularly if he senses some problem at work. With the utmost of precision and detail Feelo can create a chronological tale of woe that would make an ogre cringe. The scenarios are unending - from lawsuits to accidents to misfortunes to family problems to you name it they all happen to Feelo.

One day Feelo heard that his boss was just super pissed off at some sloppy work, so Feelo left a message with the boss's secretary right away : *"Emergency crisis at home - have to leave early"*. The next morning Feelo came in at 10:00 AM. By this time Moon, his boss, was so furious that he was ready to kill him. *"That son of a bitch hasn't even called in. I'll have his ass!"* Moon was mumbling as Feelo appeared in his door. *"Shit man, what happened to you?"* he said. Feelo's leg and arm were bandaged. He leaned on a crutch and he had band aids above his eyes. By this time others had followed him to the door, to listen to the incredible story about his kid stuck in the car trunk, the accident on the way home, a mad dog, the fire in the kitchen, and his wife on the verge of mental breakdown. A beautiful planned fabrication, but what could his boss do? Give him shit? No way, Feelo knew how to cover his ass.

MISERY DOESN'T LIKE COMPANY like ROLLY GROWL

One way to shut the rest of the world out is to just be a miserable old bastard. With some people this sort of thing is quite natural. The trick is, however, to be anti-social with some and miserable with others. They leave you alone. Lets look at Rolly Growl.

Rolly is the Budget Coordinator. Here, as an Accountant, he coordinates numbers because numbers don't get pissed off at him. In most other cases, Rolly snarks and grumps at anyone in his vicinity. Although he is a fairly capable individual, Rolly has an overzealous affinity to details. If given half a chance, any general question like *"How much have we spent to date?"* will yield armfuls of journals, file folders and papers, with a rambling soliloquy on why the computer and the department heads screwed them up. Clearly, his AQ is too high and for this reason he has not been able to progress position wise. Rolly just can't understand how the rest of the world can be so stupid and can't see the solutions as easy as he does.

So anytime he gets the chance he captures victims to bend their ears for hours at a time. And yet Rolly's boss hasn't fired him. *"I feel sorry for the miserable son of a bitch"* his boss would say, *"I don't have the moral constitution to place this guy into a soup line. Who the hell would ever hire him? Anyway he only has 12 more years to retirement."* And so Rolly sits in his office behind a clutter of papers and file folders, muttering in a cloud of cigarette smoke, peering up over his bifocals to capture some passer-by with *"Hey Frank, have you seen this stuff?".* If Frank enters the trap, he gets growls and bitches and complains about "stupid goddam system" and "stupid goddam people" - in endless profanity and profusion.

Understandably, Rolly is naturally anti-social since no one cares to be associated with the grumpy old fart.

DREAM, DREAM, DREAM like JAYBIRD WARPMATTER

Some people have the ability to transfer themselves into a fantasy world which is more realistic to them than the real world. In a research environment where a constant flow of results is not expected, such a world is quite possible. In an assembly line job where intense productivity is expected, this is not the case. But then there is a large gap in between these extremes. Consider Jaybird Warpmatter.

Jaybird is an Engineer. He likes to create problems for which only he has an answer. In this manner, Jaybird proves to be invaluable to the Company - and his boss. This fellow has a huge mouth which flaps in a continuous monotone frequency *"now theoretically"*, he would say, *"we can reduce the problem to a set of symbolic representations"*. Upon scribbling some triple integrals with most of the Greek letters after them upon some scrap of paper, he would peer over his glasses and *say "now if we can solve this set of resultant partial derivatives we could benefit the operation quite extensively. If you don't mind, I'll take this home with me to see if I can work out a solution"*. (He was asked to reduce friction on one of the conveyor belts. It did not strike him that a good lube job could be the answer).

So Jaybird goes along with great fantasies on how this solution will not only cause revolutions in previously published material, but will impact the Corporate balance sheet. The next morning typically results in an ecstatic *"Man, I solved the sucker, now lets try it"*. Needless to say, Jaybird gets the time to test the theory. But the results are typically disappointing, with a new cycle of revised equations and dreams set before the supervisor. In this way, he is able to do what he likes to do - mainly nothing - and still be employed. Not only does no one understand what he is doing, but he always appears to be totally dedicated to improving the Company by solving all the real tough problems. *"Christ,"* his boss would say in defense of another Jaybird failure, *"Those are tough problems. How can we discourage his keenness and dedication? Just think of the economic benefits!"*

COURSES AND PAPERS like LOU KABBAGETOP

There are those who get their gratification through the Company, not within the Company. External recognition and the opportunity to develop one's mind sometimes has a more soothing satisfaction than those reviews, positions and perks. Lou Kabbagetop works within such a world.

Lou is the Senior Planning Advisor. This position is hardly one of prestige since Lou suffered one of those lateral re-positioning strategies that Corporations use to punish people with. As a senior advisor to the planning function, Lou has very little responsibility - particularly since the Executives like to operate on the 'seat of the pants fire fighting planning principle. Lou has his PhD in Micro Macro Econometrics. Here he specialized in the application of "Fuzzy Caterpillar Scatter Correlation Principles" to financial planning. Lou is also a chronic gossiper. He is like a nattering old lady, seeking out and dispersing gossip and hearsay, with an uncompromising tenacity. In the past Lou would actually sneak around, listening through walls and doors, reading secretary log books it went on and on. This is why Lou was re-positioned.

But Lou doesn't mind his position because he has more time to work on his caterpillar theories and get them published. He has, over the years, published and presented and impressive list of eccentric esoteric papers in economic journals, periodicals and you name it. And he just loves to appear at seminars and luncheons - to awe the audience with his research. Of course everybody at Steadfast meats views him as a nut case but he really doesn't care. "*Quite obviously, this Company is not quite as intelligent about these findings as the rest of the world*" he would say with a cool contempt. In addition, the need to publish creates the need for new material, so Lou is always taking courses. And this only adds fuel to even stranger theoretical papers like the "Explosive Recursion Method for Moving Averages" for example.

Lou is actually quite content since he got his new position. He has no responsibility and he feels important. On the other hand, he serves a PR function for the company - makes them look progressive with the research papers - and it keeps him out of their hair.

SOME KIND OF A WEIRDO like MOON FLASHER

If you recall, Angus Steadfast did not make it to the presidency because he had a weird little habit of leaving his fly at half mast. The act itself wasn't quite as much of a problem (to the judging president) as the reason for doing it. Although Angus made it quite a distance up the ladder before his little habit stopped him, others, like Moon Flasher, use such idiosyncrasies for other purposes.

Moon is a Design Engineer and he wants to be left out of the usual groping and climbing. He doesn't much care for people around him but he hides his distaste. His AQ Disequilibrium is hidden by the false smile and occasional attempt at idle chatter. Moon basically believes that one job is as bad as another "*So what the hell is the sense of moving to another job with new vermin*" he says. The more Moon is left alone to do his work, the better for him. In fact, Moon has so much contempt for the two faced plastic A's, as he calls them, that it is better that he keeps away.

So Moon, a rumor has it, flashers in the park on weekends. He has also been known to hang his ass out the window as he and his buddies drive by the Burger Hangout. In reality Moon doesn't really do this, he just had a buddy `drop' some juicy information into a few key gossip groups and let the SIC Network do the rest. The occasional reinforcement of the news is enough to keep the news hot and widely scattered.

The result, needless to say, is quite predictable. Moon is weird! Although no one has seen him actually flash or moon, he has a silent reputation that keeps others away from him. And as long as Moon does his work, smiles and doesn't grab anyone by the ass, he is left alone. To hear people whispering about him gives him satisfaction, for he knows it just helps to keep all these Corporate parasites away from him - just what he wants.

DETAILS AND MORE DETAILS like CIRILLA GORILLA

If you think about the fact that information has a tendency to deteriorate in its upward journey, you may appreciate the idea that the further away on is from the facts, the more one believes what he hears. Some people can take great advantage of this, like Cirilla Gorilla.

Cirilla is a Senior Systems Analyst. She is a little squirt of a woman with an insatiable desire to put her feet in her mouth - both of them. On top of this, she thinks she is pretty cool and only listens to what she wants to hear. This unusual "filter system" has a tendency to get her into trouble quite often since she doesn't hear someone say that *"there are problems"*, or *"someone doesn't like you"*, or *"the job you did wasn't so great"*. Despite this tendency, Cirilla has managed to keep her position of a Senior - primarily because it is difficult to trap her.

"She really pisses me off!" says a user, *"I know bloody well that she screwed the whole thing up ...but when she goes through all that mumbo-jumbo, I have no defense...".* Cirilla knows that most of her superiors and her clients do not know the details - otherwise why would they need my services, she says. When confronted, she lets out a flurry of bits and bytes, program procedures, operating malfunctions and whatever possible - together with user stupidities to justify the problems. Any question results in further deluge of irrelevant details. Worse of all, Cirilla actually believes the dribble that flows from her mouth so it is very difficult to convince her that she screwed up.

For years it has been impossible to get rid of her, even though most know what her tactics are. No one has had the patience to set a trap for her or enough knowledge of details to trip her up. This way she has continued for years.

278

COMPLAINTS TAINTED WITH TEARS like BERTHA BITCHALOT

Some people can be the most rotten creeps imaginable, and then, just at the critical moment, melt your opinion (and your wrath) which has taken days to build. An extreme case of this is shown in Bertha Bitchalot.

Bertha is a Sr. Filing Clerk. She clearly has a chronic case of bitchitis, and being located in a central service area of the company, has ample opportunity to bitch and complain to just about everyone. There is very little that Bertha likes. She complains about others, about policy, about benefits, about the weather, about equipment, about anything and everything.

She can be seen pouncing upon some poor employee who has come in to locate a file *"Have you heard the news?"* she would ask. *"They are going to change the color of toilet paper. Why would they be so stupid? Don't these turkeys know that we like black? Pink is not aesthetically appealing. I suppose you agree with them?"* Any poor unsuspecting person who answers her is sure to eventually get embroiled in the verbal diarrhea which follows.

Now since Bertha is a Senior, she is not in a position to call or tell people that they are assholes, so she has been in Disequilibrium for some time. But when some senior or peer gets pissed off at Bertha and takes it up with her boss, there is always a different story. Just as the Boss begins to scold Bertha for her performance, she breaks down sobbing. *"Oh, Mr. Strutland, that mean old man took it all wrong, I was trying so hard to get on with him... He just kept complaining about...."* Just about the time those big tears turn into screaming hysterics, the boss starts to panic. Christ, he thinks, they will think I am beating this woman! So he wilts his anger and consoles her - just to stop the sobbing. *"I'm sorry, Mr. Strutland, I tried so hard, I don't know what to do".* Well more to the point is that Mr. Strutland doesn't know what to do.

JUST KILLING TIME like GRIM RECTUM

At some point in time, your AQ interferes with productivity and attitude. No matter what you do, you face the inescapable conclusion that you must go to a new job before you get fired so you kill time while you hunt like Grim Rectum.

Grim is a Planner. He has been a planner for three years and he just can't agree with his boss, the bosses above and everyone else in the department. His AQ is in bad shape and he is clearly in Disequilibrium. Grim thinks that his department is a holding area for old has-beens, piss-tanks and unwanted corporate lepers. He is at the bottom of the heap and is the only one who does any work - even though the work is useless. Unfortunately, Grim is correct in his assessment but he is trapped, unable to move within the Company and unable to change his AQ. It is not surprising to see Grim's attitude extremely morose. "*The only reason the old bar flys don't fire me is because none of them knows how to do it*", reasons Grim.

Grim changed his attitude the day that he decided to get out. His brain tuned in to finding a job somewhere else and it is totally immune to the jerks surrounding him. He simply produces what he must even if it is pure crap. He looks forward to his day of escape and he focuses on that objective. Every day Grim looks to seeking out interviews or reading books on job seeking. The grim tasks at work are now secondary since he is just killing time.

13
THEN THE LAST RESORT

THE LAST RESORT STRATEGIES

In the last example involving Grim Rectum served to illustrate that when all fails and there is no escape within the Company, an escape path outside the Company may not be as bad as one thought. Just making the decision to get out was enough to change Grim's attitude - as if a great weight had been lifted off his shoulders. The point of the matter is that changes outside the Company - as dreadful as they may seem to someone not used to finding jobs - may be the best alternative that ever happened. The consequences of AQ-Disequilibrium are normally much more damaging if left to take a natural course. Nevertheless, as anyone approaches the reality of AQ Disequilibrium and the possibility of having to get out, there is a natural tendency to resist the truth. Then what about Moose Baxter who was able to simply rise above it all? And Lou Kabbagetop who found salvation outside the corporation?

The Last Resort Strategies are for those people who can't stand it any longer. Clearly, the best way is to zero out that AQ and get out. The last resort strategies are therefore fairly limited but let us consider a few new cases.

GET OUT FOR A WHILE like FANNY BUMWIGGLE

Although it is not easy to lower an AQ once it has grown, there are ways, as we have seen, to ignore its presence. A temporary measure can sometimes be activated by escapism. Fanny Bumwiggles is a good example.

Fanny is a Legal Secretary. Unfortunate for Fanny is the fact that she works in a department with some exceptionally repulsive characters. Dork McPork, Horace LaPrick, Gross Fartly, Barf Chapstick and Lardo Billogroin are only a few gross contenders for the most obnoxious person title. Fanny, very much unlike her boss and the other members, has a nice clean personality and a quiet disposition. The end result is that her AQ is not so good but she has to bite her tongue or she will lose her job. Anyway, being a quiet soft spoken person, Fanny ends up containing her frustrations - sometimes building up to considerable anxiety. *"It is really hard to describe these creeps"* she tells her girlfriend, *"they could create their own wax museum if they wanted to"*.

Fanny takes a different tact when it comes to AQ Disequilibrium. She firstly spreads her vacation out over every long weekend possible! Since she gets 3 weeks of vacation per year, Fanny can add a vacation day here and there to create a 4 or 5 day vacation almost every month. Any spare days are neatly assigned to Christmas and New Years holidays. Fanny then plans a series of inexpensive trips with her girlfriend. Each year, they plan out a scenario that would impress an expert in Critical Path Scheduling. And their savings strategy is equally impressive. In addition Fanny has a reserve fund for one month leave of absence without pay, so her total days away from work is around 150 days.

In this way, Fanny has a chance to forget her AQ at an average of once every three weeks. This then makes the situation a bit more tolerable, never letting her AQ Anxiety build too much. But if she feels that her anxiety is increasing too fast, she kicks in a quick trip with a sick day thrown in. Even though Fanny can't zero out her AQ, she has learned to "refresh" herself on a regular basis to minimize the effects.

GET A TRANSFER like SPASMO MOVER

The next strategy down the last resort list also does not zero out the AQ. It is a last ditch effort to get the hell out to another segment of the Corporation - if you can. Spasmo is an Industrial Engineer who knows when he has been in one place too long. And Spasmo also knows that a good career growth path is through operations and into management. He believes that he should not stay in anyone position for more than 18 months. This leaves one year to leave your mark and six months to leave your post, as he puts it. "*Takes me about a year before the shitheads around me bother my effectiveness - leaves me six months to find something new. But that's ok, cause it takes me about a year to lose interest in the job and about that long to prove myself. After that I spend six months making sure I don't make any mistakes*".

Spasmo began his career as an Engineer in training at one of the Meat Plants. For a year he was keen and eager - just his enthusiasm was enough to make him look productive. After that he just got more and more embroiled in disagreements on operating procedures. So he put his tentacles out to search and even asked his boss to help - so they could ease tension between them. Within four months, a position at one of the other plants came up and Spasmo asked his boss if he could put in a good word for him.

For one year Spasmo moved in with zeal and enthusiasm. At about the 13 month mark, when he figured he had run out of new ideas and momentum, he went to his boss (who was still impressed with Spasmo) and asked for a transfer - to head office if possible. With his ear to the ground and inquiries everywhere he realized a new position in the Industrial Engineering Section was being created. Once again Spasmo made the move with the help of his boss.

Each time Spasmo avoided staying too long in one place - unless his position changed upwards. Here he could once again work vigorously for a year to prove himself. But if a change was not available to him at the end of a year, out went Spasmo's tentacles in search of new places. In this way he could maximize productivity and his bosses support in relocating. He would move when his chances were best - each time lowering his AQ. So now Spasmo has moved into senior status in the Department, with an eye for a supervisor's job within a year. If this does not come about, his recourse is clear: *"These jerks obviously do not recognize my efforts and since they have been my best shots, things can only go down hill and I will lose support as well as efficiency. I will therefore spend the next six months finding a position outside the Company".*

GO DOWN IN FIRE like BANG LOUDMOUTH

The next strategy down the list may be an alternative when things have perhaps gone too far. In other words productivity is down, line AQ is high and there is no escape except outside. Lets follow Bang loudmouth.

Bang Loudmouth is a Systems Analyst. He used to work as a junior programmer in one of the plant operations. Here Bang worked fairly diligently until he started to disagree with the office manager who was his boss. It seems that this jerk and others around him would never ever make up their minds on system changes. Just at about the time that Bang had moved into the testing phase, in came old Snark Warflespecs with other staff members, to tell Bang that they had changed their minds. On top of this Snark would only remember the first time estimate so Bang would constantly receive verbal abuse for being late. By this time, Bang's AQ was in trouble and with the job market fairly poor, Bang figured a new strategy. He would keep notes on all his instructions and he would buy a good tape recorder which he could hide in a cigarette package. This he could activate un-noticed at an instant. He then made up a list of changes to systems that he would need direction and approval on.

At the same time, Bang went to the Plant Manager and asked him his opinion on what he could do about these wishy washy specifications and why he was always getting shit. Needless to say the Plant Manager went directly to Snark to ask him what the hell the problem was. This only pissed him off more. At this point Bang was after evidence, he had put the next line supervisor on notice of something being wrong, and he set up his supervisor to make him more emotional in his dealings. Bang then phoned Clepto Superbyte, the Director of Information Systems at Head Office, explained his problem and asked for his opinion on what to do. Of course not knowing the real situation, Clepto had to choose his answer carefully. So he asked Bang to simply discuss it with his boss and let him know the outcome. Now Bang set up another pawn by alerting Clepto at Head office.

Then Bang made a list of disagreements and went into his bosses office, listed them out and recorded the answers. "*Why you fucking pipsqueak*" said the boss, "*who the fuck do you think you are talking to? You just do as I say!*" "*But Mr. Warflespecs, we are just not being efficient. Wouldn't it be better to spend a bit more time laying out the requirements, first ...?*" replied Bang, trying to antagonize him further. *"Look, kid just stop trying my patience - fuck off and get to work!"*

Bang could hardly contain himself but he had it recorded so he got up and left. About a month later, with some good records and tapes at hand, he once again talked to the Plant Manager, and the Personnel Director - to ask them what to do about an intolerable situation. He then walked into his boss's office with a list of evidence and said "*Snark, you and your cronies are the greatest examples of juice brains that I have ever seen. I have a list of 10 items that you have screwed up by indecision. It has cost us an extra 10 days. You should lose your job immediately*". Then he turned on his tape recorder and said "*You caused delay, confusion and extra cost. Can you justify your actions?*"

After the steam disappeared and boss's voice died down to a low roar, it was obvious that Bang no longer had a job. He just walked out of the office, made an appointment with Clepto and the Head office Personnel Director. After a discussion of the evidence, the Plant Manager was called in, with the Vice president of Operations. On the third day Bang got a Systems Analyst job at head office and Mr. Warflespecs "fell from grace".

JUST GET OUT like CRASS FARKLE

As we continue our travels down the list we get to more desperate measures. Sometimes things can get so bad you just can't stand it any longer. Lets follow Crass Farkle.

Crass is a Project Engineer. Being a fairly outspoken individual, Crass has a tendency to have his AQ out-pace his position very quickly. Being fairly spontaneous and reactive, Crass likes to tell people, including his boss, just what he thinks - whether he has thought it out or not. In the beginning, Crass lost a few jobs over this attitude, so he has a simple strategy. He has what he calls a "Fire Cushion". This fire cushion consists of a savings account sum that would cover 6 months of his operating costs - in the event that he did not have a job. This way Crass is free to feel that he can mouth off if he so desires.

Therefore Crass tells it like it is. When his AQ is giving him a problem he vents some steam and gets it even higher. If he gets into a large disagreement he just tells his boss to go piss up a rope and walks out.

Crass finds that there is nothing like hitting the street without a job to get the adrenalin moving. *"Just quit and get your ass out there!"* says Crass, *"Why take shit from a bunch of jerks you don't like or agree with? If you can't find a job within 3 months you got to be a klutz!"*

A FINAL NOTE ON STRATEGIES

You will see that the strategies have become more and more extreme as we have pressed onwards down the corporate pyramid towards the lower reaches of AQ Disequilibrium. For those people who happen to be in a lower level than those that they look up to, just think about some of their strategies and tactics. In many cases they are manipulative dishonest and even despicable. So before you try to enter that sphere of what they call "Excellence" it may be useful to see if you really like or believe in those little arsenals.

If you do, then it is useful to understand the corporate processes in the nitty gritty terms identified in these previous chapters. Even though the characters and situations may seem a bit absurd and far-fetched, there are truths within these exaggerations.

But be aware that the rules of corporate climbing - the rules of professional advancement. The nature of the corporate playgrounds are not as they are taught in ivory tower educational institutions. Nor are the rules picked up in management or career publications.

As a final note, one last section is provided. It deals with a termination kit. Whenever ones AQ gets anywhere out of line, a termination kit is an essential item for everyone.

TERMINATION KIT IS A MUST

Whether anyone likes to admit it or not, there comes a time when matters can get out of control and you could well become a candidate for unemployment. Your AQ may be so obviously high that you are hardly tolerant of your work, your associates, your subordinates or your superiors - you want to get some peace of mind and quit - but you want to make sure that you get those bastards for the wrongs they have inflicted upon you and you make right from wrong. When you get to this state, things are indeed severe and it becomes more and more difficult to hide your attitude which affects productivity. Remember the productivity slides? As your line AQ increases you begin to live on more and more precarious ground. You should therefore prepare and maintain a "Termination Kit".

Termination Kits are simple in principle but effective in use. They are designed to give one either a defense or some protection should there be a move to terminate one's position.

There are two parts to any kit. They involve the defensive and offensive strategies. This is like the rattlesnake - he uses his rattle to give one a signal of a good offensive strategy mostly a visual sign to warn an attacker of what may be in store should confrontations occur. The defensive strategies then involves the snake's bite - his ultimate weapon if the attacker chooses to ignore the offensive strategy. So a kit involves certain key (usual) items which are strategically placed and displayed for potential attackers (bosses) to see so that they do not get the idea that they have "easy prey".

The other segment of the kit involves the key ingredients which one needs to strike with, if necessary, and get away (without financial injury). The use of these and whether the offensive part is displayed or not will undoubtedly depend upon how vindictive one is and whether the kit is just a survival tactic or a true means of vindication. That is, one could choose not to display the offensive segment, using surprise to strike with. First, let us look at the Offense part.

OFFENSIVE ANTI-TERMINATION

The principle idea is that a good defense is a strong offense. What one needs to do is to display various items in an obvious attempt to dissuade anyone who may be contemplating some vile action against you. This you do by letting them think that you are well informed and capable in matters which pertain to dismal and termination.

BOOKS   There are usually many books that are available which deal with items such as Corporate Law, Business Ethics and Wrongful Dismissal. It is a good idea to place these in an obvious place where anyone entering your office or domain can see them - Intersperse them with other books and leave markers sticking out. A book on "Wrongful Dismissal" will stop dead in his tracks, the most awesome opponent. The key is to issue a warning that you are informed in these matters.

POLICIES These are also good items to have if you can get them. Such things as the firm's layoff procedures and employment benefits - all that great stuff that the personnel department is glad to give to anyone interested. They may even have salary and performance review procedures and so on. You need, therefore, a nicely bound volume on these Company matters sitting close to your other books. If possible, this should also be a part of your defensive package. This material informs people that you are aware of internal Company practices.

DIARY A book marked "diary" should form part of your normal desk clutter. It is simply displayed to let one know that you keep track of something. It is up to their imagination to decide what it is you have kept track of.

AQ METER Keep your AQ Rules handy to help keep your sanity and sense of humor. Keep your AQ Meter on the wall beside your desk with a means of keeping it current.

DEFENSIVE ANTI-TERMINATION

This portion is what you need should someone either ignore your warnings and confront you or you actually get fired. Needless to say, a good kit, depending upon how one chooses to use it, can serve to achieve a good settlement, get some of your hit list candidates in trouble, maybe even postpone firing, get you ready for exit and so on. Your kit should be kept in a secure place at work - you may need it in a hurry - mark it as personal. It is made up of Ammunition, Evidence, Exhibits and Contingency.

AMMUNITION This is the stuff you need to get someone else up shit creek with and gain their paddle. Your diary is your ammunition, its contents the bullets. The principle is fairly simple in that if you have documented dates, quotes, names, etc., it is very unlikely that any of the guys on your hit list have done the same and can even remember anything you can quote. So you can rattle off or list numerous items and dates which show that the other guy is bad, has done you wrong, has misguided you, is incompetent, etc. Whether wrong or right matters not, for he is at a distinct disadvantage where the burden of proof is on him - not you! So your ammunition is a good diary of hassles, disagreements, encounters (with reference to memos, correspondence, witnesses, etc.) that you have been involved in. Such documentation should present your side of the case as wells as, and in rebuttal of, that of whomever criticized you. If you are working in a community of A's, it is usually quite easy to get vast supplies of notes describing conflictive orders, subjective interpretations, misdirections and stupid comments which you can bend to your own way.

Any direct confrontation makes them look fairly stupid and if it ever comes down to court action (where the employer is already a bad guy in the eyes of courts), he doesn't have a hope in hell of catching you unless he has purposely set out to trap you instead. Another bit of ammunition includes documented evidence of superior performance on your part. Again these can be statements made by others, actual performance appraisals, etc., etc., with references to physical reports, memos, documents, etc., where possible. Keep also a list of all things that you have accomplished for the Company or for whomever with dates, times, comments by others, etc.. We saw Bang Loudmouth use the method.

EVIDENCE Evidence is exactly what it implies. Not only is it supporting information for your ammunition, but it is also the formal relevant copies of stuff that affects you and could be used in a court of law. Here is a short list of evidence items.
:

- performance reviews
- copy of lay off or firing procedures
- copy of any contracts you have signed or agreed to
- list of items in your office which are yours
- published information which reflects on you in any way
- copies of any things that you have designed or developed

In many cases it may not be possible to get some of the above as a copy in fact some Companies make you sign agreements which prevents the removal of information to your home. Your personnel file and all other information are however available to you while you are employed. Where such items cannot be copied a list of items, dates, etc. which identify the appropriate material may serve as useful references to be pulled by the court if necessary.

EXHIBITS These are not always easy to get and usually take the form of contracts, agreements, etc. Here are some examples :

- Job offers: letters of employment, etc. This is usually the stuff you don't keep when you get a new job.
- All of the correspondence between you and your employer.
- Employment contracts (signed) if one is involved.
- Statement of cause for being fired, laid off or dismissal. You should attempt to get this in writing and as such your kit should involve your own form. Make up a simple form which identifies who is terminating you and what for, along with reference to the lack of conformity to what organizational or government policy or rule. Have it signed. If there is a refusal then make a statement that such is the case and make notes on why you think you were fired. sometimes this may even work better.

- Termination agreements which are signed upon agreement of some settlement - i.e. a promise not to bother the company thereafter.
- Special agreements as to how you are to be phased out. This should include how much and when., i.e. severance pay, services, settlements patents, copyrights, conditions, etc.

CONTINGENCIES Contingencies are items, lists, notes which are required to assist you in your plan towards a new job and financial security.

An up to date resume along with some book or advice on how to write a good resume.
- Notes on how to collect unemployment insurance in your area and a list of requirements etc.
- Details of any job insurance scheme, pension plans, medical schemes into which you may be paying and will either be terminated or continued in some manner.
- Details of government agencies, contacts, etc. which are charged with looking into violations of human rights in employment matters.
- Details on employment agencies that specialize in placing people with your skills. Names and phone numbers of contacts, friends in your association who are likely to know of job openings.
- Financial contingency or list of savings, resources that you have against which you can borrow. An emergency plan.
- Details of attorneys who would act for you in the event of unjust termination.
- Check list of items to be addressed in "phase out"

AND ONE MORE TACTIC FOR THE ROAD

There is yet another little gem that you may want to keep in your sack of goodies. Most Companies, being competitive in nature, have tendencies to sometimes be hostile to direct competitors. Many firms have an "unwritten constitution" about their mortal enemies. As such, even though the Executives of two similar companies may "rub shoulders" together at professional associations, they have a dim view of anyone who would leave their company to go work for a competitor. It is quite often the case, therefore, that one may be given as short as 15 minutes to pick up his things and leave, after he has quit. This may also be the case with "sensitive" positions, such as security jobs, etc.

On the other side of the coin, an employer is pretty well obligated to conform with the termination date which is placed on a formal resignation. This means that if you have given your employer a formal notice to terminate at a certain date, he is obligated to pay you until that date unless he can prove fairly gross negligence on your part. So even if he gives you 15 minutes to get out, he must still pay you up to your termination date. The obvious conclusion, therefore, is to give a 3 to 6 month notice and give the indication (not formally) that you may be working for the company's mortal enemy. You may be able to walk out the door with six months pay!

14

THE BOTTOM LINE
A ZERO AQ

THE DEEP LESSON HERE?

When you read about all these Corporites and their AQ's, the Arsenals, peculiar habits, striving for power and position, you begin to wonder why it has to be so. And you think about yourself, and how you may be affected as well. Why do we tend towards seeing and being assholes? Why do we choose to engage in these darker corporate ethics to protect and climb towards the perception of "success"? In a company full of these people, it seems the contagious aspect of being an asshole increases substantially. I would challenge you to say you have not seen many of these people and that you have not been affected, and infected in some way.

For me, the greatest lesson came when I began to understand that the vast majority of CEO's, Founders, VP's, Managers, and the likes that were deemed to be "successful", especially the ones that were the experts in the brutal AQ tools, also at some point fell from grace, lost their fortune, company went bankrupt, etc., etc.. So many lived through a boom-bust cycle of rise and fall, profit and loss, happy and unhappy. In retrospect, I cannot recall anyone in my business life that did not go through this cyclic process; just as I did myself. Eventually, I had to get out completely because this "cause and effect" process culminates in ill mental and physical health which take the brunt of this emotional roller-coaster ride on this corporate gopher wheel of life.

My lesson was that I got what I dished out. I received what I perceived. I chose these ways and I received what I gave out. What I had not figured out was how come? I never made the correlation of **Cause and Effect** and the **Law of Attraction** because it was never clear or obvious that something like this was happening.

Of the AQ Laws, it is the 8th Law that I should have paid most attention to. It states:

8th LAW OF AQ'ISM: AQ's have a tendency to be reciprocal in motion.

In other words, you get what you project. "*Ask and it shall be given*" or "*That which you sow you shall reap*". It is not hard to understand that is you do something aversive or bad to someone, that there will be some reciprocal actions. The only problem is that you don't always know you are "asking". And you don't know when or how the "given" will be "reaped".

In the AQ process, we learned that the way you **think, infer, call, tell, and treat** other people has a direct correlation on the corporate position and the way in which you carry out your duties to maintain order, focus and company mission. There is a choice as to how this is done; nice or not nice, good or bad. You can tell people they are assholes and better get with the program or get fired, or you can feel the need to help them get with the program to improve. How you engage in the thought, emotion and deed is always a choice.

In the AQ process, we learned that we have a tendency to put people on our AQ lists because we feel they are assholes. That feeling is again, a choice which arises from a fear, hurt ego, a loss, threat, and so on. Whichever way you look at it, that feeling is determined by one's choice of perception and thus also the potential engagement of emotion. It is that process of thinking that leads to the infer, call, tell, and treat action that you engage in. Regardless, that is a choice that you alone make.

Can you live in corporate life, or climb into executive positions maintaining a zero AQ? Of course you can. It happens when you start a new job, regardless of position. It happens early in corporate life when the CEO and others are one big happy family. It happens when you are passionate about the work and simply accept others, and forgive them for their idiosyncrasies.

So why is it so difficult to maintain this posture to become immune to the AQ Virus?

THE LAW OF CAUSE AND EFFECT

My big lesson was that what has been portrayed as corporate life in this book, does not have to be that way. And I did not have to choose to use these negative tactics. Why? Because it was my choices that created the Cause energies that returned to me the Effects. But so many times, I did not even know I was doing it. And fear of loss creates a lucrative energy ground of panic and helplessness for doing stupid things.

Regardless of what choices we make we are engaging in a natural Law of Cause & Effect which states that absolutely everything happens for a reason. All actions have consequences and produce specific results, as do all inactions. The choices we make are causes, whether they are conscious or unconscious, and will produce corresponding outcomes or effects. Here is a big lesson; **even the choice of thinking has an effect!**

The Law works the same for everyone at all times. Distilled down to the simplest possible terms, this Law states that for every outcome or effect in one's life, there is a specific cause; poor diet and exercise habits result in poor health, constant and uncontrolled spending results in debt and money worries, not putting effort into your key relationships results in poor relationships and all of the associated issues.

Remember that this law is not the same as the Law of Attraction, this is about what you put out (cause) will have a result (effect).

The trick is to know which one you are using at any one point in time, and when you do to use it properly.

The law can also be applied in the physical sense through examination of Sir Isaac Newton's third Law of Motion, which states that "*for every action, there is an equal and opposite reaction.*" If, for example, you were to hold your hand over a candle's flame (the cause) the effect would be that your hand would burn and it would hurt! While this is an extreme example, it serves to illustrate the point very well.

At the point of making this idea of putting your hand over the flame, you made a decision to act on it (cause). You made a choice and then got the result or (effect). The decision you make becomes the cause and the effect is the result of the decision. The same holds true with your personal relationships. If you treat the important people in your life with respect, love, compassion, dignity and honesty (cause), you will experience loving, solid relationships – which lead to happiness, fulfillment and peace of mind (effect). If you use the AQ Tools (cause) on others, what would you expect the effect to be? Kindness? Gratitude? Respect?

The Law of Cause and Effect is the foundation of Buddhism made up of three essential guidelines:

Good deeds bring good results.
Bad deeds bring bad results.
Your own deeds bring your own results.

Every effect has a cause and a condition. A cause and a condition combine to make an effect. All effects have a cause. All effects have a condition. There are no exceptions.

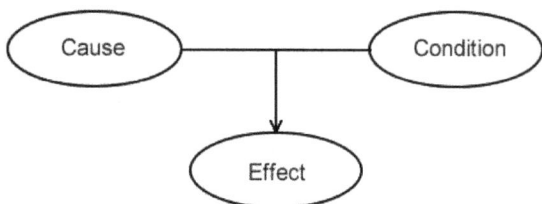

The condition is like planting seed of corn. The corn (effect) will not grow wheat and it will not thrive or grow in a desert. Those are the conditions or nurturing ground for the effect. In the corporate world, the condition is the corporate growing ground.

Think about how this works in the your physical world. Try pissing someone off with your words. Try hugging someone who is pissed off at you. What you give out comes about. So give your brain (and ego) some leeway here and let go of the idea that it does not work the same way with the other energies you create constantly, like thoughts, images, and emotions as well as words.

WHAT IF?

It is not difficult to understand that if you do (cause) something to someone that there will be an effect. What if you suddenly found out that your thoughts, images, and emotions created energy signatures that once you gave attention to, became projected into the empty space around you to find similar energy (The Law of Attraction)? And what if what it attracted was reflected back to you in the form of new thoughts, people, events, situations, whatever reflected the type of energy signature you projected?

Now what if you realized that the energy you projected is simply behaving according to some natural laws but require you to really energize them – charge them like a battery before they start their quest? And what if the size of the charge is related to how much attention you place on it, **and** how much emotion you attach to it?

Would you think and act differently? And if you knew that the Cause and Effect law does not distinguish between good or bad, would you try to minimize the bad and stop emotionalizing them?

Would this lead you to start managing your thinking differently? Would you be much more attentive to focusing on more positive thoughts and emotions instead? Would you be careful about using these negative AQ Arsenals?

If so, would you be paying a lot of attention to the content of these thoughts? Would you spend a lot of time thinking about things that you don't have or would you think about things that you would like to have – like more money, a healthier body, better life, better job satisfaction, more quality time, and so on. Would you begin to appreciate the subtle difference between *wanting* and *having*?

And what if the *having* the *effects* was like the Genie and the Lamp? Rub the lamp and out pops Mr. Genie ready to manifest your wants in some ways best defined by the wish!

Does this sound a bit far-fetched? Of course it sounds crazy – this is not part of your belief system. It is a fantasy - like a Disney movie – a fairy tale, not reality.

So what if in your corporate life you are constantly creating energy signatures of fear, of vengeance, of assholes, occupying your mind with survival and power, even in the way you think and imagine things? You are deploying the law of cause and effect to manifest or create your reality.

So how do you manifest and attract now? Well, first you determine a need by *placing your attention* on it. It is in your target range. Now you work like hell to attain it, to make it, to buy it. But the other process you are not paying attention to is the other energy you create, especially the negative ones of fear, worry, lack, doubt. Every time you think or feel poor, useless, sick, unworthy, angry, create an asshole, guess what? And if you supercharge this with the emotion this is like a command for this energy to get its shit together fast and find a fit. And what happens when something really pisses you off and your energy levels hit the roof? A big flag goes up and live energy starts waving for a mate. What about hatred from the past, an enemy, the boss, fear of the future, the tax man? And what about wanting more? Have you ever considered you are creating the energy of wanting and fear? What about wishing and hoping about great things? Great things are ok but what happens when it is counteracted with hoping? It has no power to manifest, it is just hope. And what do you think about most? It is not abundance because you lack. That is the energy you create to go out and hunt for a mate. You give it life and purpose.

Now here is the kicker. What do you occupy your mind with in regards to plans and wants? Is it the work needed, the assholes in your life, the effort required, or is it the completion itself? If these are negative energy then they attract more problems. If it is positive energy it will attract positive solutions.

Regardless, here is where the mind shift is needed. The universe works the opposite of what you think. Sure you can struggle away on the Gopher Wheel and make it happen. But the better process is like assertions that successful business people follow. Create the energy of solution, of completion and energize it with emotion, see a vision of it completed. That is the energy you need to have out there and let the Laws of Attraction and Manifestation deal with the situations. People who know this know about how suddenly a deal just comes to them, something happens from nowhere and that dream becomes manifested into reality because the energy of the solution has been activated.

We will delve into this later, but the bottom line to "success" to those in the know of how this works, is they continuously re-enforce the thoughts and visions of completion over and over with thoughts, and emotion, with a knowing, a faith, and a trust that this is the way it works.

If you look at your 24 hour day there are 86,400 seconds. It is said that we can generate 50-70,000 thoughts in a day. How would you classify these? And if every one of these critters is energy with purpose, what do you suppose the reflection would look like as an expression of your current life? Of course the vast majority may be mumbo jumbo energy because they are not clear or with purpose so they never mate. But what about those strong ones that do? When you are on the Gopher Wheel, you do not make any correlation between the energy you create upstairs to the experience you get downstairs. So perhaps it is time to become more aware of how you think and act.

A NEW (OLD) WAY OF GETTING YOUR WAY

In the 30's a fellow named Napoleon Hill was consigned to write a book about why some of most wealthy men on the planet were wealthy. His book, *"Think and Grow Rich"* became one of the best-selling books of all time and was even used as a bible in getting a Harvard business degree. Since then, what he found and printed, not only has made thousands more successful but it has formed a foundation for a lot of other Guru's wisdom about success. In a book I wrote called *"Morphic Energetics"* I studied the "wisdom" of the following Gurus:

Napoleon Hill: Laws of Success

Wayne Dwyer: Power of Intention
Joe Vitale: Attractor Factor
Jerry & Ester Hicks: Law of Attraction
John Kehoe: Mind Power
Gregg Braden: Power of Prayer

These give us a picture from Ancient times to the great depression and to now, the wise keys to attaining desired effects or results. They convey a certain pattern about becoming "successful" and living your dreams:

The bottom line: Be clear, positive, know what you want, **see it already achieved and be passionate** about it. Each one of these gurus has put a new marketing twist to the same process. For example as a businessman, if I wanted to make a million dollars, I may choose to do as follows:

1. We form the thought of making a million dollars
2. We form a vision of a company that sells chairs
3. We make a business plan of the company and product
4. We get emotionally excited about the plan/company
5. We launch the intent to execute the business plan
6. We engage others, money, etc. to make it happen
7. We create the chairs/company that enters our reality

Notice however, these top sellers of these have injected a more and more spiritual aspect to the process. Notice that we have moved also from "doing the hard physical work" to "letting the universe" bring the result to you by knowing it is already done.

Do they all work? Have people achieved results? Yes!

All the time? No

Why?

The gurus haven't figured it out.

Figured what out?

How to create a true law where it works all the time.

Of course the degree of clarity, emotion, belief, determination, complexity all make a difference. But that is the same in business. Some fail, others don't. Why? because of clarity, emotion, belief, determination which are all personal energetic matters. Why? Perhaps the AQ has some Effect?

What seems strange here is that all these gurus admit that we *already create our own reality*. And there is no distinction to "the Universe" as to whether this is bad or good, positive or negative resultant reality. The estimates on the number of thoughts per day is 50,000-70,000 thoughts! Over a year that around 18 million and over 50 years we are near a billion thoughts. If thoughts create reality wow, that a lot of things to happen!

The truth of this matter so far is that there is really nothing new here at all. We all certainly choose our own perception of reality. What about physical reality? It has always been the clarity of vision (thoughts, visions, words), the passion of the mission (emotion), the drive of the individual (intent), the building of relationships (engagement) that determines the success or failure of the end reality. And no matter what secret process one may attach to this process, there is no law that guarantees it will work.

Soo... here is the big question.

Do we create our own reality by choosing the thoughts, visions, plans that become a passionate drive to achieve the resultant reality by *hard effort*?

Or do the thoughts, visions and plans, once energized *attract* the resultant reality?

And the big question... Can we really get the Universe through the Law of Cause & Effect to pay our bills?

WE DO CREATE OUR REALITY

This is what I have found: In our world of reality we create things all the time. In the most simple cases, let us use a simple example of creating a chair. Usually we follow certain steps:

1. We form a **thought** that we would like to make chair
2. We form a **vision** of what that chair will look like
3. We make a **design** or description of the chair
4. We get **emotionally** excited about creating the chair
5. We launch the **intention** to act on its construction
6. We **engage** with wood, saws, nails, etc to make it
7. We **create** a chair which physically enters our reality

These seven steps are typical of anything we create in our reality. What I have also found is that these 7 steps correspond to the key functions of the 7 chakras but that is another book! This is our physical world. This the way we do things. Even in the more complex situations, like making a million dollars or building a corporation, it is the same process, as in our previous example.

1. We form the thought of making a million dollars
2. We form a vision of a company that sells chairs
3. We make a business plan of the company and product
4. We get emotionally excited about the plan/company
5. We launch the intent to execute the business plan
6. We engage others, money, etc. to make it happen
7. We create the chairs/company that enters our reality

Now here is the big question.

Was it the thought process that actually first manifested, then created the end result? Or was it simply the idea and then the physical effort that created the end result by some unknown way of attraction? The examples serve to show how we create first mentally through the thoughts, visions, words, then we create physically from the intent, relationships, and materialization.

The reason for this question is that either way, the 7 steps reflect what is alchemically known as "As Above, So Below" Although this term has been bantered around for thousands of years and interpreted many ways, it reflects a well known process of creation.

In the seven steps, the first "above" would be in the thoughts, images, words that are not yet reality. It is still all mental. In the last three steps of "below" would be the intent to act, engagement, materialization that bring it into reality. In the middle is the emotion that is the catalyst that actually creates the conversion from above to below; the passion and emotion.

Now, you have to ask, in the more complex business cases, why do some succeed and others not? Well, we have developed many aids and tools and techniques to assist in this process. For example the level of emotion, of focus, clarity, passion, attention, of action, of intent, dedication, all go towards the success of the end result. The attraction of the right people, money, resources, events, all need to be in alignment with the plan; all attracted and acted on to create the infrastructure of the 3D process. Some use assertions to drive them. Some us prayer. Some are so passionate they are driven to completion. Whatever we use, the truth is that the clarity, passion, dedication all affect the time and the exactness of the end result vision. And of course, depending the complexity, size, and time to do it, the result and the probability of success varies considerably. The vast majority simply fail. So whatever process we use, we cannot guarantee the final creation.

If we go back to the questions, one could say it was just idea clarity, passion and hard work that brought the result into reality. The other ways was that when the idea and clarity was created, it attracted the rest of the below elements that came forward to choose the relationships with others that would create the end result. This process is suggested in the proliferation of stuff around the Law of Attraction.

But either way, sometimes the end result does not come into reality. Our business plans fail and the Law of Attraction does not work all the time.

And if something does not work "most of the time" or cannot be explained, then it is not a law and it is discounted as no sense or nonsense. It is not part of our reality.

The most obvious is the millions of healing miracles that occur around the world. Because they cannot be replicated or explained, they simply become discounted and cannot be "statistically significant" to enter the reality of the medical world. So although they exist, they do not exist. For those who have had or engaged in the creation of miracles, they certainly exist; even though they can't be explained - try to convince them otherwise.

But what if these miracles or this Law of Attraction, or the process of creation from above to below is simply not understood, or not executed or engaged in the way it was meant?

Let us extend that for a minute. Do you believe that the events in your life are there because you have drawn them to you? And further, do you believe that what you choose to do with these is entirely up to you? Do you believe that what you resist will continue to persist? Do you believe you have the power to manifest events – and anything else you want, including miracles? The answers are all YES but do you believe it?

The fact is that you may already know this to some extent. But you may not be aware to what degree you can begin to plan out your life, just like the party - and everything in it. So it isn't a matter of believing it, it is a matter of believing that you have much, much more power to control experiences, events, and your future more than you are willing to acknowledge. It is a matter of the degree.

The fact of the matter is that your body is a very special generator of energy and that energy likes to find similar energy. This energy is what we call subtle in that it is energy that we do not usually see, read about, is not readily measured, yet it is always being created by you.

So try to look back. What have you been preoccupied with and really focused on for the last few years? Is there any correlation with your life now? Have you been focused on wanting something but thinking a lot about how tough it is to get it? Do you think about how hard you have to work, or how it is going to be a pretty tough slog? Then you have asked for more of whatever you have. Have you focused your attention on the outcome or the process of getting there?

How much time have you spent thinking about why you don't have it rather than enjoying the feeling of having it? Because you say: *"this would be a fantasy, it isn't real and I don't have it so why would I fool myself? We all know that it must require hard work, effort, sometimes sacrifice, doing things we don't like, blah, blah, and maybe some luck thrown in."*

THE PROCESS OF ENERGETICS

In our world, we see the power of words and images all the time. If you don't believe this, look at some despicable, or some beautiful picture. Look at the word IRS, or Collections Agency. This brings about the topic of energetics. what about a thought? Can it make you blush or make your hair stand on end? What do you suppose those words in your memos do? Have you ever felt the "presence" of others energy in a room? Or get repulsed or attracted to others by being near?

In general, energetics is concerned with seeking principles that accurately describe the useful and non-useful tendencies of energy flows and storages under transformation. 'Principles' are understood here as phenomena which behave like historical invariants under multiple observations. When some critical number of people have observed such invariance, such a principle is usually then given the status of a 'fundamental law' of science. Like in all science, whether or not a theorem or principle is considered a fundamental law appears to depend on how many people agree to such a proposition. The ultimate aim of energetics therefore is the description of fundamental laws. Philosophers of science have held that the fundamental laws of thermodynamics can be treated as the laws of energetics. Through the clarification of these laws energetics aims to produce reliable predictions about energy flow and storage transformations at any scale; nano to macro. Regardless, energetics of some kind is a work here attracting and repelling people, events, etc.

Although we do not really understand the process of this transformation of energies, science certainly agrees that everything is energy and it vibrates at specific frequencies. They agree that energy cannot be destroyed but it can transform.

When you see an image or a word, it can rapidly create a reaction in you as an emotional return. If it is a horrible image, or a word or words that something terrible is attached to, then it draws forward a similar response emotion, and possible action. Its energy signature solicits a likeness most of the time. Think about what a word like IRS or CRA conjures up in the reaction and emotion. It does not have to but in most cases it is so because there is a connection we create between a word, image, symbol and what it means to us. Then this causes an engagement to trigger emotion or act in a certain way.

If the words or images carry a peaceful or heartfelt energy, the result is much different. The response has a likeness which is expressed through us. Similarly when we speak these words, or create images carries. Call someone an asshole and see the response that it creates. Send someone a letter of hate or threat and see what the response is.

When we act in deed, it is the same process. A good deed usually solicits a good response. A bad deed usually solicits a bad response.

These processes are energetics at work. You my say that this is no big deal but these images, words, deeds are energy and they carry this energy to others even though you may not have expressed them directly. The working of this energy begs the question as to how and why this is so.

And the much bigger question is: If we create an energy pattern this way, how does it, and why does it usually draw a likeness in reactions or expressions or even actions?

If you stop and think about how many times you have received what you gave out, you have to start thinking about why you would ever think, write, see, project anything that has any evil or negative energies. The reason it is not seen this way is because the time of when, and how are not clear; so there is no correlation to the Cause and Effect.

Furthermore, at the top of the "above" process is thoughts. Remember in our seven step creation process we came from a thought, to image, to words, to passion to action? How many times have you heard "change your thoughts and change your world"?

Is thought, or anything else we create, energy? Quantum physics says it is so. And there are endless sources of research confirming this. Thoughts come from synapses from axons in neurons in the brain. Energy is released from the brain into certain areas of the brain or body (depending on the thought) and releases energy in order to bring the thought to that part of the body. The energy is converted in each neuron the impulse passes through. This energy passes through each neurotransmitter. This is why thoughts are technically energy.

The brain uses energy and uses synapses in neurons to make thought. Thought is a philosophical matter not tangible. So where do thoughts go? They simply end when the brain stops sending synapses to certain neurons. Where does all this energy go? What does it do? What are the laws surround this process of creating and transforming that it abides by?

So in creating the 3D "real world" those seven steps were creating energies. Did these energies once defied as a vibratory signature attract the people, situations, resources and events that you chose to create the result? Or did you alone go out and seek all these out?

Think about how you create your desires—you want to find a new friend, or find something and you think about it, dream about it, feel it in your heart. You are creating waves of energy that create a field. It is actually a morphic field alive with purpose and it permeates other energies. It is like a swirling vortex of energy which builds a stronger charge depending on how much clear energy of desire you create.

Think about your TV set and the particles that form images. Think about how these particles that create emotions in your physical body are nothing but specs of light, color and intensity that your senses interpret. These dots or pixels could have a magnetic pull that either individually, or combined, created a specific pull signature that looks for like energies and attracts them. Do these dots sometimes draw you? Yes, a hologram that can draw others! This is not a difficult concept except that it is not supported by our scientific wisdom.

The Law of Attraction (covered later) suggests that what manifests is what your experiences draw to you as energies that have likeness. It draws to you the energies that you generate through your thoughts, visions, words and emotions. The speed of manifestation is determined by the clarity of the desire. The alignment of these subtle energies dictates how rapidly the energy that you create draws or propels you to the like experience. This process is simply manifesting the experience of something desired by drawing the people, situations, things that already exist.

Think about how you may do this in two ways that you are used to. First, you may want to create something, or do something to have an experience—say it is flying or climbing a mountain. You simply plan it and away you go to have it. Sometimes it may be more complex, so you create a business plan and follow the activities you have outlined to make this experience occur. It may result in the creation of something as a result—like a business. You are used to this.

But consider another way and that is to create the energy of alignment with desire and watch how you draw others into your energy field. You may want a house, or new TV, or new opportunity; then suddenly it is there as a choice for you. This does not mean the TV suddenly materializes in your house. It could mean that the TV may be seen at a store or it appears somewhere for you to make a choice on. Certainly you have to buy it and you may not have the money—so manifest the money as well. Clarity and alignment are vital. Remember this as this is an easier way, as you are letting the Law of Attraction work for you after you clearly define what it is that is your desire and continue to energize it by reinforcement. It is done from the inside.

Think about this. Sometimes, you may be drawn into others energies as well. This is the way of it as you may have a need to sell something and someone else has a need to buy something. All that happens is that the two needs attract each other. How? Well, your energies penetrate everything depending on the strength and because all that exists is within you all, it is a matter of matching the energy signatures and drawing them like those little TV dots. This may be a local morphic field or a larger one. It may come from anywhere—an ad, a TV show, another person, but it is this drawing within the fabric of all matter.

Now you are doing these two ways automatically all the time. That is how you create your world of experience and perception whether you know it or not. This way is not particular to the need or the type of energy you create. It is simply energy the laws respond to, negative or positive. Most are used to such strong alignments when it comes to fear that permeates your thoughts, visions, words and emotions. Most of you are good at this already. Clarity and focus are the key and continued attention reinforces the energy to make it resonate stronger. What kind of thought and emotion permeate your life in a corporation?

It is like a musical note. It has a specific tone or vibration when played. From 7 notes, you can create a song. These 7 notes can be combined into new patterns that are each unique. These can be played by different instruments making different tones and this can be combined into a magical concerto. These are all energy signatures looking to attract others of like sound. You are the orchestra playing the music. Your chakras are the original 7 notes and they can create any concerto you want if you use them. What are their musical sections? Thoughts, images, words, and emotions, brought about by your perception of your experiences.

ON THE LAW OF ATTRACTION

There has been much publicity on the Law of Attraction (that which is like unto itself is drawn). The Law of Attraction maintains you created the energies which attracted the events, situations, people that were brought to you from the quantum soup of limitless possibilities like energies. In fact, it goes a step further; It suggest that the end result can be attained without all the work!

The Law of Attraction, however has not been confirmed as a Law because the process by which it is alleged to operate has not been proven to be consistent in its results. Let us review this law as expound by the experts Ester and Jerry Hicks:

1 Relax your mind. Meditate for 5 to 10 minutes. Doing this will increase brain power and have your mind at that relaxed state. This step is optional but recommended.

2 Be sure about what you want and when you do decide don't doubt yourself. Remember that you're sending a request to the Universe which is created by thoughts and therefore responds to thoughts. Know exactly what it is that you want. If you're not clear/sure, the Universe will get an unclear frequency and will send you unwanted results. So be sure it is something you have strong enthusiasm for.

3 Ask the Universe for it. Make your request. Send a picture of what you want to the Universe. The Universe will answer. See this thing as already yours. See How to Visualize. The more detailed your vision, the better. If you're wanting that Nintendo, Wii, see yourself sitting down playing a game on it. See yourself feeling the controller, playing your favorite game(s), touching the console. If there's that person you have a crush on, see yourself walking with her/him, touching or caressing the person, or even kissing the person. You get the idea.

4 Write your wish down. Start with "*I am so happy and grateful now that...*" and finish the sentence (or paragraph) telling the Universe what it is that you want. Write it in the present tense as if you have it right now. Avoid negation terms (see Warnings for more on this). Every day until your wish comes true, close your eyes and imagine your desire as if it's happening right now.

5 Feel it. Feel the way you will now after receiving your wish. You must act, speak, and think as if you are receiving it now. This is actually the most important, powerful step in using the Law of Attraction because this is where it starts working, and sometimes if you do this you don't feel like you need it anymore because you

FEEL like you already have it! and then the universe will manifest this thought and feeling and you will receive it.

6 Show gratitude. Write down all the things the Universe has given you. Be thankful for what you already have and be thankful for all the things the Universe has given you. The Universe has done a lot of things for us. Paying the Universe back with some gratitude will motivate the Universe to do even more things and will draw more things into your life. If you were once bullied and that person stopped, that's one thing to be thankful for. If the person you're crushing on likes you back, or doesn't but she/he didn't send their lover out to hurt you, that's another thing to thank the Universe for. You should also thank the Universe for this process too. Showing gratitude will turbo boost the Universe to manifest your request faster.

7 Trust the Universe. Imagine an alternate dimension that is almost exactly like the real world but whatever you truly desire comes true in an instant. See yourself in that dimension, where whatever you ask the Universe for comes to you in an instant. Don't *look for* what you asked for; this is where people tend to mess up. If you have to keep an eye out for an event that manifests your wish, it's only telling the Universe you don't have it and you will attract...not having it. Be patient. Don't get upset if these things don't happen immediately. Don't stress the "how" of things. Let the Universe do it for you. When you take the Universe's job of worrying about the "how", this says you're lacking faith and that you're telling the Universe what to do when the Universe has far greater knowledge and power than human mankind.

So the Law of Attraction states that a concentrated focus on what we really desire, added to taking action when the opportunity arises, will always give us what we want? That is a good strategy for trying to get what you want, especially the taking action step, but this is a pretty interesting addendum to the Law of Cause & Effect because the Law helps qualify the when and how the effect may be realized... if it is aligned with the energy of the Cause. In other words, the Attraction may bring before the people, situations, events that you can choose to act on but they cannot be misaligned. If the cause is bad, and you are attempting use good image it ain't gonna happen! The big mistake in deploying the Law of Attraction is that it alone will "create your reality"—in other words, what you want will not "just manifest" no matter how intensely you focus or how much action you take—if you do it in a reality that doesn't permit what you are seeking. It is like trying to grow wheat when you plant corn in the desert. Moreover, it won't even occur to you to take action in a reality where what you want is impossible. And you still have to make choices and act on them to get to the result.

Now Napoleon Hill we mentioned before. He was the Author of "***Think and Grow Rich***" one of the best-selling books of all time where he stated the secrets to hundreds of the most wealthy people success was to follow these rules:

First. Fix in your mind the exact amount of money you desire. It is not sufficient merely to say *"I want plenty of money."* Be definite as to the amount. (There is a psychological reason for definite- ness which will be described in a subsequent chapter).

Second. Determine exactly what you intend to give in return for the money you desire. (There is no such reality as "something for nothing.")

Third. Establish a definite date when you intend to possess the money you desire.

Fourth. Create a definite plan for carrying out your desire, and begin at once, whether you are ready or not, to put this plan into action.

Fifth. Write out a clear, concise statement of the amount of money you intend to acquire, name the time limit for its acquisition, state what you intend to give in return for the money, and describe clearly the plan through which you intend to accumulate it.

Sixth. Read your written statement aloud, twice daily, once just before retiring at night, and once after arising in the morning. AS

YOU READ, SEE AND FEEL AND BELIEVE YOURSELF ALREADY IN POSSESSION OF THE MONEY.

It seems basic, but if you actually compare this to just about any personal finance guide out there, you'll find exactly the same simple steps. They just come with a lot more bells and whistles.

What is Hill saying as the bottom line? Begin with thought and make it very clear in your mind as to what you want. Know what you are going to share with others as a result, create a clear plan, then **see, feel and believe yourself** already in possession. Firmly entrench this into your mind by reading this daily. Who does this translation of unreal to real? Some of the wealthiest people on the planet at his time.

What is the lesson here with regards to AQ and AQ'ISM?

1. Get out and build your own personal vision
2. Change those perceptions and result energies
3. Deploy thoughts, images, words, emotion to create positive acts
4. Make sure the 4th law of AQ'ISM returns good results
5. Manage the Cause

THE FOLLY OF FOCUS

All of us, all the time, "create our own reality" via the beliefs we form. Let me explain. A belief is a statement about reality that we feel is true. I say "feel" rather than "think" because we may logically know that something we believe is not true and still feel it is true. And as long as we feel it is true, it really is true for us.

So if we believe *I'm not good enough*, or *Life is difficult*, or *Relationships don't work*, or *work is the shits*, or *those people are assholes*, then we live in a reality in which these

statements are "The Truth" for us. As a result we deal with reality as if these statements are true.

If, in the reality you have created for yourself, you really are not good enough, then everything you do, don't do, or even think about doing, are significantly affected by the "fact" that you are not good enough. The same is true for any other belief you might hold.

So our reality is comprised largely by our beliefs **So what projects you take on—if any—and how creative you are in pursuing them, is largely determined by your beliefs about yourself and life. In addition, each of us forms specific beliefs about what can and what can't be done.** Anything we say can't be done really can't be done (it's a "fact") in our reality, which would prevent us from even trying to do it.

If *Change is difficult if not impossible*, how hard will you try to change something, even if change is necessary to get what you really want? On the other hand, if in your reality *Change is easy when you know how*, then potential barriers to you getting what you want are only temporary roadblocks until you tear them down. If change were necessary, you would change anything that got in your way.

If you believe that something is impossible if an "expert" tells you it is impossible, it would make sense to accept the expert's advice and not waste your time trying to do something that is impossible. If you believe *Almost anything is possible; just because an "expert" says something is impossible doesn't mean it really is impossible*— then you will ignore pronouncements from experts.

Although there is a physical reality that must be dealt with, much of what each of us considers to be reality—and virtually all that stops us in life—is a function of our beliefs, not what's really out there. And because we create our beliefs and can eliminate them at any time, it is an accurate statement to say we, for the most part, create our own reality. Or to put it another way, we create the reality we interact with daily.

And because each of us "makes" his own reality, it is possible for us to change our reality if it gets in the way of us getting what we want.

Although there is a physical reality that must be dealt with, much of what each of us considers to be reality—and virtually all that stops us in life—is a function of our beliefs, not what's really out there. And because we create our beliefs and can eliminate them at any time, it is an accurate statement to say we, for the most part, create our own reality. Or to put it another way, we create the reality we interact with daily.

In corporate life most live in a different world than we think we are making. It is filled with negativity, fear and these AQ Arsenals that create a constant viral air of morphic energy. And because each of us "makes" his own reality this way, it is possible for us to "change" our reality if it gets in the way of us getting what we want.

The bottom line is **"be careful what you wish for"**. The folly is occupying your mind, belief, activities and emotions with what you **do not want** when you do not even know this is the wanting that you will attract. **What you think about, you bring about** is hard to swallow as what you are creating as your reality. But can you afford to ignore this?

INVESTING IN YOUR ENERGIES

The important thing about the Law of Cause and Effect is that much of the cause can be unconscious. And when thoughts and images and words and emotions add to creating a cause, you can never be understanding of when the effect comes back to you. This is especially so when you are not even aware of a cause been given energetic life. With the number of thoughts and visions and emotions going out every day it is a pretty awesome task to make any correlations. It is only when you make a conscious effort to desire or achieve (like in Napoleon Hill's wisdom) that you can monitor this progress and even influence the result. And even when we cause and effect numerous times in a day, it is not believed that we are actually creating the energy to seek out mates, and, what about all the stuff we have created in the past that make be coming into effect now, or about to?

When AQ'ISM hits, are negative thoughts and needs closely related to the desire for either protecting, acquiring or maintaining power, profit, and ego in front of your actions and decisions? Does it need to be this way? No, but when shit is given to you, you give it back. It's ok because it's just business does not really stop the similar effect from coming back.

Do you have a choice as to how you talk to, tell, or treat people? YES. Do you have a choice as to how you tell them what to do? YES. Do you? Probably not.

Before I said that one has four options:

1. **Raise your AQ to be in line with your position.**
2. **Raise your position to be in line with your AQ.**
3. **Leave and zero out your AQ.**
4. **Don't engage in the AQ'ISM addiction**

The first three only add to the AQ Gopher wheel to create more of the same energy that you will eventually get back. It does not really break the cycle.

In a simple sense, it's like you have been creating an energetic ledger that balances itself like karma that is keeping track of the entries over your life (and maybe other lives too) that need to be balanced to close the book. It took years to face and neutralize mine!

So the 4th option is what I learned and it is what the best solution is. Whether you get out and chase your own vision, or whether you decide to climb in a corporation, or whether you decide to stay in a corporation, the best solution is to proactively balance the books in a conscious effort to open your own passionate visions where AQ'ISM has no energy to keep alive.

CHANGING THE AQ BALANCE

There are four main types of energy which are **proactive** and **reactive.** When you are engaged in a Corporation, it becomes a subset of your larger environment but nevertheless, the energies are the same. The fact is that 8-10 hours a day of negative corporate life **does** have an impact on your health and wealth.

The reactive ones come from what you let into your attention—media, TV, news, others opinions, etc. That is probably the majority. What are the usual thoughts you create from a world full of bad news and conflict? And 8 hours at the office?

Then there are events that happen to you in and out of the corporation. How do you react to these when you disagree or become angry, or spiteful as to why they happen to you? When you work in a corporation, much of the information and energy is coming from the corporate culture environment becomes a powerful influence on how you react to create energy.

Then the proactive ones come forth. These are the ones you simply generate in your own space. Do you ponder on lack, fear, problems, or issues?

Then there are the ones that are your desires and plans for a better life, job, pay, position, etc. Do you think about a solution or the lack of one? These are the critters of life that need to be muzzled and directed through the heart. These are the energies that create your perception and your life. Can you remain in that positive space of the heart? The trick is to stay there.

But most important of all is the need to change the balance from creating negative energies and reacting to situations in a negative way. If the energy you create is there to find a mate, it makes sense to pay more attention to creating positive energy. Secondly, if the energies strength of attraction is dependent upon the added emotion, then it would make sense to start creating strong positive emotion and start a program where you proactively choose what it is you want to attract and manifest. Third, if the negative energy plays havoc with your physics and your physiology by creating disease and disease, it would make good sense to avoid creating these.

The best way for me to explain this is like making an investment portfolio of energies like the four above. The following is taken from a book (**Return to the Future**) I wrote years ago when I left the corporate world as CEO and Director. It is about a fellow Michael Carpetbagger whose life has become so horrid financially, he tries to commit suicide and while in limbo (out of body) meets his angel Shea-Ri) who gives him some guidance while he is still mumbling about all his woes:

Shea-Ri sensed she must try to relate this information to his old ways. *"Michael, you are thinking about your life as Mr. Carpetbagger."*

"Well, I can tell you, this would not be so easy in Mr. Carpetbagger's life! He has had so many disasters and has probably got a big shit load of this karma to work off. It is all just such a negative world. I don't know where I would even start."

"Dear Michael, it starts by understanding and believing those pillars of wisdom. Every day your mind generates perhaps in excess of 30,000 thoughts that you seem not to care about. If you believed they were the culprits in creating your life would you change them?"

"But they are automatic. How do I do that?"

"Michael, you are an investor. It is your current way of life. Why would you not invest some time in following an investment program in a new life. What about investing in your own energy to change these old habits of yours? What would it hurt?"

That got Mike's attention instantly. "Investment?"

"Look at it this way. You have 24 hours in a day like everyone else that creates energies. Let us call it your energy fund. You are going to take responsibility for managing this fund a different way. Within this fund are four portfolios. You are going to take the management of the fund away from your broker—namely your ego and take responsibility for managing it yourself. You, through your mind are going get a new advisor to four energy portfolios in the fund. You will let the heart be your advisor to what makes up these four portfolios and how to make them grow."

"I see where this is going," replied Mike, "I am going to let the heart manage my thoughts, images, words and emotions!"

"Not exactly but you are partly correct. There are rewards for this, remember. Your portfolios are made of four different assets. These relate to the way you create the energy. The more positive the energy, the higher the value of your investment. The more negative the energy is, the lower it falls."

"Hmmm, that's pretty interesting, go on."

"Your initial investments in the four portfolios can be apportioned into four types of energy generating activities. The first two portfolios are reactive energies. One is a result of your thoughts you create from the news, the media, your television, papers, what others tell you is truth. Let us call this group media. You, listen, *hear, see, read and you react. Perhaps 60% of your total time in the 24 hours is of this nature, is it not?"*

"Maybe even more."

"Your purpose is to not react in a negative way. You do not think negative thoughts, you do not add negative emotion, get angry or say things, or do things that are not in alignment with the heart."

"Hmmm, that could be hard given the state of our world."

"Remember it is there to teach you what you do not want, and focus on it, not the reverse. If you react instantly in rage, it is your ego. Simply stop the thought for three deep breaths and you will find the ego subdues and the heart takes over. Then create a new reaction that sees a good reason for the issue, or do not react— keep it neutral. Recall that you are investing in a future life of goodness, so the more goodness you can energize, the more you build up the value of that portfolio."

"Ok, positive grows the asset, negative diminishes the value. And the second?"

"The second portfolio also comes from outside of you and is part of the reactive. It has to do with events that happen to you that are seemingly not under your control. Let us call it events. You have a dreadful accident, or you get involved in a terrible situation. This may account for 10% of the energy fund. Your immediate ego instinct is to clash, react, or do something that you may be sorry for later. The focus here is to not do that. Do not create a huge energy action that is negative. Try to see some reason that this occurred to you and read something good out of it. See in it a lesson of what you do not want."

"But what if it is a terrible thing that you have to take on with a vengeance?"

"It is your choice, but if your portfolio is to build rapidly, this is the place you can make huge strides. Many of these are a result of old karma or negative energy in escrow from the past. If it is a terrible problem that puts you in fear or hatred, leave it alone for three days to get the ego out of it then you will have time to look at it with the heart in mind."

"The next two portfolios are proactive—those energies that you yourself can create in your own time. The first is easiest described as free thinking. It is the time you spend letting your mind simply generate thought about whatever is on your mind. This can be 20% of the time, or 20% of your energy fund."

"You mean thinking about people and experience, and task and stuff?"

"Yes, when you create a thought about your own personal affairs, is it about your feeling of inadequacy, doubt, fear of the future, crisis from the past, not enough money, or feeling sick? Or is it how great the world is, what you have to appreciate, what is good. What is your focus? To add to the positive investment energy in your fund, add positive thoughts. Do not let any negative like it pisses me off, or I hate this, or I feel crappy, etc. Learn to stop this and convert it. Do not give it negative life."

"The last portfolios has to do with plans. We will call it plans. You may have 10% of the fund allocated toward this. These energies are for investing in major desires, solution, passions for you to manifest. Here, rather than being focused on the problems, like not enough money, having to work hard, do this do that to get more money, change the focus to the solution. Feel the energy of completion, add the emotion of enjoyment, be grateful for it being done, and put the positive energy of completion out to the Zero Point Quantum Field to attract. Place this energy in your fund. This may be a very small part of the fund but it can have an immense effect on the positive energy of joy that can result in your fund and its future value."

"Shea-Ri, that is very smart. I really like that idea."

"You will begin to see a dramatic change in your life as your fund grows from positive energies. Your objective is learning to generate new positive energy or convert more and more negative energy until there is no room for negative events and experience to enter your day. It is like your own business where you take old energy companies that are failing, then put new energy into them to be successful."

"Hey, that is cool. What about all the old shit that is maturing from before?"

"Of course, you will have residual energies in escrow that are looking to materialize. These are there as your lessons that through the Law of Grace you are converting. Celebrate them as a great opportunity to create a big impact in your fund. They are indeed great opportunities. That is your challenge, is it not? Is that any different than the challenge for you to find a company that than can grow nicely for your clients?"

"I see your point."

"Then?"

"Yes, it makes sense. It is something that I would have to work at."

"New habits to break old habits?"

"Hmmmm."

Mike pondered this. He was imagining how this portfolio worked. It certainly made sense, but it did not get the demons away quickly, or solve his monetary issues. It seemed that while he was loving himself and loving everybody, he was putting his guard down and getting screwed by others.

"Dear Michael, I know it is a hard reality for you to accept. But where are you now? Are you not already screwed. What have you to lose now? It appears that you have already lost it. Do you think that more worry and fear will serve you better?"

"Yes, I guess you are right."

"Michael, you will learn to be aware of your inner and outer world to manage the energy better. This is simply taking responsibility, working with the heart to create deliberate management and guidance. It is your key to the joys and passions. Your fund will reap incredible profits to you."

"This is how I can follow a passion that I prefer to do and enjoy, isn't it? But is it still not the ego that is instigating selfishness?"

"Your inherent philosophy should be to take care of yourself first. Be selfish to satisfy your joy, passions and desires. If you want perfect health, prosperity, great relationships, and harmony, think about choosing these, firing up the positive energy burners and feeling them. Feel the emotion which creates the strong vibration. If you are happy with yourself, and love yourself dearly, you will automatically love and help others."

"As a manager of your portfolio, you are going to be the inviter, creator and attractor of what you want as well. But understand that there is no list of right or wrong. What one deems right, another deems wrong. Everything begins in a neutral state until you alone qualify it by your own belief, judgment, and choices of polarity. You then become a powerful magnet attracting more of what you choose to create."

"And if I am negatively influenced by others and my own old habits which create doubt, then my belief system is out of alignment. If something does not come, it is because I am focused more on its absence."

"Yes, Michael. Focus on the end desire; the completion of the result. By managing the energy, you will bring more and more compatible events and circumstances into your experience. But you must first alter your belief system and accept you have the right to be or to have whatever you want. Learn to think about only what you want and see whatever you want to see. Those are some of the many lessons you have learned here."

"Always remember that every question has an answer. Every problem has a solution already sitting in the quantum field as a fulfillment of your request if you make it. It simply waits for you to align energies with it so it can materialize for you. It is already there waiting for your mind to complete the possibility."

"How can that be?"

"Because there is no time. All that exists is now. It is all a continuous stream now moments replacing the last. There is no past or future except what your mind records and creates. So the solution must already exist as a possibility in the quantum state. It is there waiting for your mind to collapse the wave patterns. The act of enjoying it and feeling it reinforces its manifestation. Everything is already. It simply has to be drawn to you by your actions alone. Do you understand clearly why your life has been the way it is?"

"I think so. It is because every event, circumstance, meeting, and experience has occurred because of what and how I have been thinking, wondering, pondering, seeing, and imagining somewhere in the past. I have been thinking my life into being differently than I thought, through thought. My energy fund has been focused on negative or unclear energies."

"Yes, it is a paradox, is it not? You have ordered it that way by energizing your subtle energies of the past. All your thoughts and emotions have asked for what you have received."

"Michael, what do you now think about how you control of big events—like an earthquake, or a storm, or some other catastrophe?"

"Hmmm, I don't want to be there."

"You are funny. Understand there is a global consciousness that is a composite of your local consciousness and everybody else's. These are at work manifesting larger things. Although the dividing line between the local and global events are at best difficult to rationalize, the point of it is that whatever these events are, you have a choice on how you perceive, and react to them. And you do have a choice of being part of them."

"Oh. How does global consciousness work?"

"The same way as your personal one. This financial purge that you see on your Dow Jones stocks is a mood withdrawal from supporting it. It is a mass change towards selling not buying. Is that not a mass consciousness?"

"But you are talking about manifesting things. Like big events."

"Understand that within a framework of what appears solid—like the planet—that is also a conscious living thing, the consciousness of all people interact for the purpose of experience. That energy, depending on the strength and focus, can rearrange matter, and attract certain events that reflect the type of experience. You all evolve and interact together and individually within this changing energy framework."

"So mass consciousness creates larger global events and the Earth itself creates her own events?"

"Yes, it is so. There are four main Zero Point Vortexes of Energy, each one being inclusive of the other, like a hologram. They are all swirling vortexes of energy in a shape your scientists know as a

328

torroid. The smallest is a photon, that which everything is made of, even you. The next is the heart that can be 8 feet in diameter, the next is the Earth and the largest is the universe itself. Each contains the information of all that exists. Each can manifest into a possibility that you can experience. You are all part of the same consciousness."

"So everything is simply part of that consciousness. But what is subconscious?"

"Subconscious in you is the memory of all that exists, as well as the life force that controls all your vital functions. It is the energy systems you have learned about that are within subconscious that are the life force and are always working at healing you and keeping the body alive."

"So the conscious part is like a front end filter to the subconscious. Is that where the orders for what we want energy to go to?"

"Yes, it is so."

"Then things like autosuggestion and hypnosis that can access the subconscious to create miracles and have people do things unknowingly later is the same process."

"Yes, the body simply responds to the subconscious. That is its duty. It is there to respond and keep your life force active. The subconscious knows how to heal your body. It knows how to keep you alive when you sleep or are unconscious. It is the portal to your DNA and your body as well as the Zero Point Field of all possibilities. It knows how to respond to the energies you create."

"The subconscious is also part of the greater consciousness and knows all there is to know."

"It is so. All you have to learn is how to communicate with it in your conscious state."

"Is that what prayer and miracles are all about?"

"Michael, prayer is something that religions have distorted. But nevertheless, it reflects a specific high vibration process by which the subconscious and the heart, the center of Grace, are accessed. It matters not what you call this because it is simply a matter of convincing yourself and your subconscious that a miracle of health or prosperity is within your faith. When you do that, through whatever process you choose, you instruct the subconscious to manifest the experience or result the way you request it."

"Just like hypnosis and auto suggestion. But does prayer not have a specific format? Why is that?"

"Again prayer is only a process and the rituals that are placed around it are only different ways to convince your consciousness that these things are possible. It is all part of creating faith. It is a direct communication to the heart—to Graceland. But yes the format is indeed relevant."

"Like what?"

"The generic process is based on the result and the solution already existing so you are simply drawing forward to you and having the faith that it is done. It means that first you acknowledge that such power and results exist, second stating exactly what it is that already exists, and then showing gratitude for having it."

"So I would say I am alive on a wonderful place of abundance, money comes to me easily, and thank you for providing me with a million dollars?"

"Precisely, but what else have you learned about it?"

"That I think this, visualize the result, speak it and feel the emotion of it being done and me enjoying it, then it becomes so!"

"Yes. if you do that several times a day, then you are reinforcing your belief and confirming your faith."

"And the stronger the faith, the more you can create miracles like healing."

"Your world is already filled with evidence that this is so, regardless of whether your best scientific minds want to admit this or not. But there is one more key in this, the joker in your deck so to speak. Do you know what it is?"

"Yes, belief. It is the joker. It can sabotage all of it, right?"

"Correct."

"Shea-Ri, I am confused about this now thing; that time does not exist."

"Your life is simply a record of memories held in your consciousness. It does not exist once it passes except in your mind or in your cameras. It is no more real than a set of frames in a movie that sit there on a DVD waiting to be played. Anyone can edit, erase, or change it. It does not sit somewhere as any physical thing. It is in your mind that can also change it. What you have not yet experienced sits as a possibility waiting to be called out by your mind to experience. It simply sits as vibrating waves of Zero Point Field as a potential something that has not yet been formed. And any possibility you can think of can be created, so it already exists. That is why there are infinite possibilities."

"So now is like filming a movie, each frame being a moment. The next replaces the previous to form a continuous string of moments that are created or attracted as we move moment to moment."

"And that is entirely up to you as you have free will. Dear Michael, I have only shown you what you already knew. But what you must *know now is that you must never forget the power you have but need to wake it up. It is your way of thinking and your belief in yourself that must change."*

"I can see that. I need to think like I am prosperous, or I am healthy, I am happy?"

"Yes, you are what you say you are."

"Yes, I do understand that."

There was silence now as much had been said and so much had been learned. Shea-Ri was pleased.

Michael was very quiet. Shea-Ri knew what was next.

"Shea-Ri," asked Michael quietly, "what is next? What am I to do now?"

"You must make a choice."

"What choices are those?"

"What would you like to do?"

"Will I ever forget what I have learned here?"

"Only if you do not intend to remember."

"What do you mean?"

"You are simply used to going into a dream state during sleep and not remembering. That is your status quo. If you create the intention to change that then it will be so."

"You mean it is like a day dream state where I remember all that I imagine when I snap out?"

332

"Exactly."

"But I am not in a dream state. I am in some sort of limbo."

"True."

"Can I go back to my body?"

"Yes."

"I cannot die?"

"You are eternal. Have you not seen this yet?"

"And you are always with me?"

"It is so."

"What do you think I should do?"

"It is up to you. I cannot interfere with your decisions."

"You said I had a different destiny. Can you teach me about who I was when I learned those codes of wisdom?"

"It would be my pleasure."

"How do we start?"

With a big smile on her face, Shea-Ri said: "My Dear Michael, why don't I take you there."

THE ENERGY MANAGEMENT PLAN

Well, it's a good story, right? But the proactive management of these human subtle energies that you give life to may be governing your life - and they are most certainly infecting one with the darker side of the AQ Virus. Incorporating an energy Management Plan like the one suggested by the angel to Mike, as a new habit will dramatically change the balance of negative-positive things in your life.

As you pay attention to managing the subtle energy, get your body and mind tuned up, you will build a resilience that quickly converts negative to positive. This will naturally head towards a more positive based existence that puts excitement into everything you do, think, want, and react to. And the corporate AQ will have no effect because you see, perceive, and feel things differently.

You will begin to look for challenges from experiences that you were previously afraid of. Life will become a patchwork of fantastic adventures, experiences, and good emotions, regardless of what you encounter.

There are five critical changes that will result from the practice of managing your subtle energies the way proposed.

First, if you try to see the good in experiences arising from some uncontrollable events, you will avoid falling victim to negative energy, activating the intent to create more negative energy that further attracts other situations.

The second thing that happens, assuming that you can monitor the ego and its rebellious, protective, angry, conflictive thoughts, is to stop these thoughts from being projected out to find more buddies of the same mind. You will find that you will be attracting more positive energy in the form of people, events, and opportunities. They will simply begin to appear from nowhere.

Third, there is a proactive component where you purposely engage in positive situations, positive people and work towards creating positive manifestations as you move forward. You can also engage in forgiveness to cleanse past energies.

Fourth, you will be deliberately transmitting more positive energies and you will be training your energy systems to generate positive energies while they are on autopilot. You will be training the ego to take orders from the heart. It will eventually begin to snowball for you as the dark side gets more and more light into it.

Fifth, you are launching a plan of coherence between all your subtle energy centers. This will grow, improve your health and longevity as your reasons to live expand. The physical, physiological, and psychological aspects of your life will harmonize and respond as they were designed to do in the first place

The result is to pay attention to these and you will build a wonderful resilience that others will notice and your body, mind and Spirit come into a wonderful balance of harmony.

By managing this human subtle energy that creates the AQ Virus, you are going to take control and begin to create the life you want – not have a life that reacts to everything by default of residual negative energies of the past.

There is no reason to fall victim to the current balance of thoughts bombarding your life through the day if you begin to change the channel. It is estimated that 85% of thoughts are negative as they are responding to the negative world of media, news and situations around you.

Make an effort to change the balance from 85% unchecked and 10% reactive thoughts by simply paying attention to your thought process and "*stopping the thought*".

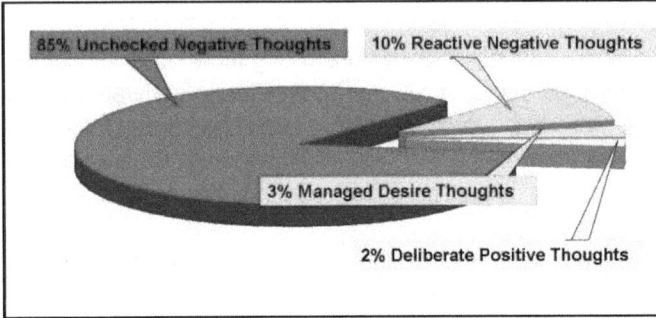

These are like snakes looking for a place to strike. Don't let the snakes out of the sack! Is it any wonder that the low number of deliberate positive thoughts you may generate simply get lost in a sea of negativity and defaulting experiences that you learn to accept you have no control of?

You have to make a paradigm shift and believe this is hogwash. You can change the balance to have 85% managed desired thoughts.

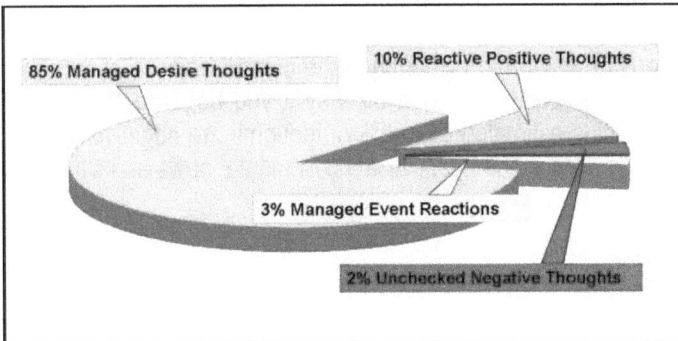

By changing the balance through managing the subtle energies, you will make that paradigm shift. The change in belief and a daily change in habit will unfold a new life – the one you design, not the one you default to. That means you can start creating a better life RIGHT NOW and it can only get better and better. It will get better beyond your comprehension. You will simply take control and begin to create the life you want — not have a life that reacts to everything. Proactive management of Human Subtle Energy will insure that your current limited comprehension, and limited physical state, does not inhibit what you can really do.

There will be no room left for _any_ unwanted experiences.

Change your point of perception.

Take charge of your subtle energies.

Become the Genie and the Lamp that you already are.

All you have to lose is fear and poverty.

The choice is yours of course… it is as simple as that.

What about AQ?

It's just a funny theory!!!

Have a great life.

Ed Rychkun

Be sure to get my first book to better understand how you may have caught the virus and how to measure it.

Corporations Stripped Naked 1: Exposing the AQ Virus

July 5, 2014 ISBN 978-1-927066-06-5

5X8 Paperback 223 pages

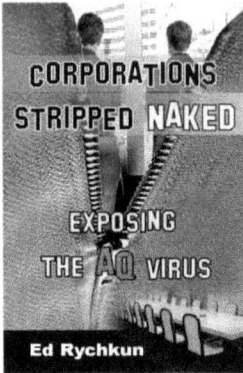

Take a tour of corporate life through former business executive Ed Rychkun's view of his lifetime of climbing corporate ladders. This provocative and hilarious expose' shows what really goes on behind those boardroom walls. It reveals the flip side of a company's naked underbelly by showing how people universally conform to laws on how they feel about each other called AQ'ISM – a classification of "Asshole". Using his own 30 years of climbing ladders to the top, he exposes how top management falls victim to a viral cross between the Peter Principle and the IQ. Using large Fortune 500 companies, as well as smaller enterprises as his stage, Ed relates his first hand experience in maintaining positions of Managers, VP, CEO, Founder, Director, and Chairman.

Ed examines the social behavior of corporate citizens and develops his universal laws about how this feeling is quantified as an AQ, and how it can have a direct impact on how fast you can climb or fall from the corporate ladder. Ed tells it like it is, revealing how the "real" professionals - the Executives, use a set of secret AQ Arsenals to hide their incompetence and maintain their positions of power in the corporate hierarchy by making asses of others. You will immediately recognize a similarity with your own situation and derive humor from it. But beware, as one critic points out, *"Never was the raw naked truth so aptly expressed as in this earthy examination of the blatantly exposed underbelly of the modern corporation".*

www.ingramcontent.com/pod-product-compliance
Lightning Source LLC
Chambersburg PA
CBHW060322200326
41519CB00011BA/1811